IMAGES
of America

POTTSVILLE IN THE TWENTIETH CENTURY

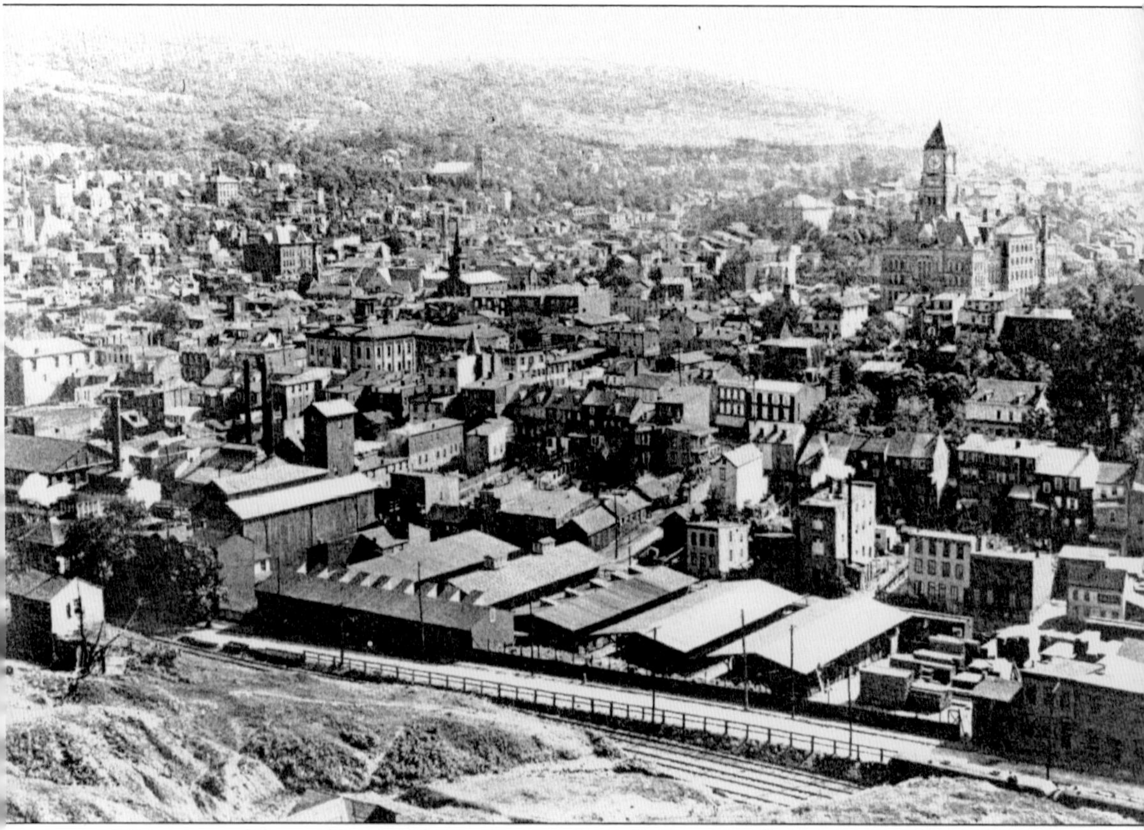

This view of Pottsville in 1900 looks west from Lawton's Hill. Notice Buechley's lumberyard on Railroad Street in the foreground, the courthouse in the upper right, St. John's in the upper middle, and Sharp Mountain in the background.

IMAGES
of America

POTTSVILLE IN THE TWENTIETH CENTURY

Leo L. Ward and Mark T. Major

ARCADIA
PUBLISHING

ISBN 978-0-7385-1237-2

Published by Arcadia Publishing
Charleston, South Carolina

Printed in the United States of America

Library of Congress Catalog Card Number: 2003105200

For all general information contact Arcadia Publishing at:
Telephone 843-853-2070
Fax 843-853-0044
E-mail sales@arcadiapublishing.com
For customer service and orders:
Toll-Free 1-888-313-2665

Visit us on the Internet at www.arcadiapublishing.com

Contents

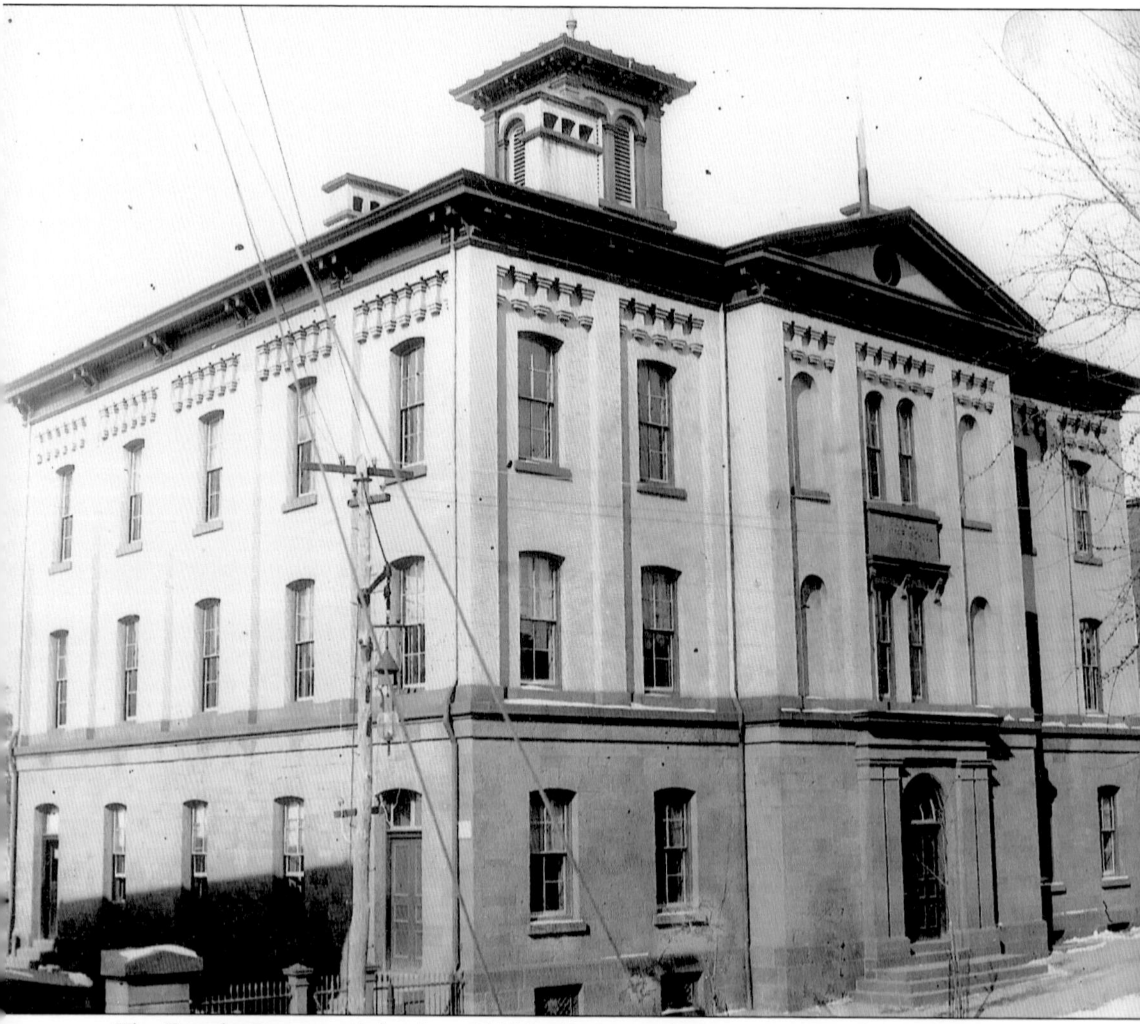

The Female Grammar School, at 305 North Centre Street, was erected in 1863. It is now the headquarters of the Historical Society of Schuylkill County. The society moved into the old school on March 13, 2002.

INTRODUCTION

The headline in the *Pottsville Republican* on January 1, 1900, read, "Farewell 1899! Welcome 1900!" The story that accompanied the headline read as follows:

> Despite the chilling weather the New Year 1900, was ushered in by the people of Pottsville in the usual appropriate manner. There were noisy demonstrations and considerable merry making throughout the town and peaceful citizens who retired before the bells rang out a farewell to the old and a welcome to the New Year, were given little rest until the new comer was several hours old.
>
> The churches were crowded at the early evening services after which hundreds took part in the Watch night services which were held at the United Evangelical, Trinity Lutheran, and Methodist Episcopal churches. The midnight Mass at St. John the Baptist and St. Patrick's churches were also well attended.
>
> The dawn of the New Year was announced by the booming of several cannon, the tooting of the bull whistle and many smaller whistles, the ringing of church bells and sweet singing rendered by many choirs from town.

Anthracite had fueled the industrial revolution of the 19th century, and the start of the new century saw a surge in the development of the national economy. Historians called the 19th century the American Century.

The United States had won the Spanish-American War and emerged as a world power. Social and political change occurred, followed by explosive technological changes. The country changed from an agrarian economy and entered "the Machine Age."

Coal miners in the anthracite mines of Schuylkill County worked in harsh conditions for low wages. John Siney of St. Clair organized the first labor union in the United States. Under his leadership, the miners fought the operators to get better working conditions and higher pay.

The seeds of the demise of the anthracite industry had been planted in the 19th century and flowered with the miners' strike of 1900 and the Great Strike of 1902. The United Mine Workers of America, led by the president, John Mitchell, closed the mines when 147,000 miners went on strike. Teddy Roosevelt was the first president to get involved in a labor strike, and he forced the operators to negotiate with the union to settle the strike. Roosevelt visited Pottsville in 1914.

What happened in Pottsville during the 20th century could not be seen or even imagined on January 1, 1900, but today, the Historical Society of Schuylkill County has hundreds of photographs in its collections to tell the story.

Robert Allison of Port Carbon bought an automobile in 1898, and the age of the automobile came to Pottsville. Trolleys were on the Pottsville scene, and in 1911, Centre Street was double tracked. By 1932, however, trolley service ended and buses were used for public transportation.

Silent movies were popular in the early part of the 20th century. When the Capitol Theater was built in 1927, talkies and the golden age of movies began. The Miners National Bank and the Necho Allen Hotel were built that year and are still standing, although the Capitol Theater has been demolished to make way for a parking deck.

Many Pottsville boys answered the call of their country in both world wars, and the Patriotic Parade of 1917 showed Pottsville's support of the country. The Great Pottsville Fire of 1914 wiped out an entire block in downtown Pottsville; the flu epidemic of 1918 struck; and telephone service, television, computers, and shopping malls arrived and changed the way people lived. The Pottsville Maroons won the championship of the NFL in 1925 by defeating the Chicago Cardinals, only to have it taken away by the league. Pottsville is still fighting to get it back.

Historians Leo L. Ward and Mark T. Major have dug into the photographic collection of the Historical Society of Schuylkill County to find pictures that tell the story of Pottsville in the 20th century. The photographs in this book, with their informative and entertaining captions, will bring back many memories for older people and reveal what used to be for the young.

One

At the Dawn of the Century

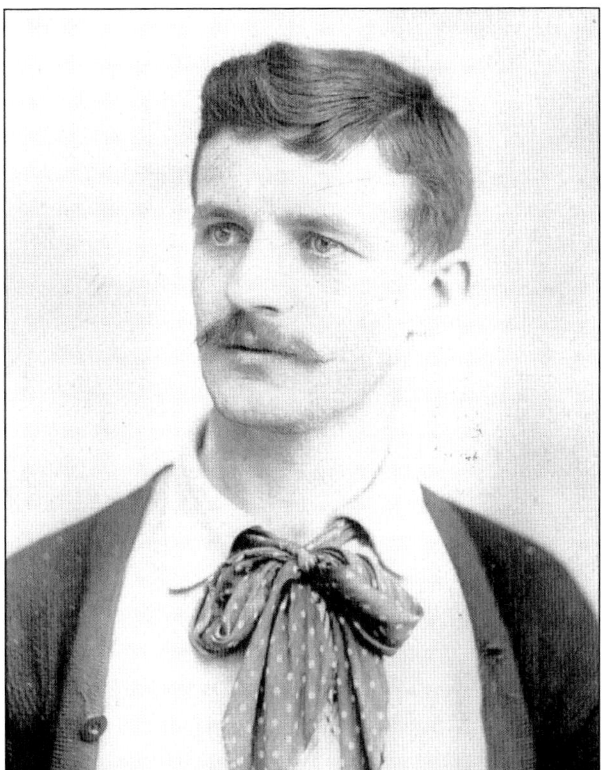

Artist and sculptor August Zeller of Bordentown, New Jersey, was given the contract to design and sculpt the Soldiers and Sailors Monument, which is in Garfield Square. He went to Paris to study art under the famous artist Rodin. Zeller's obituary lists the Pottsville monument as one of his two best.

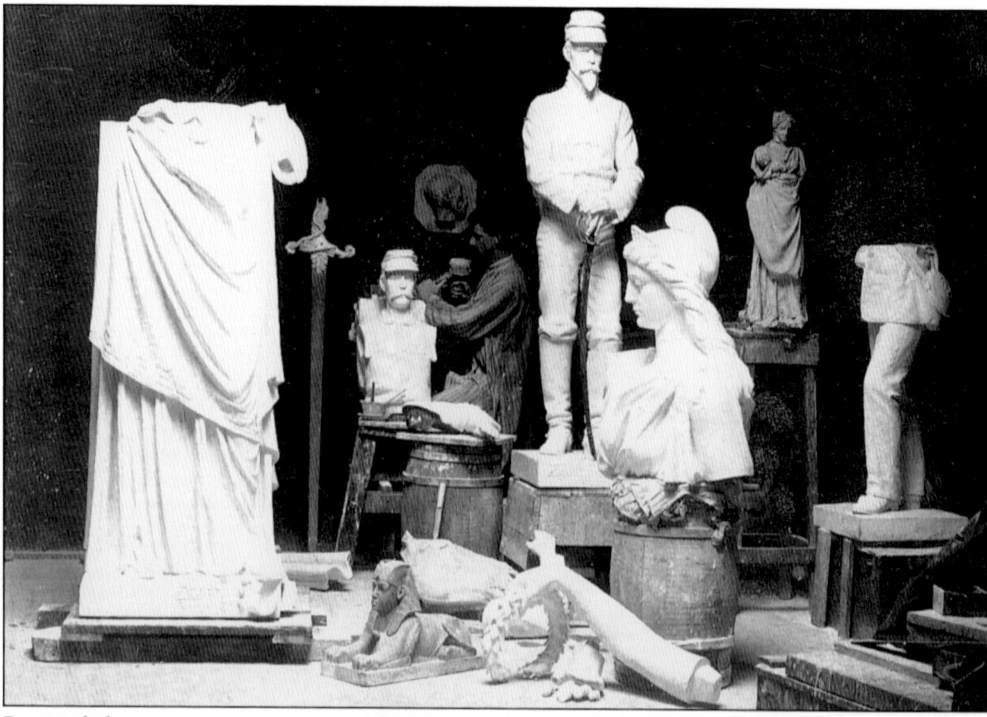

Parts of the monument as it was being assembled are shown in August Zeller's studio in Koppitzsch's Hall, on Mauch Chunk Street. In the foreground is the arm of *Genius of Liberty*.

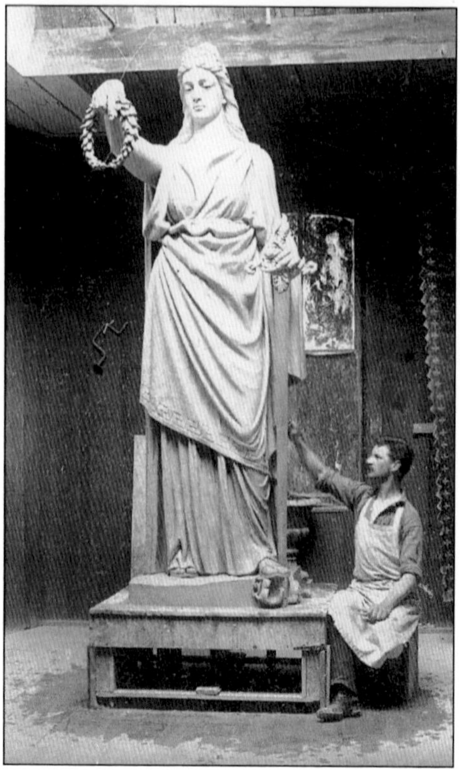

Zeller is shown working on *Genius of Liberty*. He was assisted in his work by stonecutter George L. Schreader. It was so cold in the studio during the winter that Schreader had to hold candles near the wax monument so that Zeller could work on it.

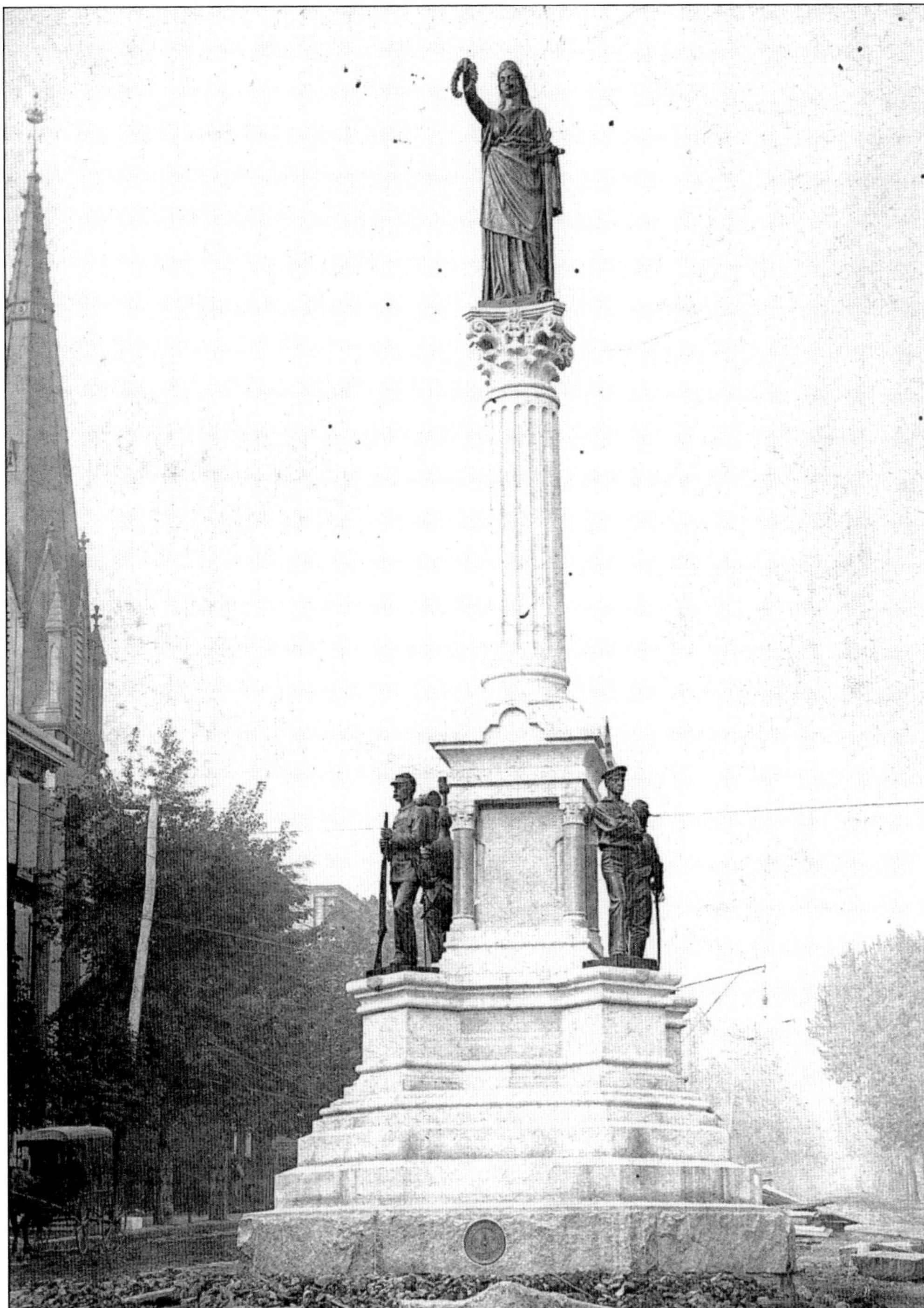

The Soldiers and Sailors Monument was dedicated on October 1, 1891, in memory of the 8,000 Schuylkill County men who served in the Civil War. The Richard Collins granite and marble yard was given the contract to erect the monument for $6,000. The marble yard was situated where Pottsville's city hall is located today.

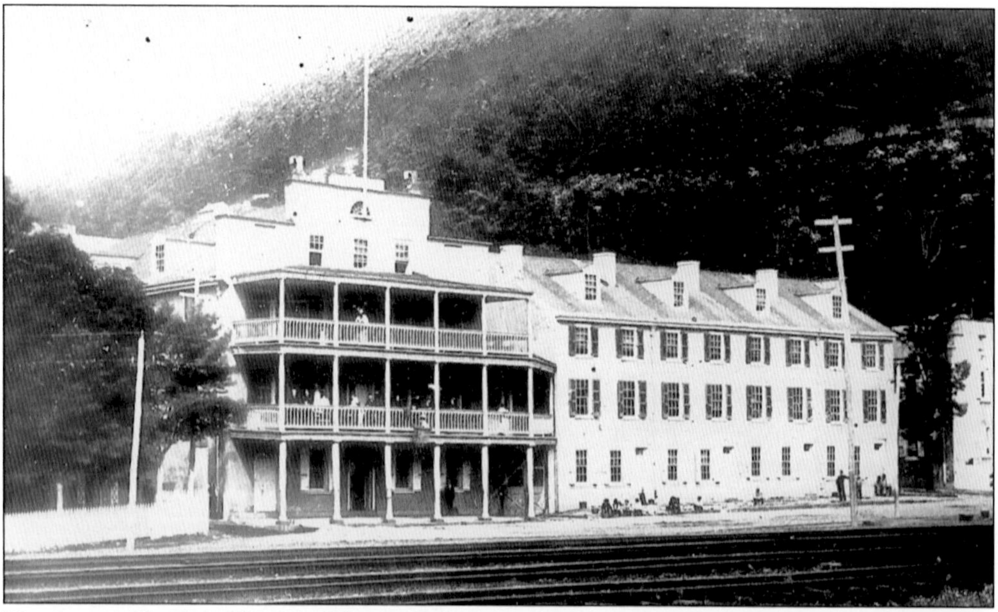

The famous Mansion House at Mount Carbon was built *c.* 1829 (the Schuylkill Canal reached Mount Carbon in 1825). It attracted many famous crowned heads from Europe and the wealthy people of Philadelphia in its heyday, when Mount Carbon was a summer resort.

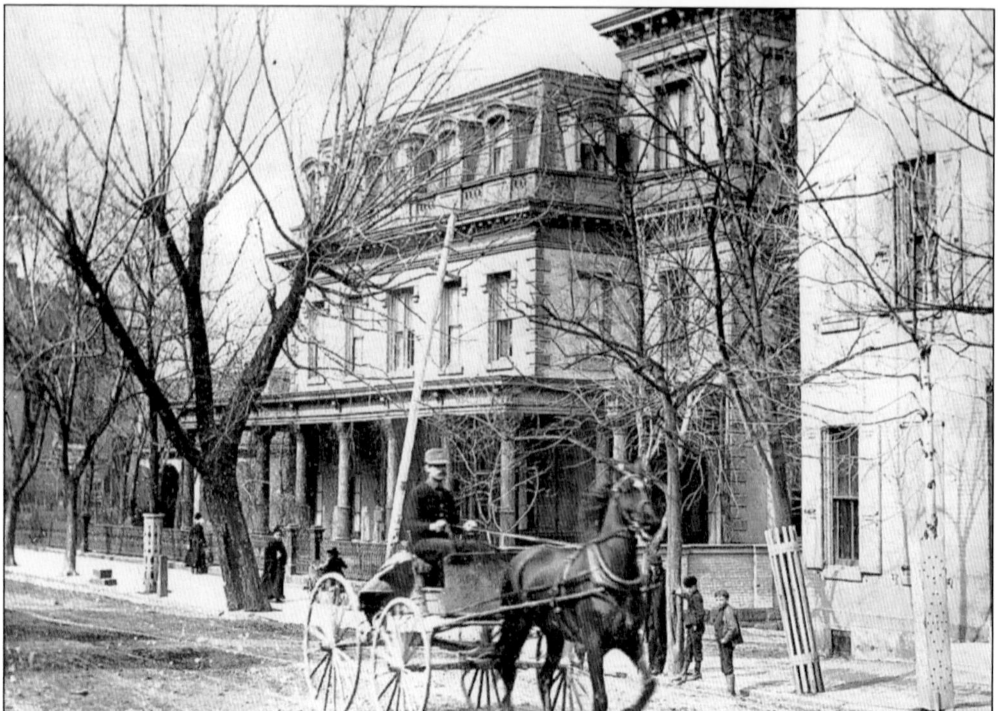

The Charles M. Atkins mansion was located at South Centre and Mauch Chunk Streets. Atkins and his brother Hanson owned the Atkins Brothers furnace, which was located in the nearby Island section of Pottsville. In 1917, after Charles's death, his wife sold the mansion to the Pottsville Loyal Order of the Moose.

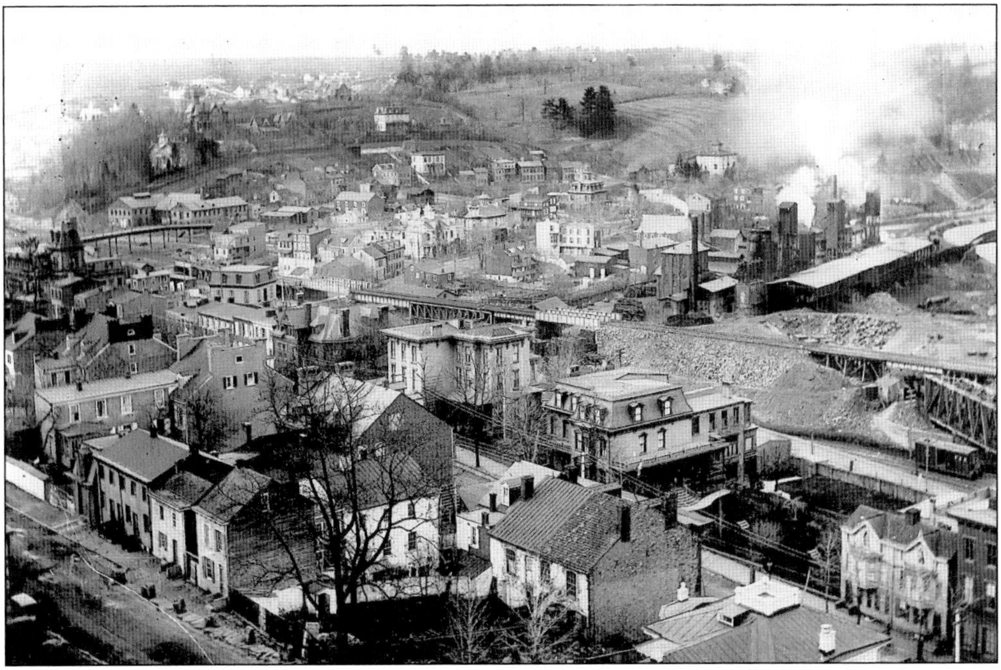

This view from Sharp Mountain shows South Centre Street and the Atkins Brothers furnace in the middle right. Notice the Washington Street Bridge on the left and a barren Greenwood Hill in the background. The Pennsylvania Railroad tracks cross in the middle of the picture.

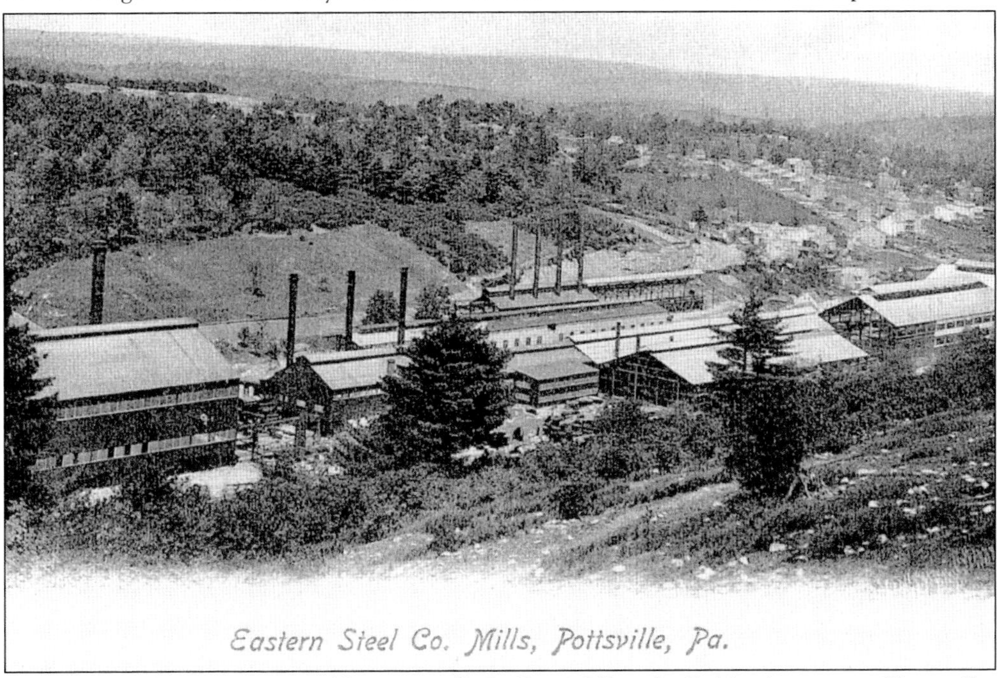

Charles M. Atkins incorporated his Pottsville Rolling Mill in the Fishbach section of Pottsville. The plant shut down near the end of the 19th century, and it was purchased by the Eastern Steel Company. The company went bankrupt in 1931, and Bethlehem Steel bought it. Bethlehem Steel tore it down and donated the land to the chamber of commerce.

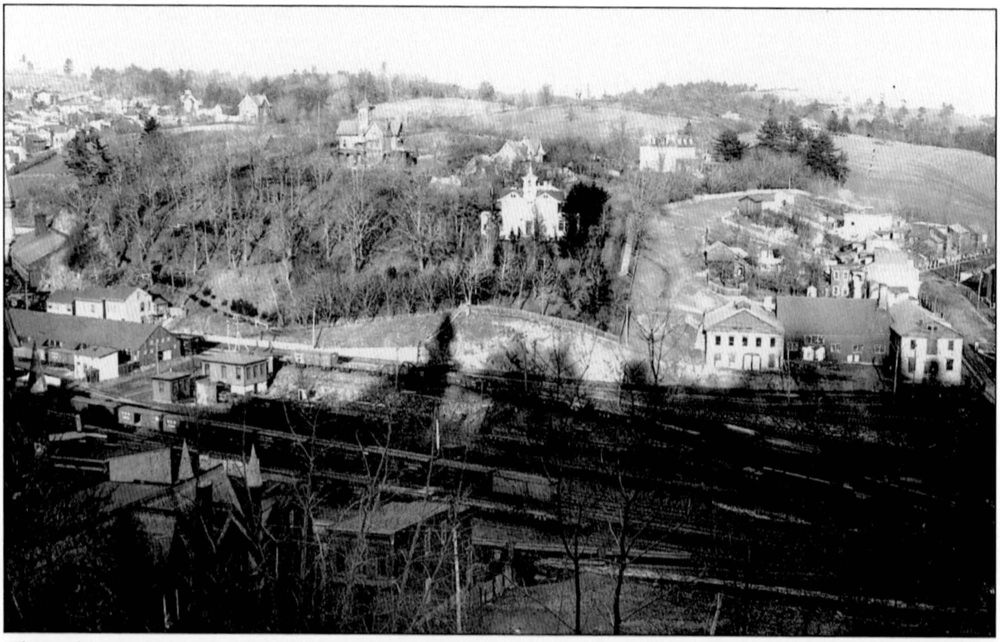

This photograph of a barren Greenwood Hill section of Pottsville was taken from Sharp Mountain. The mansion in the upper middle was the home of Benjamin Bannan, owner and publisher of the *Miners' Journal*. Philadelphia & Reading cars are in the foreground, near Railroad Street. Pennsylvania Railroad cars are in the middle of the image, next to Coal Street.

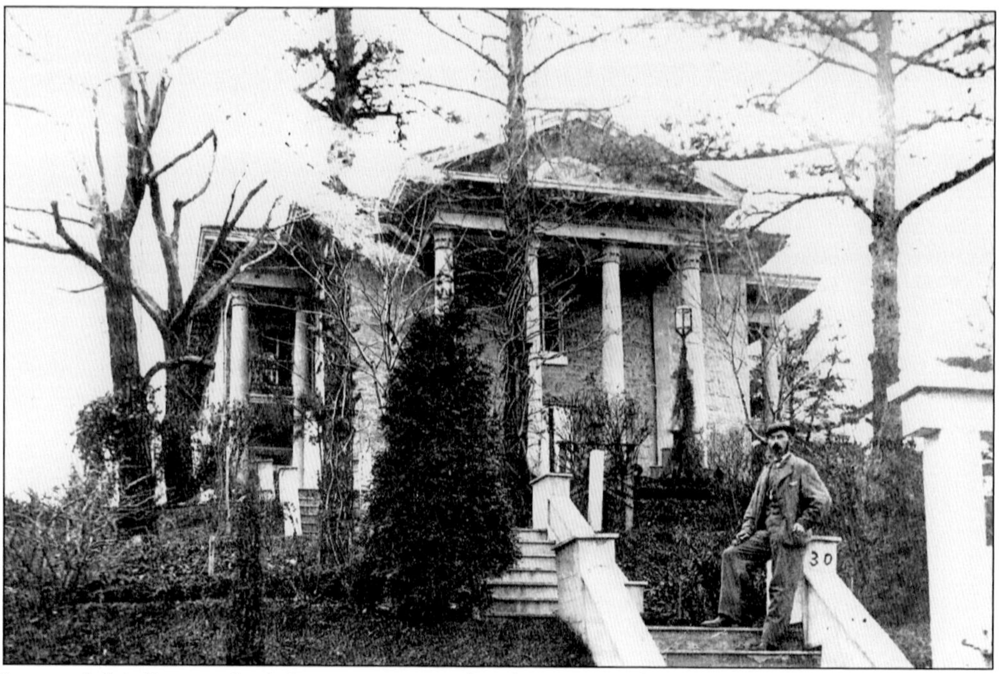

Lawyer John Bannan built his mansion made of stone on Sharp Mountain *c.* 1850. His wife named it Cloud Home because she said it was so close to the sky. It is still a prominent landmark in Pottsville today.

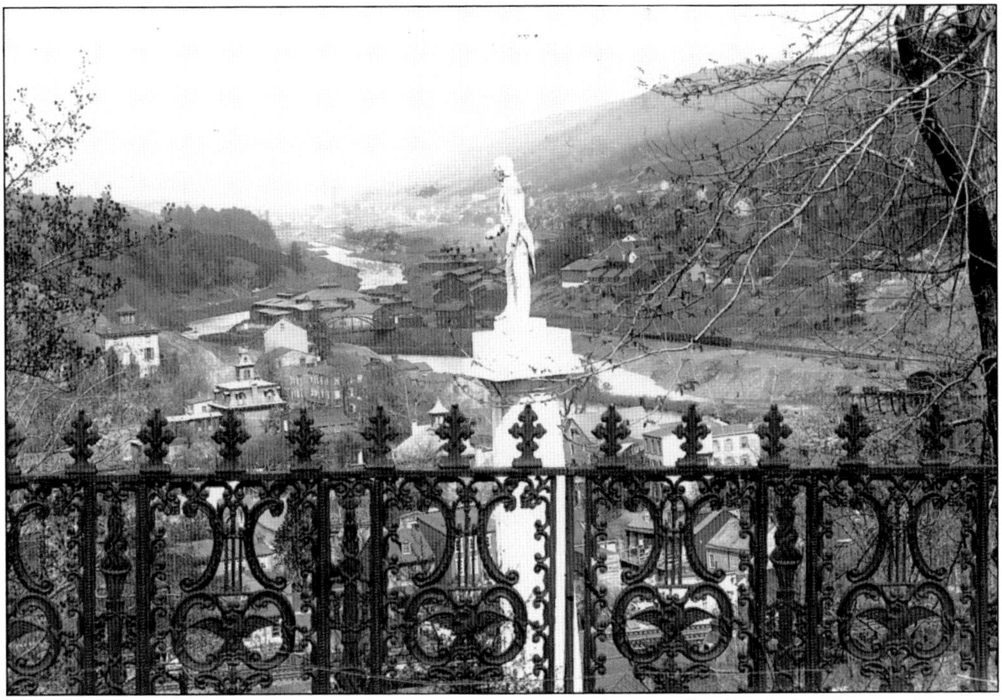

When Henry Clay died on June 29, 1852, the citizens of Pottsville decided to honor the great statesman by erecting a monument to him. The dedication of the monument was held with elaborate ceremonies on July 4, 1855. This photograph, taken from the porch of John Bannan's Cloud Home, looks up the Schuylkill Valley to the east.

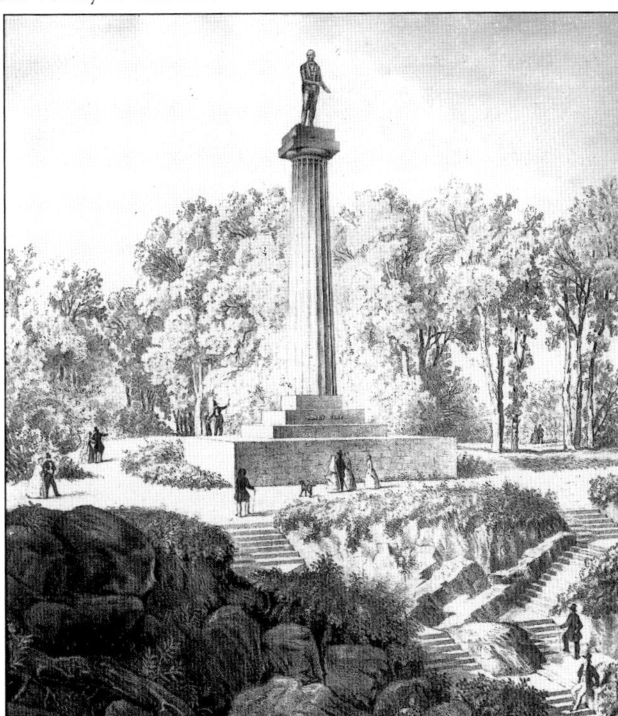

The cast-iron statue of Clay has been a landmark in Pottsville since it was erected in 1855. Clay advocated a protective tariff in his "American System" on foreign products, including iron. The increased demand for iron in the United States created a market for anthracite produced in Schuylkill County by iron foundries. This is a lithograph of a proposed park for the Henry Clay monument erected by the citizens of Schuylkill County. The monument committee wanted this lithograph to be in every home in the county. The park was never completed.

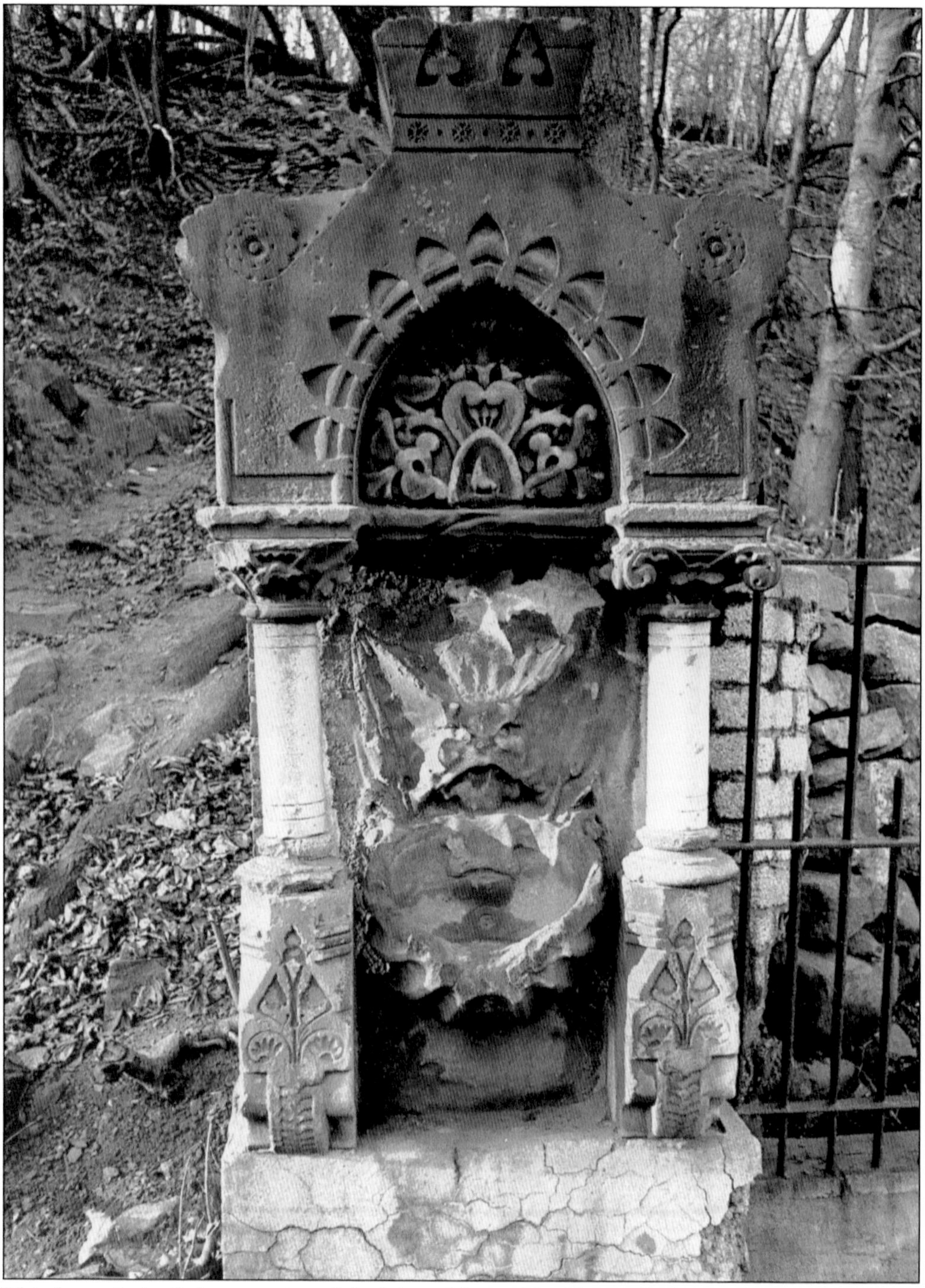

This fountain is all that remains of the *Miners' Journal* building, which was destroyed by fire in 1892. The building was built by publisher Robert Ramsey and was a model of the city hall in Bradford, England. The Sheafer Building was constructed on the site of the journal building.

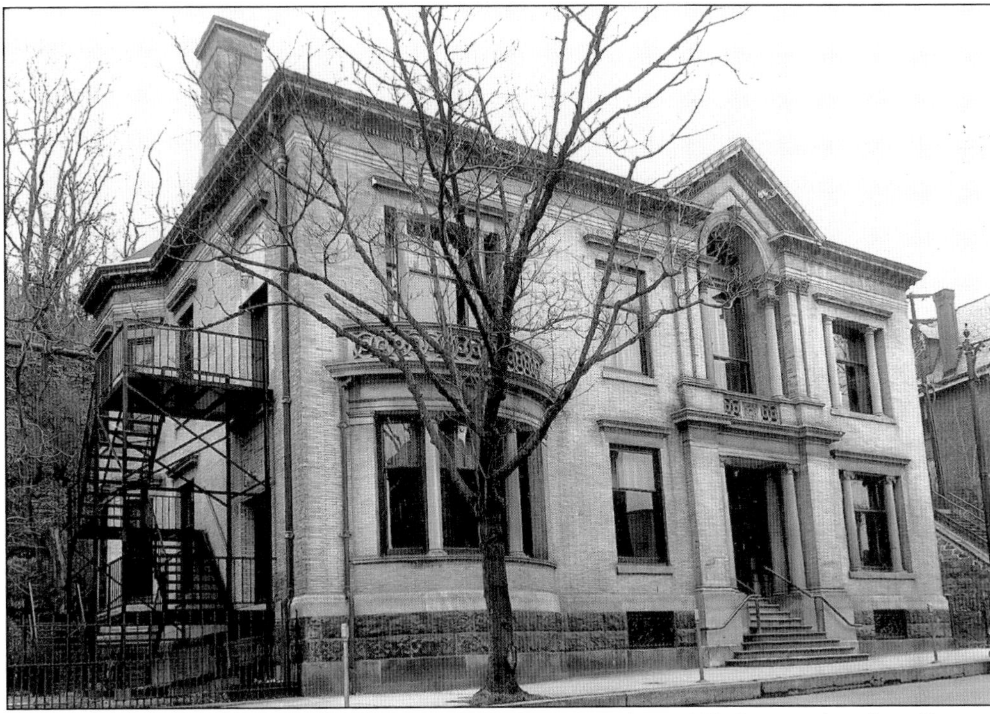

The Sheafer Building, on South Centre Street, was erected in 1893. It served as the offices of the executors of the estate of Peter W. Sheafer, who was a mining engineer and geologist. Today, it is the Pottsville YWCA.

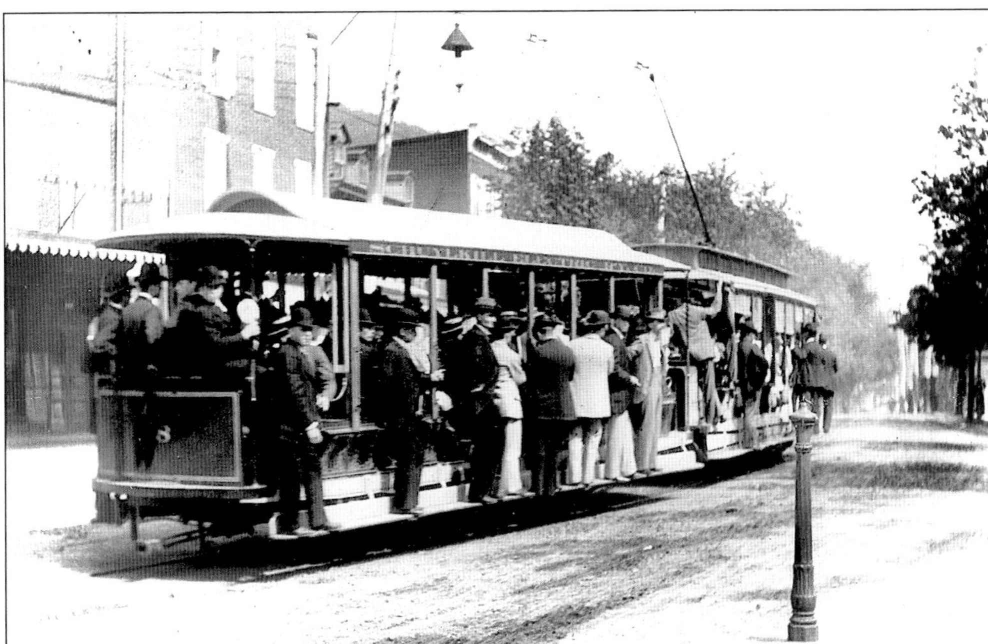

This two-car open-air trolley, on its way to Tumbling Run, is passing the Sheafer Building. Tumbling Run was an amusement park and resort near Pottsville. Notice the hitching post in the foreground.

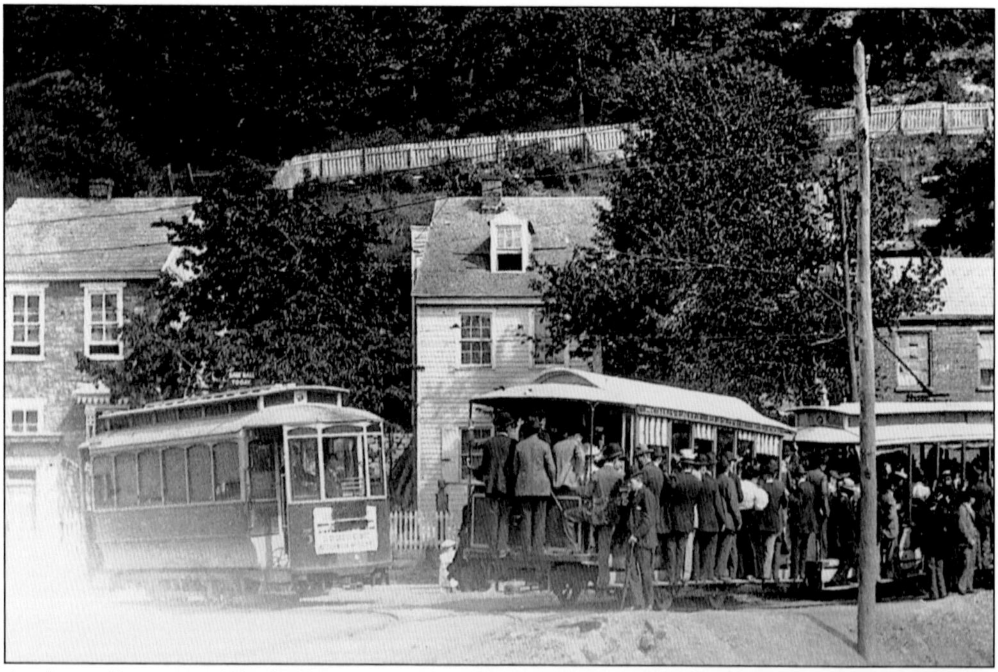

As the trolley crossed the bridge to Tumbling Run, it came to the wye in Palo Alto, where there were many mishaps with the trolley intersection. The trolley on the left has come through Palo Alto and is waiting for its turn to continue to Pottsville.

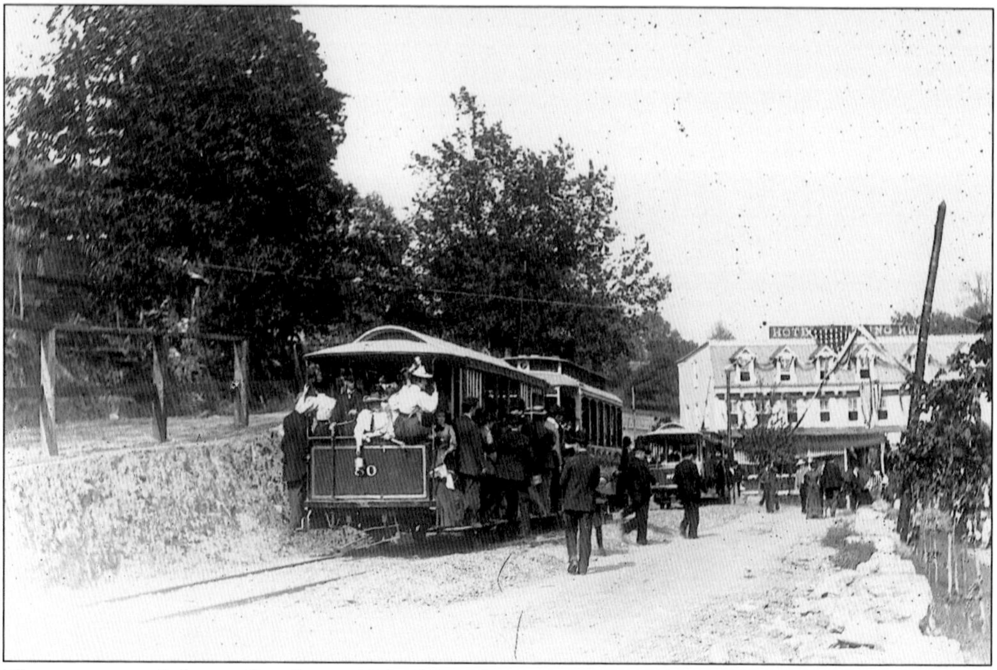

The opening of the trolley line to Tumbling Run in 1891 marked the beginning of an era of great prosperity that reached its peak between 1900 and 1912. During that period, more than one million people rode the trolley each season, which officially began on Memorial Day and ended on Labor Day.

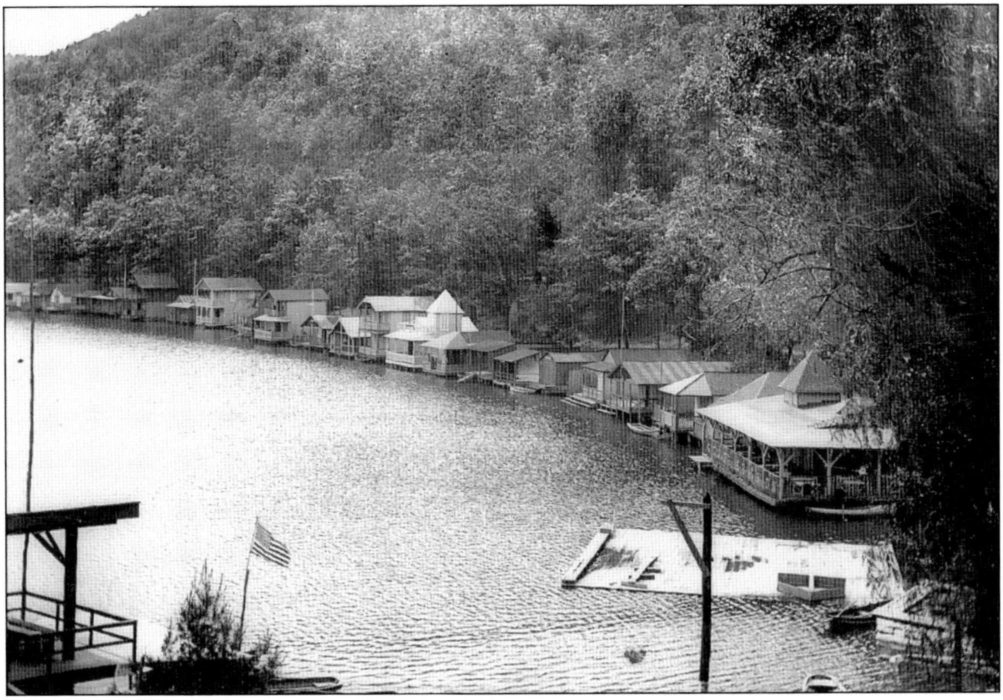

There were almost 100 boathouses along the shore of the second dam. These were the seasonal homes of prominent Pottsville families and various social clubs who came to Tumbling Run on weekends or for vacations.

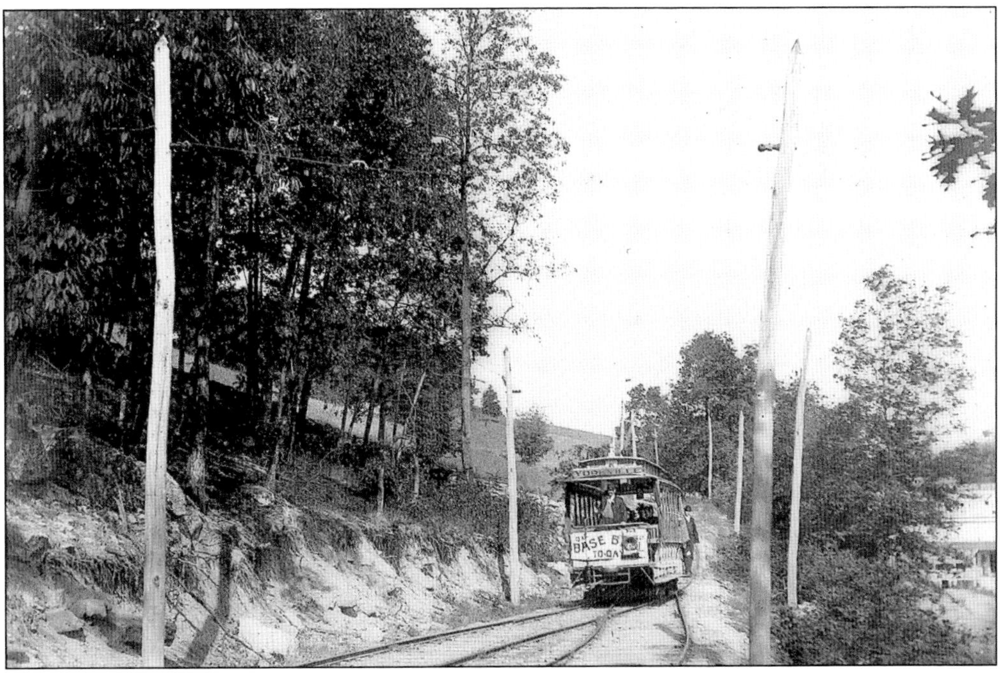

This Yorkville trolley car is returning from Tumbling Run to Pottsville with its load of passengers at the end of the day. The sign on the car proclaims, "Baseball Today." The baseball field was located behind the Tumbling Run Hotel.

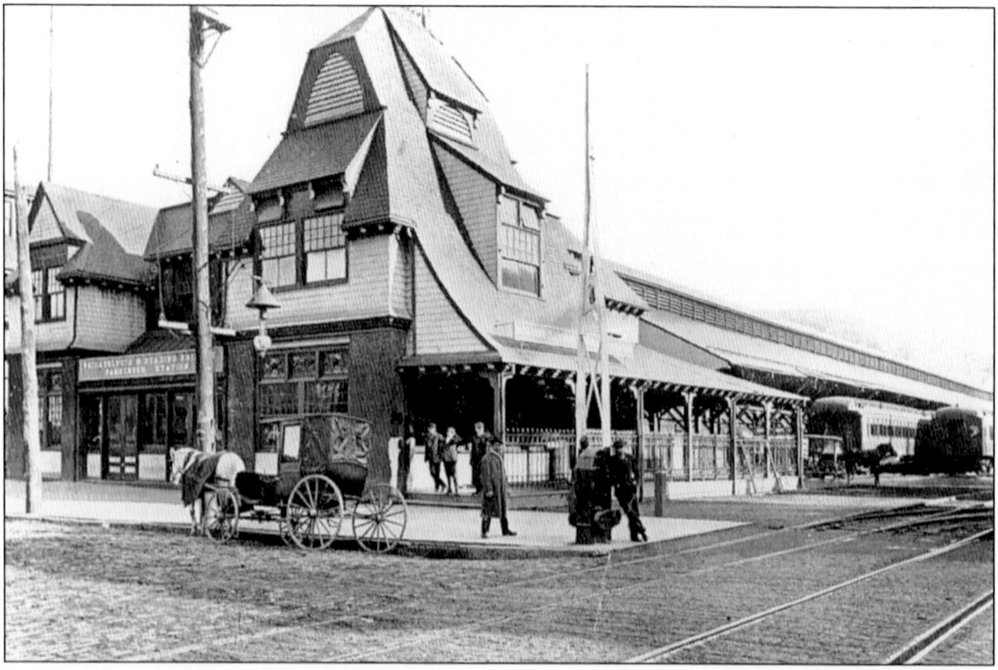

As business moved uptown in Pottsville, it was necessary for the Philadelphia & Reading station to be closer to the center of town. The new Queen Anne–style station was formally opened on June 21, 1887, on East Norwegian Street. Many Schuylkill County boys entrained from the station for military service from 1898 to 1953.

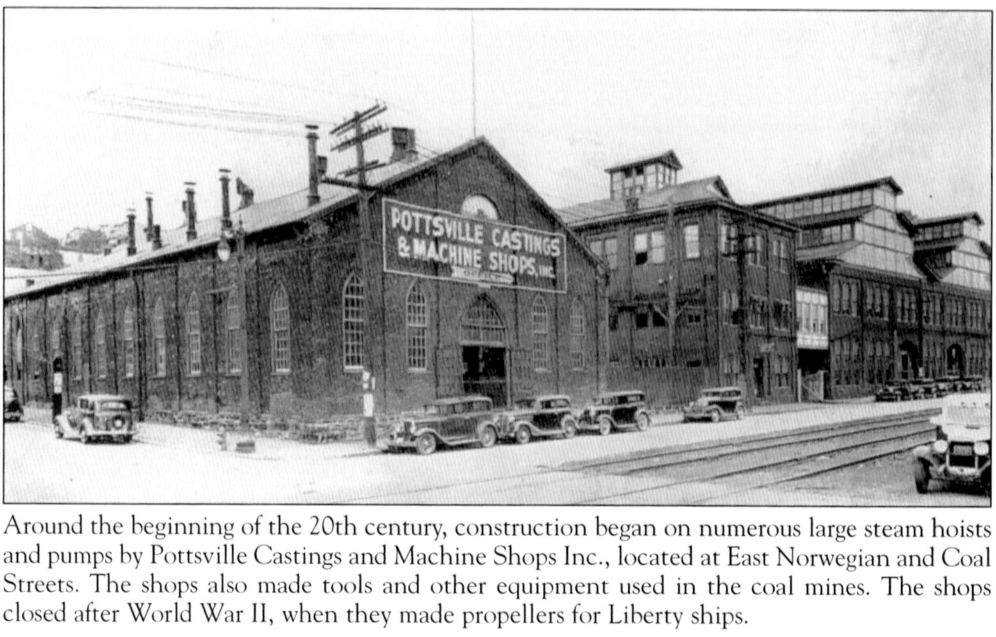

Around the beginning of the 20th century, construction began on numerous large steam hoists and pumps by Pottsville Castings and Machine Shops Inc., located at East Norwegian and Coal Streets. The shops also made tools and other equipment used in the coal mines. The shops closed after World War II, when they made propellers for Liberty ships.

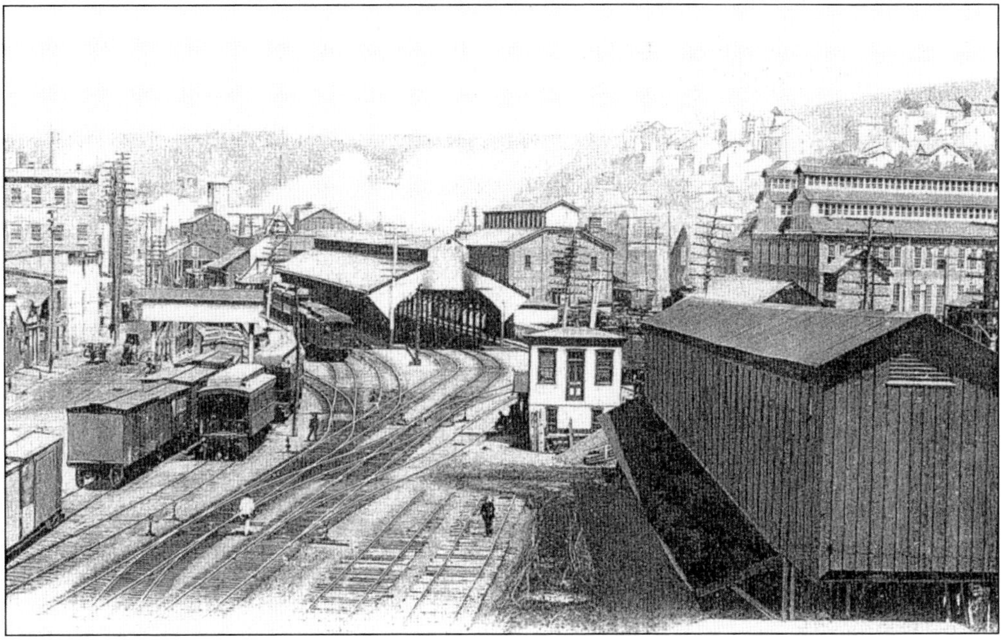

This view of the Philadelphia & Reading depot and yard is from the Washington Street Bridge. Notice the Pottsville shops on the right. The houses in the background on the right are climbing up Lawton's Hill. A narrow Railroad Street is on the left.

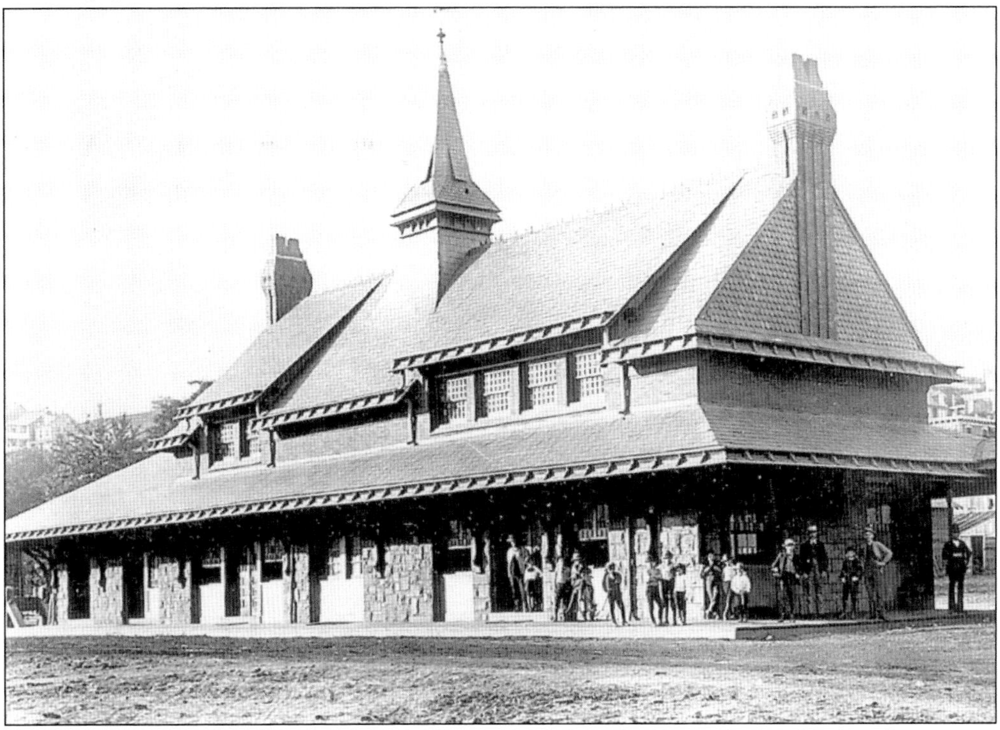

It appears from the rough ground in the foreground that the Pennsylvania Railroad passenger station has just been completed. It was formally opened on November 18, 1886. It was an elegant-looking building in its heyday.

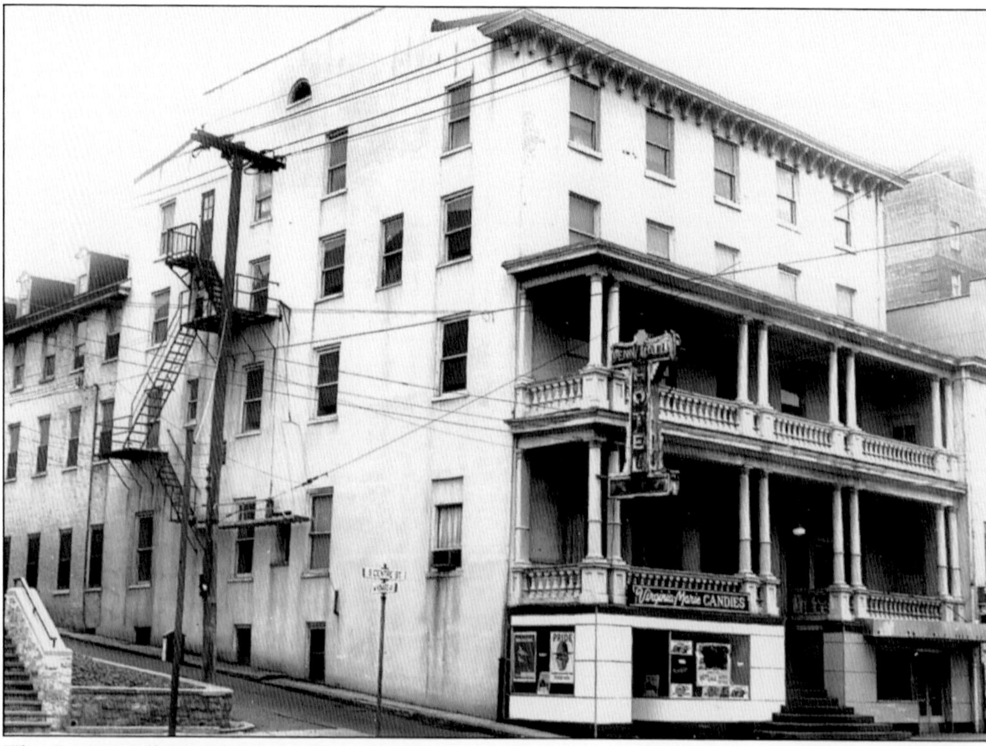

The Penn Hall Hotel was built in 1830 and was located at the northwest corner of what was then Church Alley and South Centre Street. Today, Church Alley is Howard Avenue. Many people who came to Pottsville to develop the coal lands stayed at this famous hotel. It was razed in 1956.

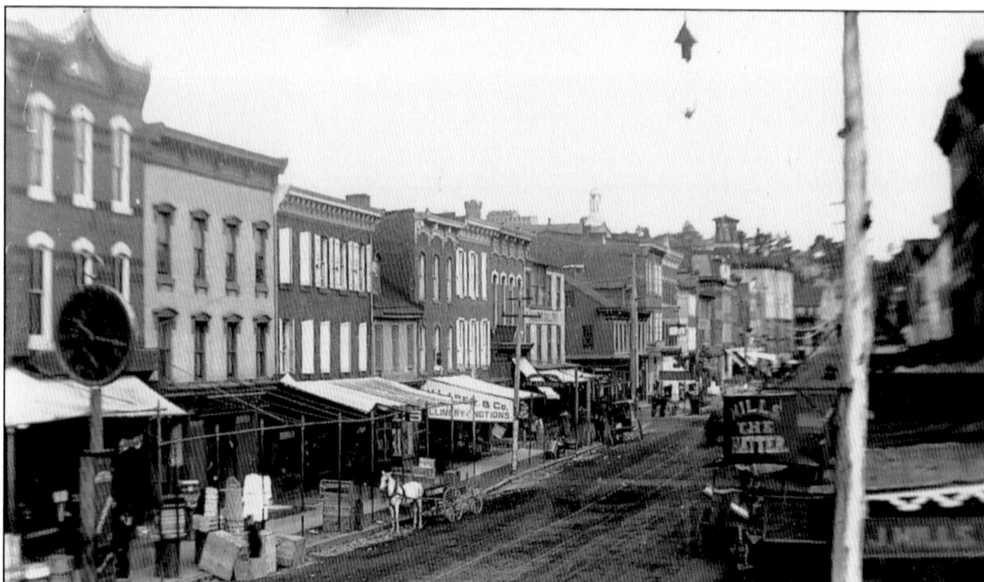

This view of Centre Street looks north from East Norwegian Street at 10:16 a.m., according to Mortimer's clock on the left. To the right hangs a sign reading, "Mills, the Hatter."

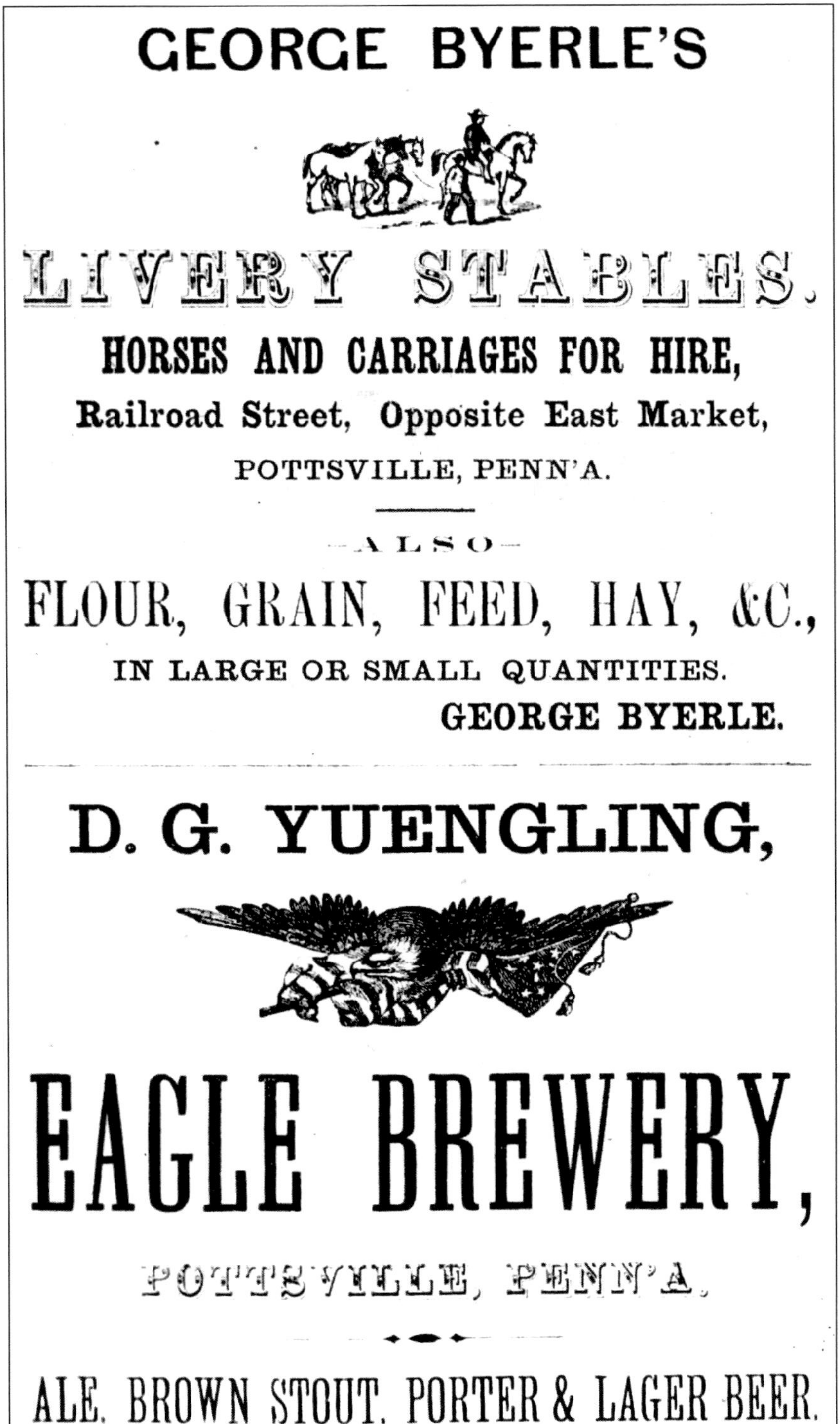

George Byerle had two livery stables in Pottsville, and both burned down. This advertisement is for the second one, located at East Market and Railroad Streets. The D.G. Yuengling and Son Brewery was located at Fifth and Mahantongo Streets when it was built in 1829. It is still there.

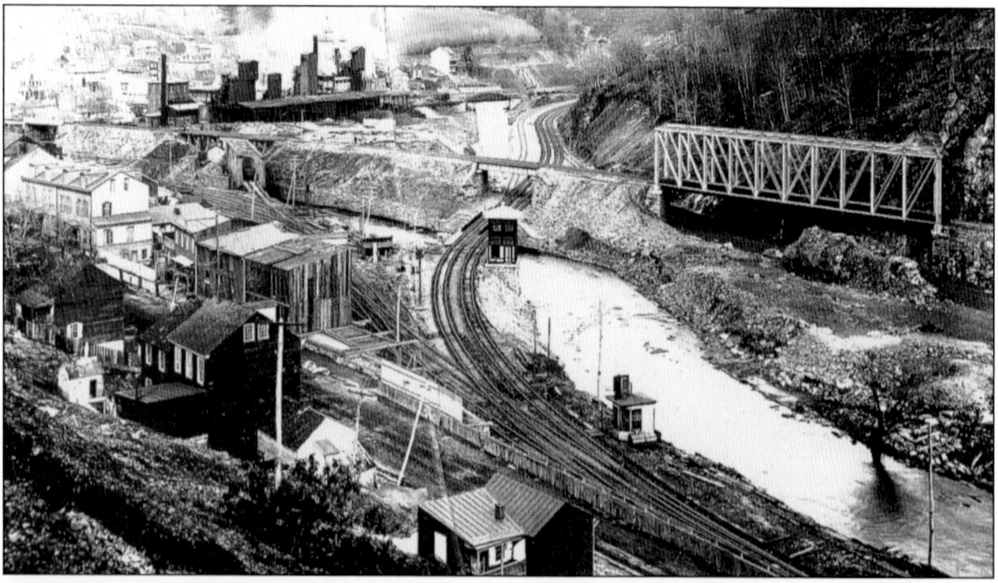

The tracks of the Philadelphia & Reading are in the foreground. The tracks on the left run into Pottsville. The other tracks cross over the Schuylkill River and go farther up the Schuylkill Valley. The Pennsylvania Railroad bridge is on the right, and the train on its way into Pottsville passes the Atkins Brothers furnace.

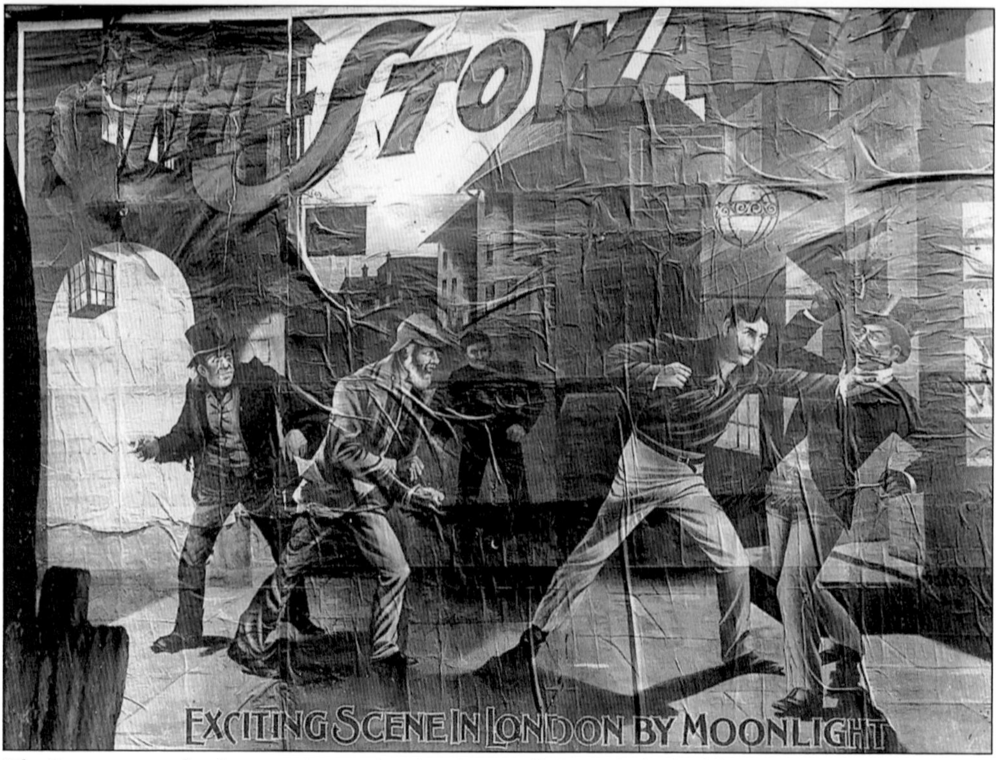

The Stowaway is the feature play at the Academy of Music. It looks like it was an exciting show. It started on August 30 and played for one week. "Paster" Dewald was the man who put up the signs for the shows.

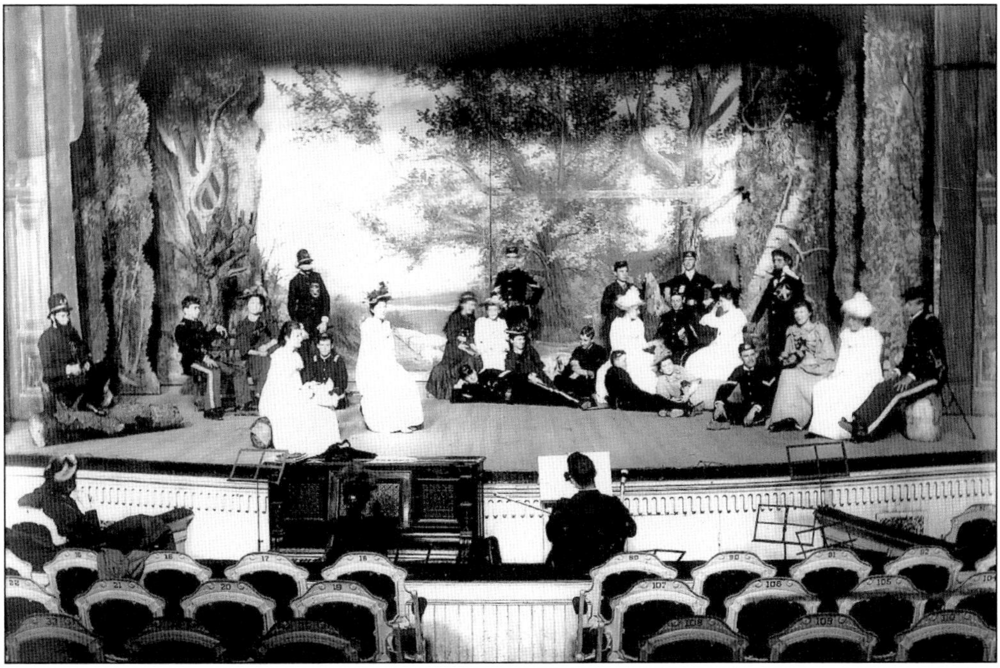

This is one of the few surviving pictures of a show at the Academy of Music. It was Pottsville's most famous showplace. It flourished from 1876 until 1914, when it was destroyed by fire. Its site is now a parking lot.

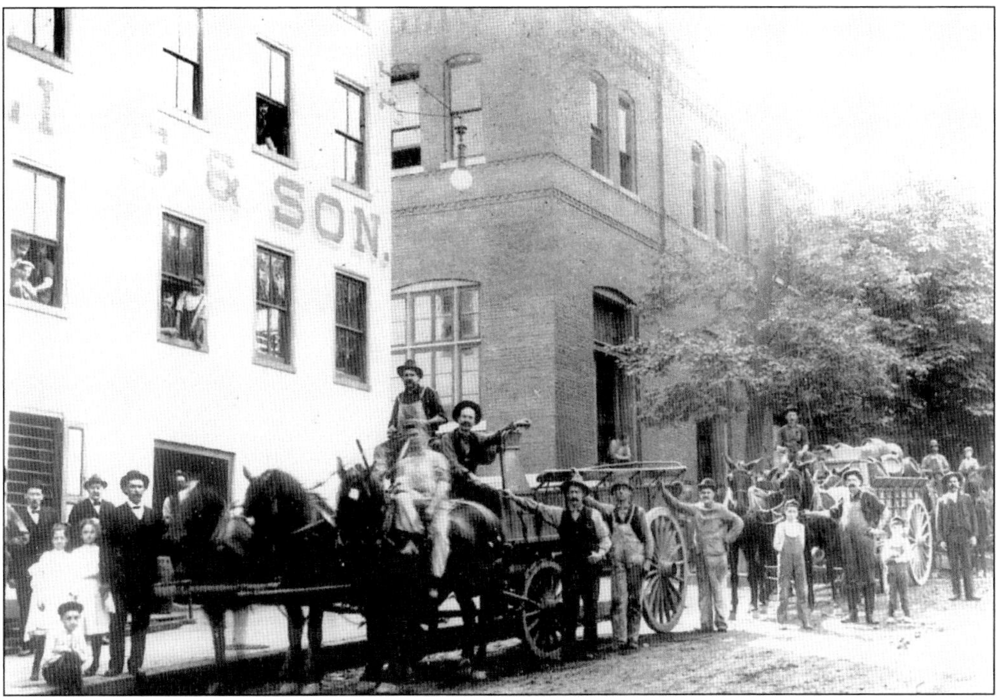

It must have been family day at the D.G. Yuengling and Son Brewery, at Fifth and Mahantongo Streets, when everyone posed for this image. Notice the kids in the windows on the second floor and the man riding sidesaddle on the horse.

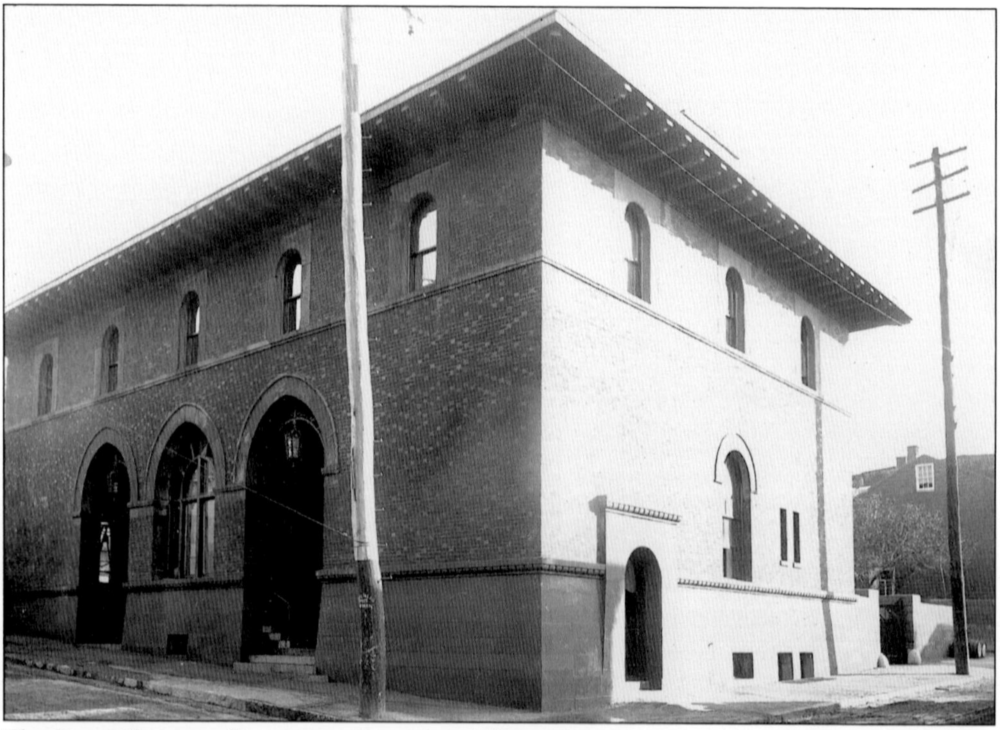

The Pottsville post office was at Second and West Norwegian Streets in 1900. This image is dated April 18, 1899. Notice the dirt streets.

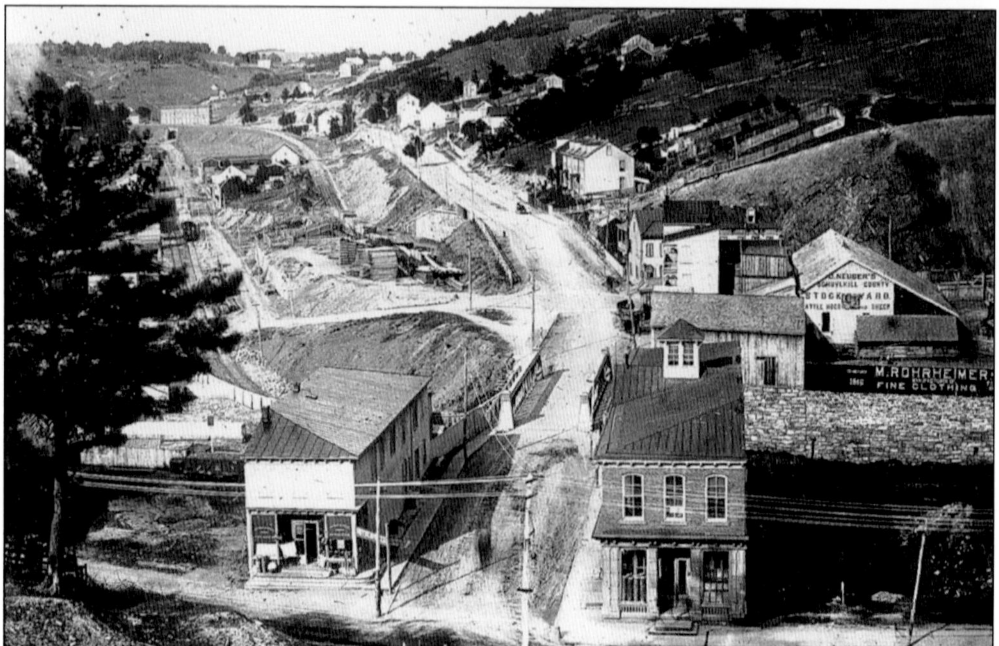

This photograph of North Centre and Nichols Streets was taken from North Second Street. G. Neuser's stockyard is on the right. North Coal Street crosses Nichols Street in the middle of the picture. The Goodwill Fire Company now stands at the corner where two poles can be seen.

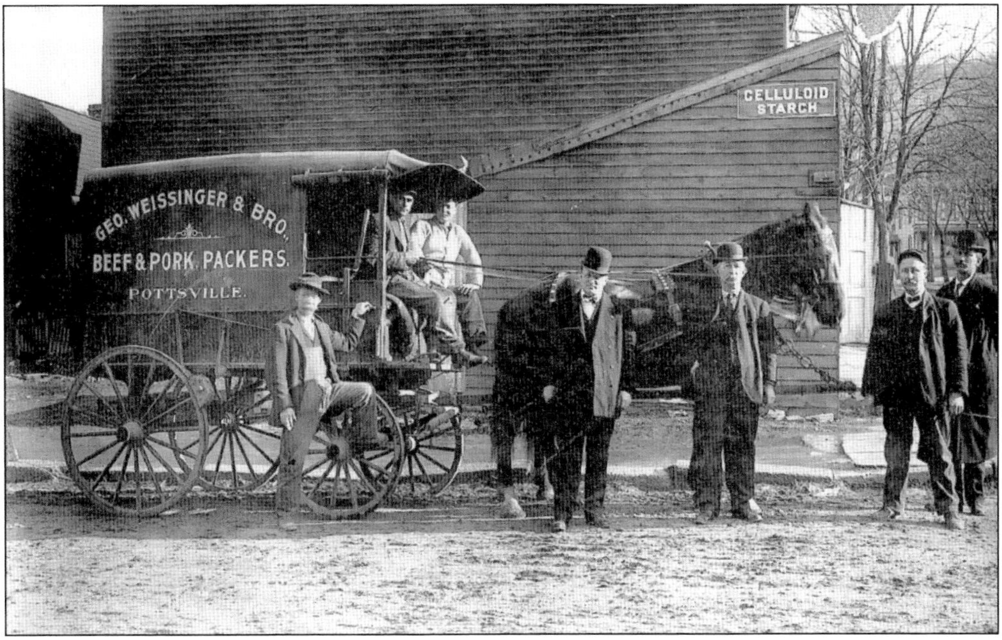

For many years, one of the leading businesses in the slaughtering, packing, and shipping of cattle in Pottsville was George Weissinger and Brothers. The business was carried on after George Weissinger's death by his sons George and Harry. The company was located in the Fishbach section of Pottsville.

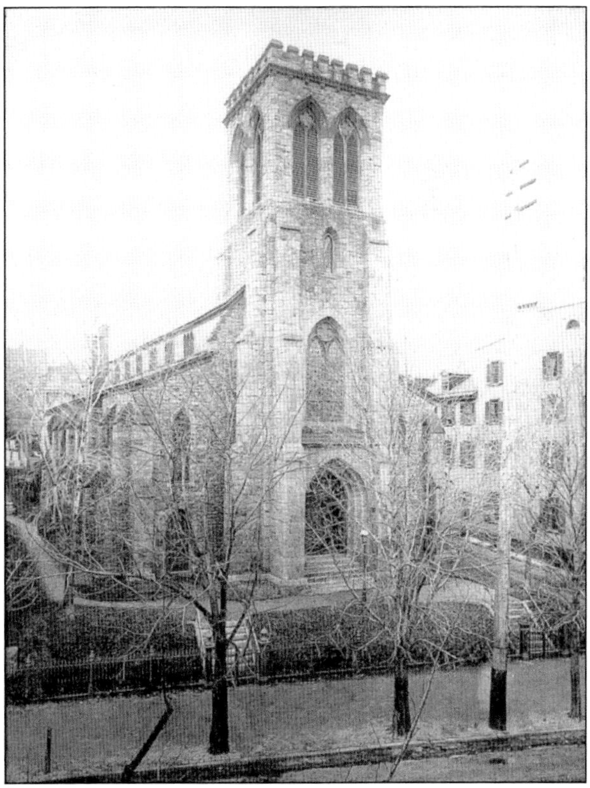

Trinity Episcopal Church is Pottsville's oldest church. It was constructed in 1830. This turn-of-the-century image shows a tree-lined street at the corner of Howard Avenue and South Centre Street. Notice the Penn Hall Hotel on the right.

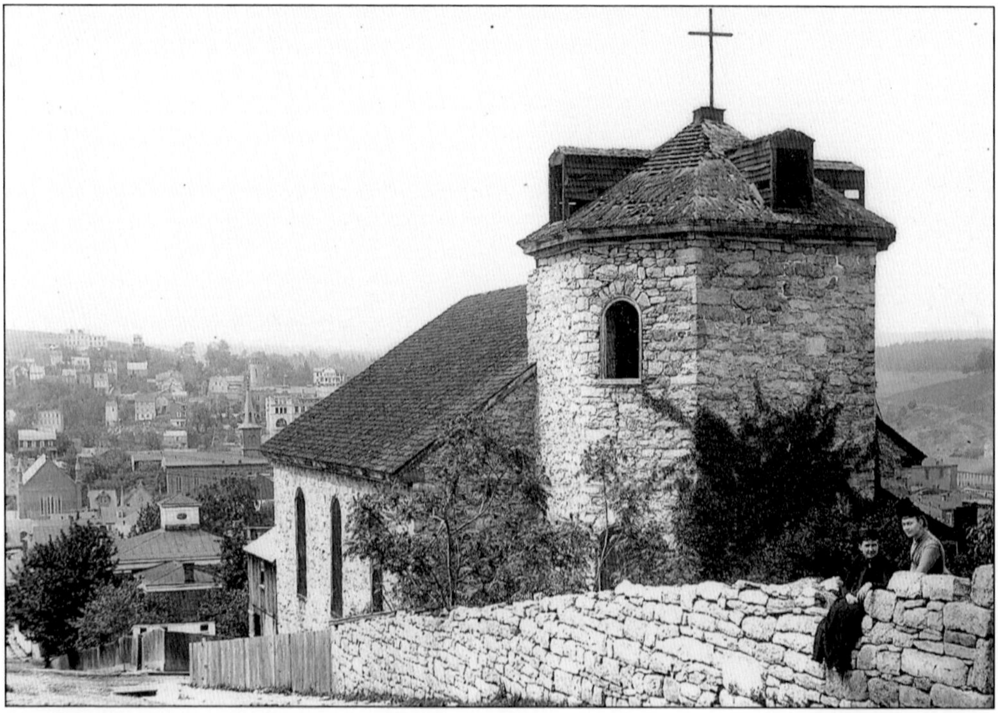

This is a rear view of the German Catholic church at Fourth Street and Howard Avenue. Built in 1842, it was the first church of St. John the Baptist and was built using the stones from Sharp Mountain. The Italian-American Church purchased it in 1907, when the German Catholics built a new church at 10th and Mahantongo Streets. The stone fence is no longer there.

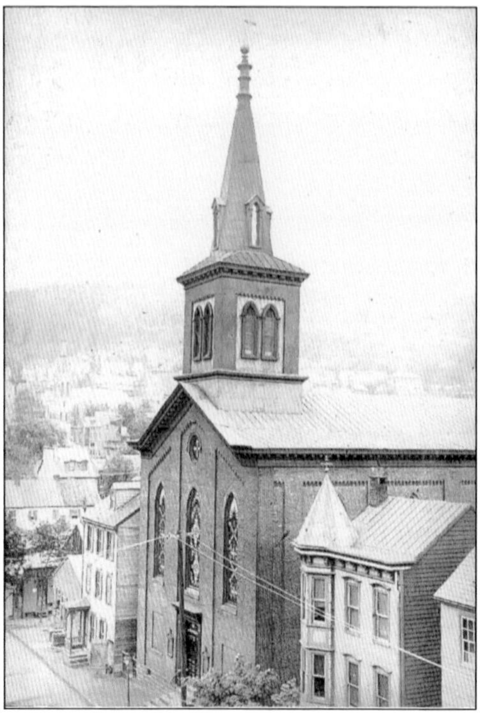

The English Lutheran church was established on May 16, 1847. The first church was a frame structure that was built at the corner of North Third and West Arch Streets. The church in this image was built in 1868 and was used by the congregation until 1912.

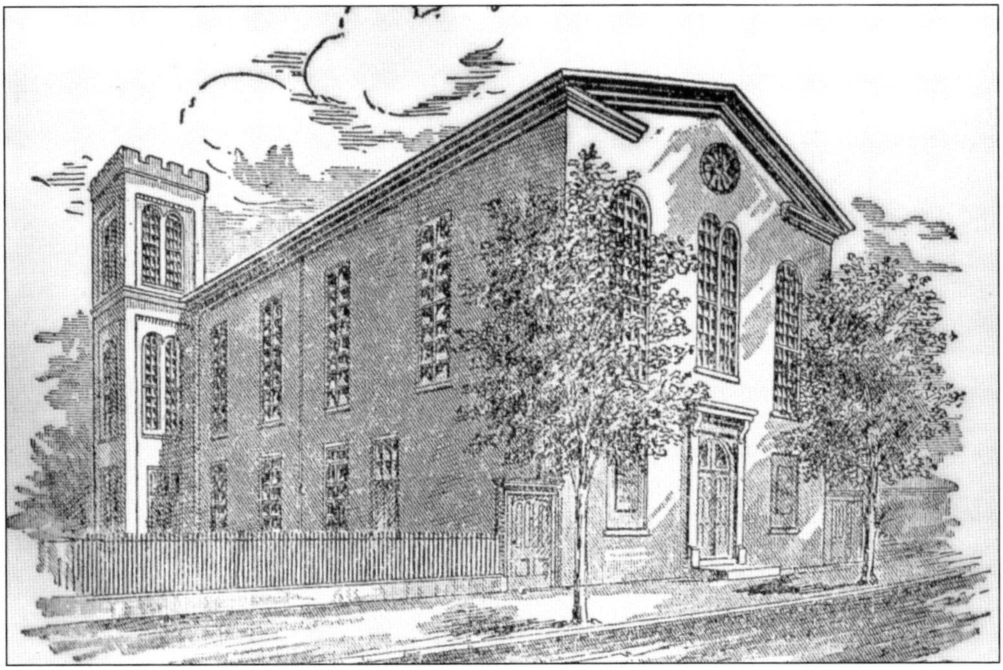

This is an artist's sketch of the Methodist church that was planned to be built on North Second Street between West Market and West Arch Streets. The church was not built there but was eventually erected in 1904 on the southeast corner of Garfield Square, at West Market and Fourth Streets.

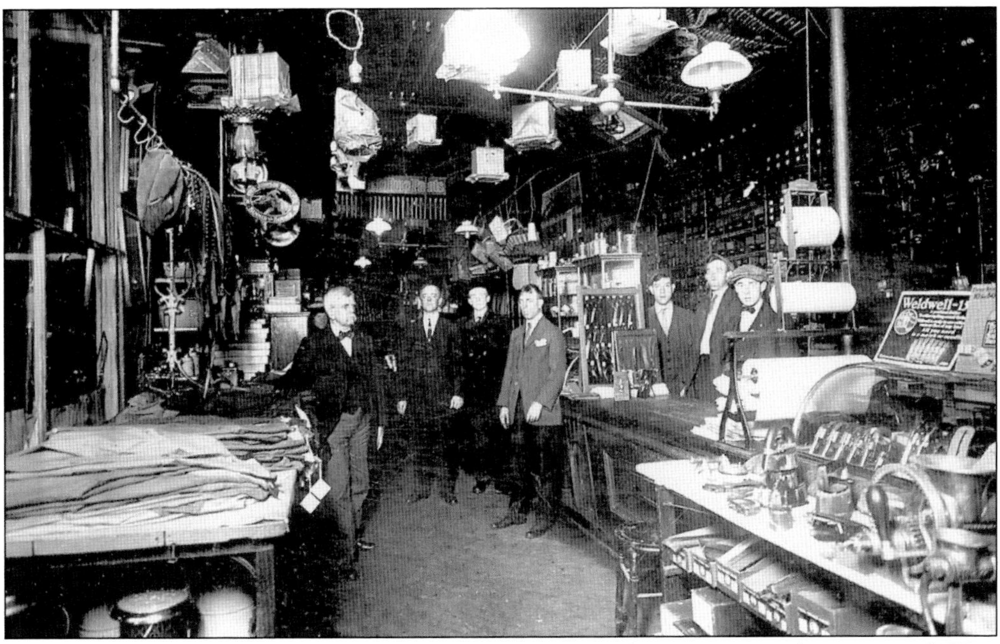

L.C. Thompson's hardware store was located at the northwest corner of Centre and West Market Streets. It supplied oils, paints, glass, cement, plaster, and many other products to its customers. Thompson is the man on the left in this image. In 1924, he sold the store to the Schuylkill Trust Company so that the bank could erect its new building at that location.

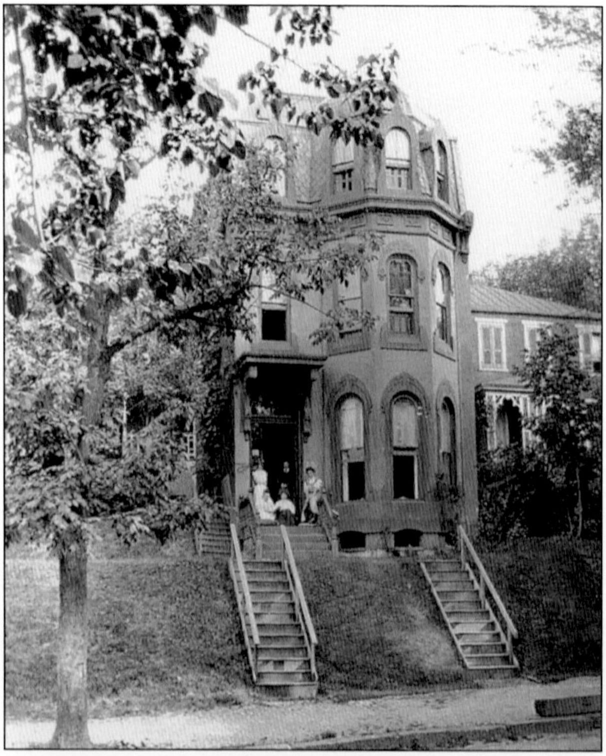

Charles H. Dengler's mansion was at 705 Mahantongo Street at the beginning of the 20th century. Dengler was a bank examiner. His home was typical of the Victorian homes on Mahantongo Street. The house does not exist anymore, but the steps can still be seen.

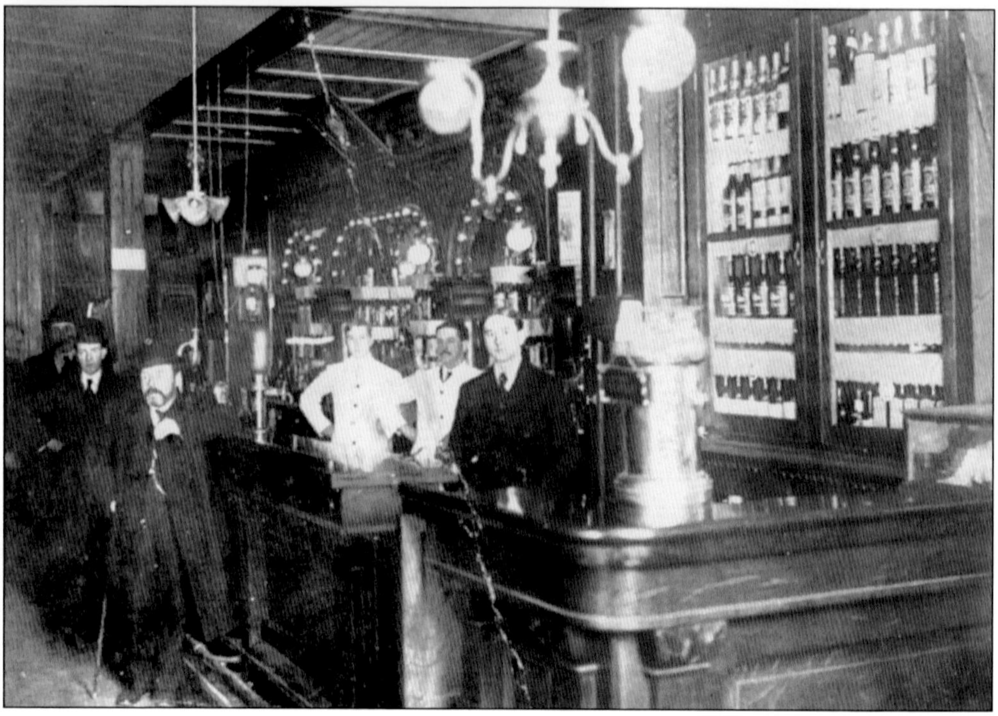

Charles F. Keeny's Café was located at 23 South Centre Street in Pottsville. It was typical of the 44 saloons listed in the Pottsville city directory of 1900.

Two

DOWNTOWN SCENES

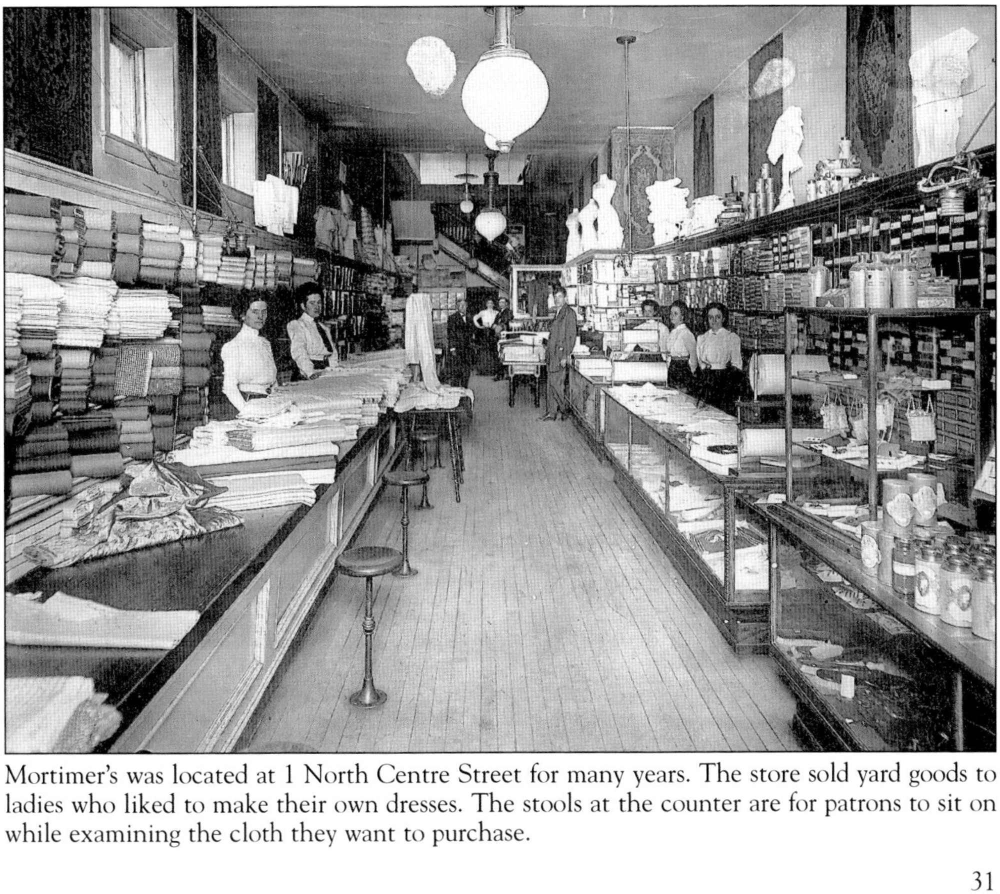

Mortimer's was located at 1 North Centre Street for many years. The store sold yard goods to ladies who liked to make their own dresses. The stools at the counter are for patrons to sit on while examining the cloth they want to purchase.

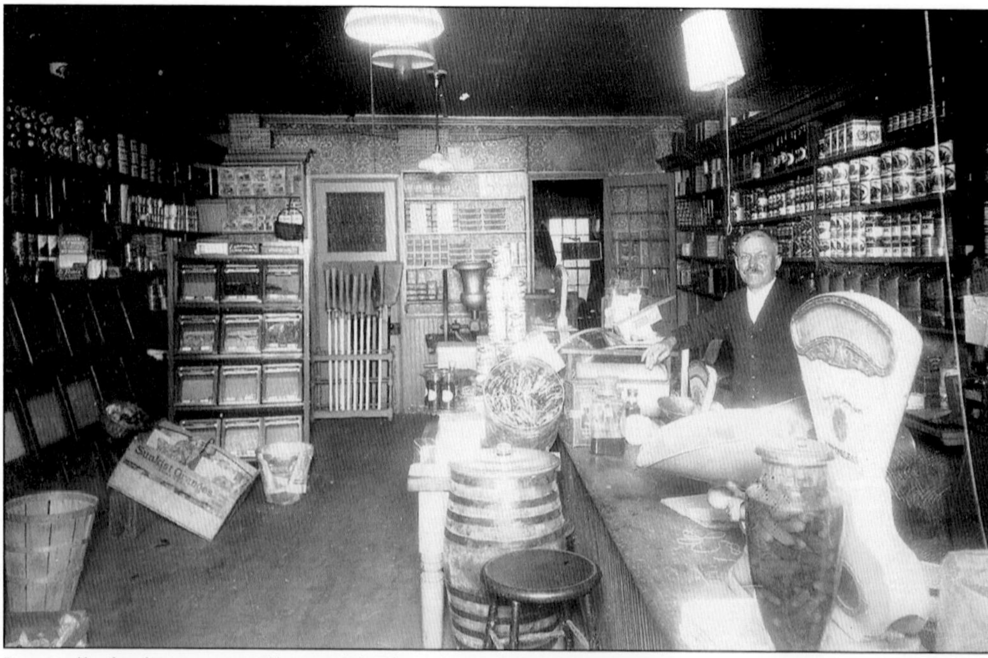

Pottsville had many small, neighborhood grocery stores before supermarkets were invented. This is Elmer Schlaseman's store, on North Centre Street, in 1920. The busy housewife would write a note for the grocer and send her children to the store when she needed something in a hurry.

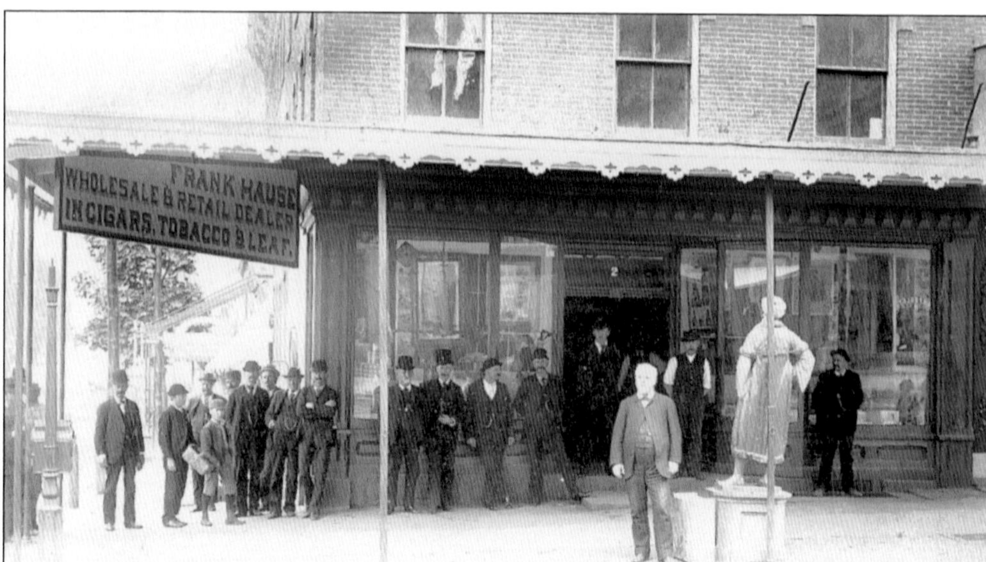

Frank Hause's tobacco store was located at the southeast corner of Centre and Norwegian Streets. Notice the cigar store Indian. Cigars were manufactured on the third floor of the building.

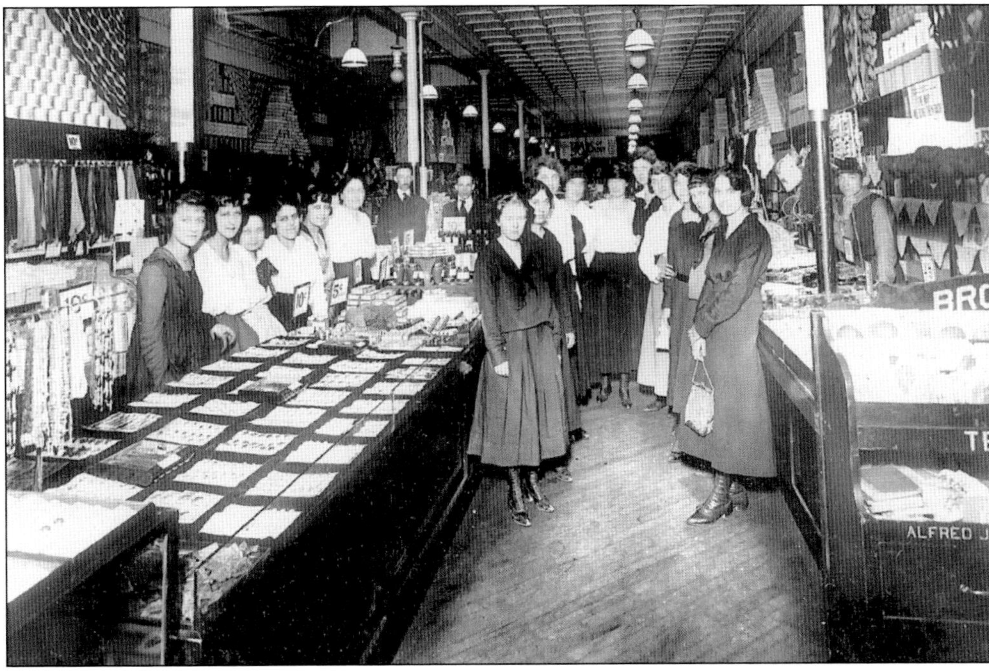

Eighteen people worked at the Kresge's store on North Centre Street in 1915. S.S. Kresge, who owned the chain of stores, was born in Pennsylvania in 1887. The S.S. Kresge Company is now the Kmart Corporation.

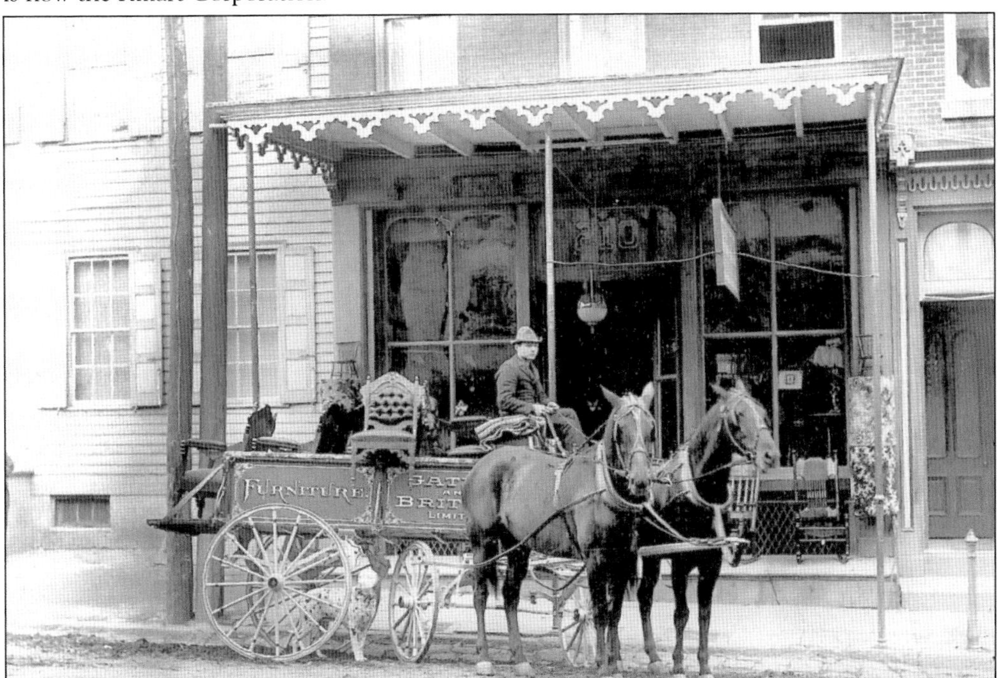

This driver with his team is in no hurry to pull away from the curb with his turn-of-the-century furniture from Gately and Britton Furniture, at 210 West Market Street. The Dalmatian under the wagon turned slightly when the photograph was taken.

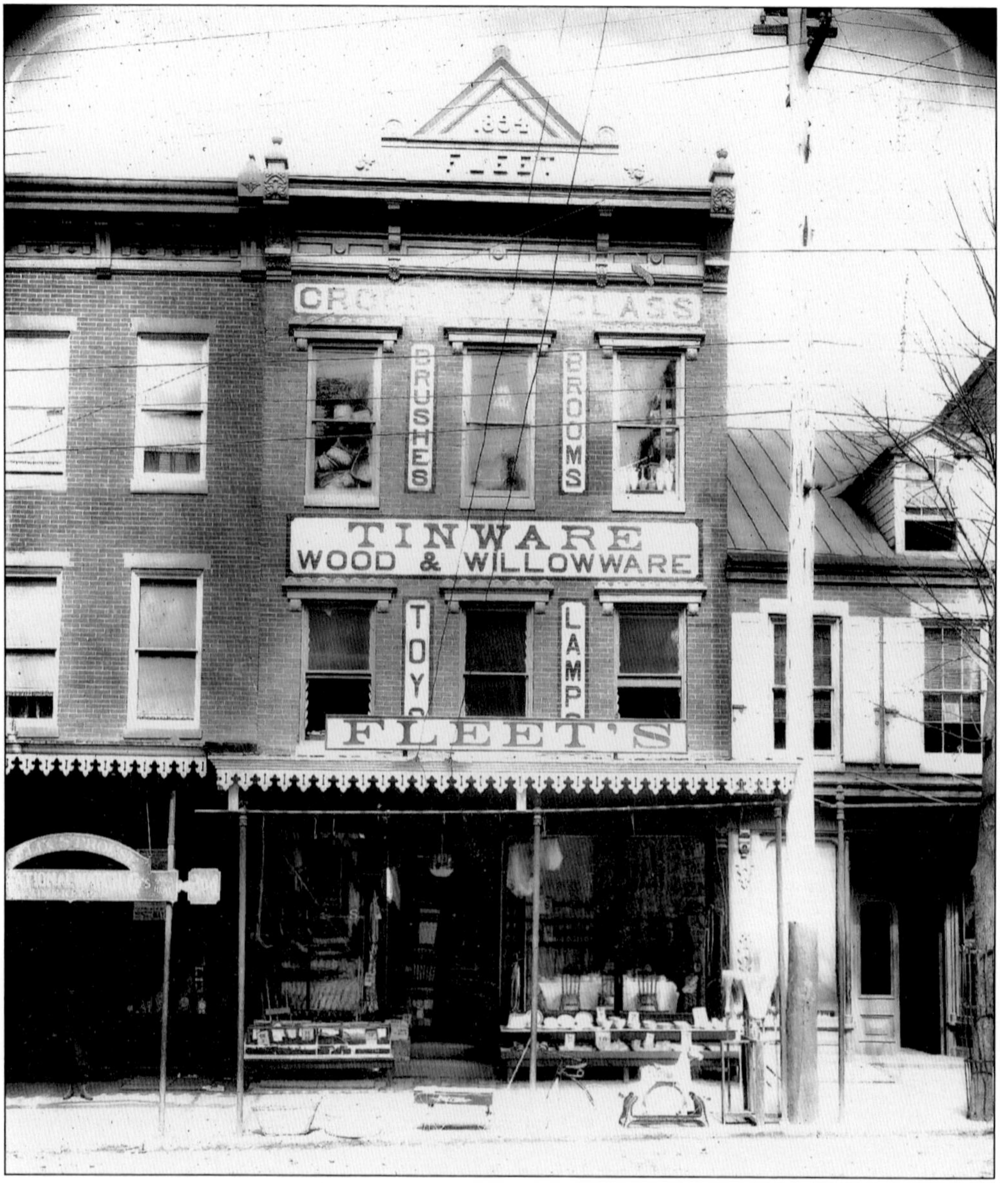

It looks like there is a sidewalk sale at Jesse Fleet's variety store, at 10 South Centre Street. Notice the variety of merchandise on the signs on the front of the store. Most stores on Centre Street in the early part of the century had roofs that extended over the sidewalk to protect people from rainy days.

The D.L. Esterly Sons hardware store was on Centre Street. A sign on the top of the store reads, "New Esterly Building." The Prudential Insurance Company offices were on the second floor.

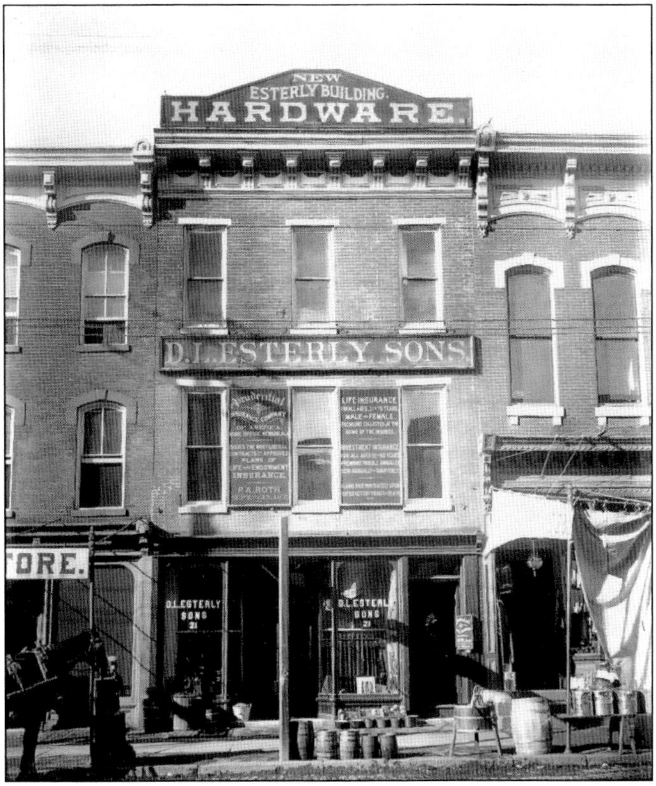

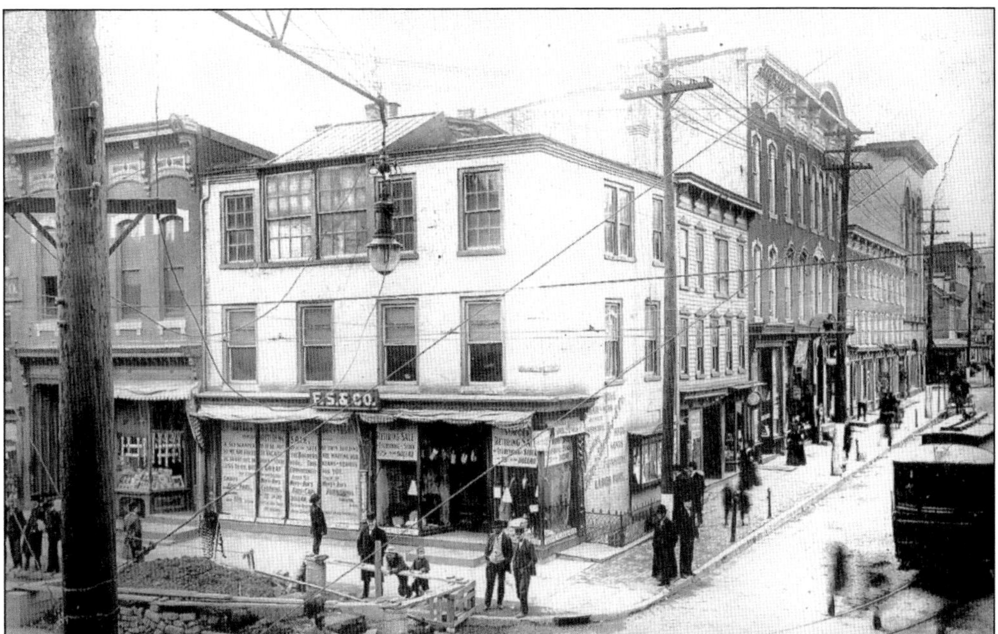

The firm of Fitch, Sheafer and Company, at Centre and West Market Streets, was sold on January 14, 1909, to the Thompson family. Notice the going-out-of-business signs in the windows of the three-story building. The Thompson Building was constructed on the site of the store.

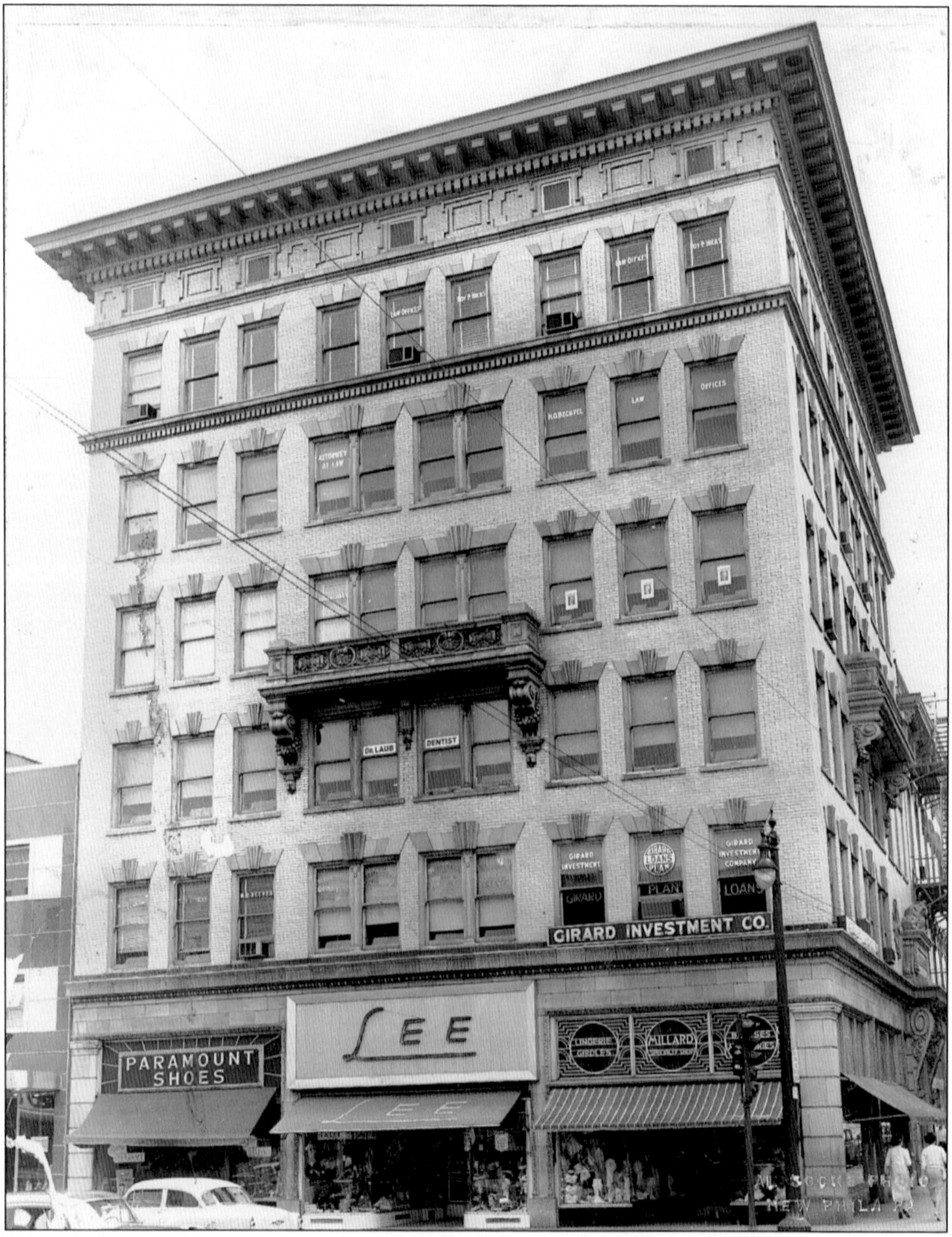

Pottsville's first skyscraper was the six-story Thompson Building, erected in 1909 at the southwest corner of North Centre and West Market Streets. Three popular stores faced North Centre Street: Paramount Shoes, the Lee shop, and the Millard lingerie store.

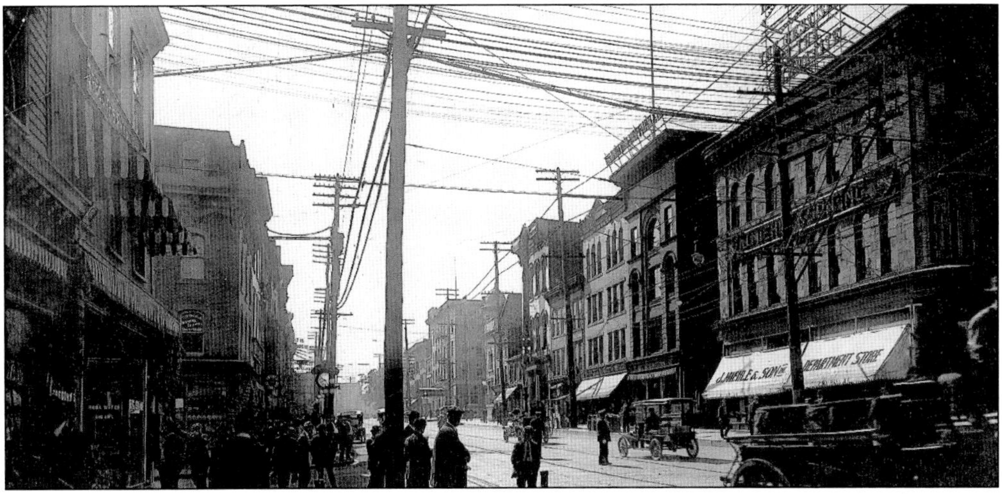

These stores stood on the west side of South Centre Street between Norwegian and Mahantongo Streets before the Great Pottsville Fire destroyed the block on December 17, 1914. Pottsville firemen fought gallantly against the blaze, but freezing weather prevented them from getting water to extinguish the flaming buildings.

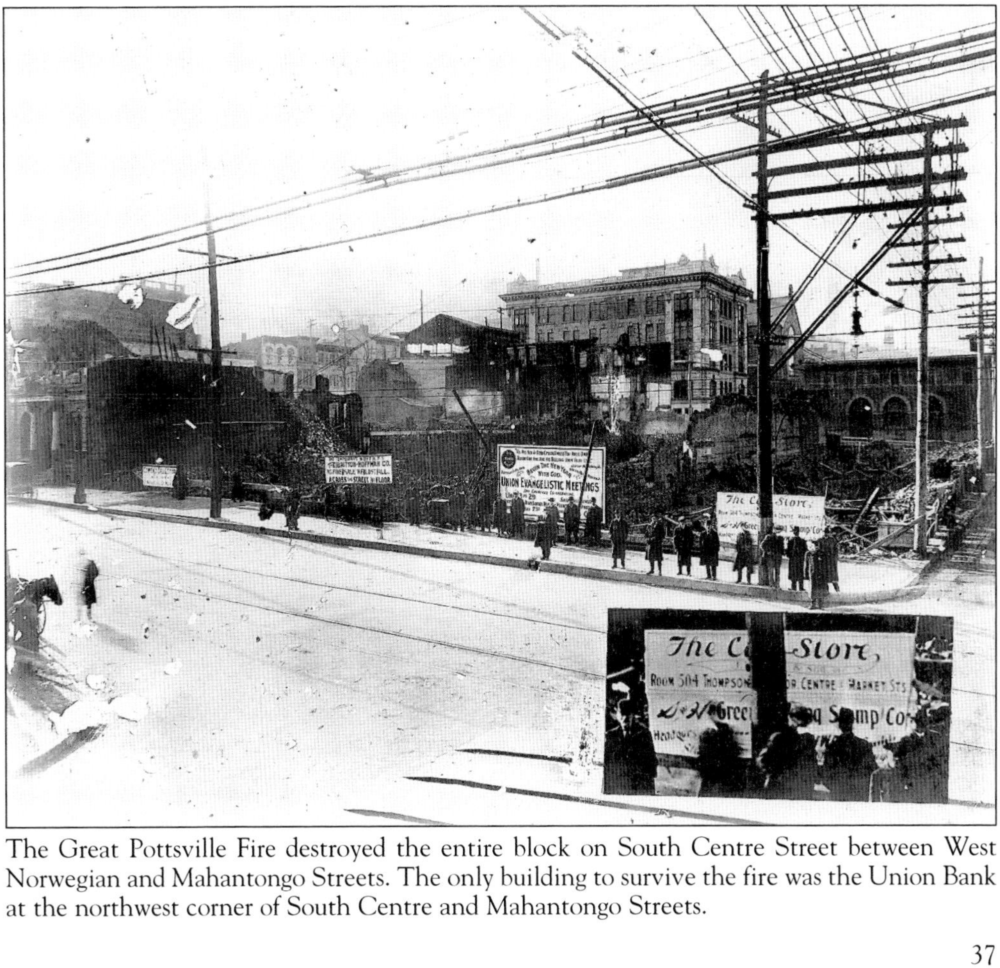

The Great Pottsville Fire destroyed the entire block on South Centre Street between West Norwegian and Mahantongo Streets. The only building to survive the fire was the Union Bank at the northwest corner of South Centre and Mahantongo Streets.

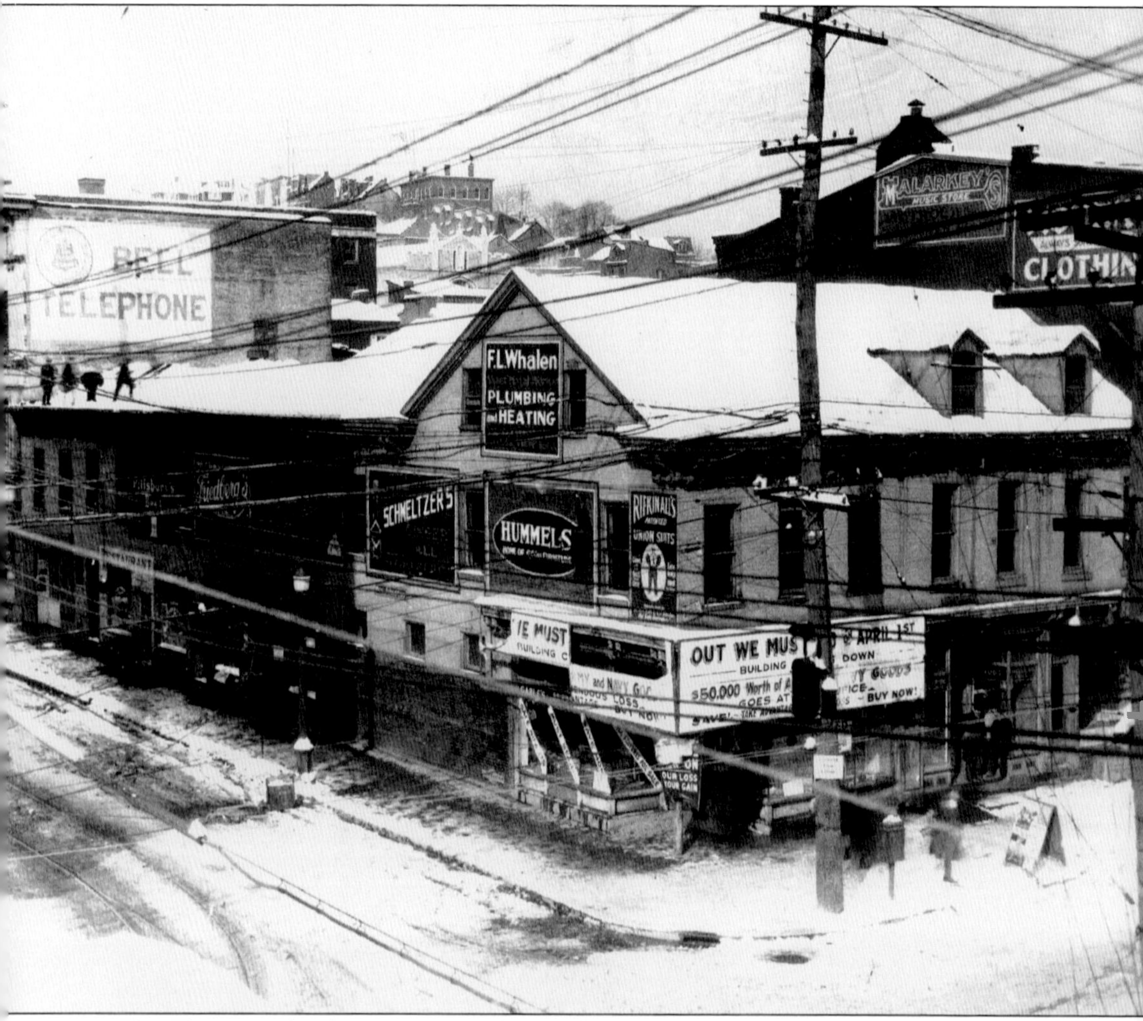

The Thompson hardware store, at the northwest corner of North Centre and West Market Streets, was sold in 1924 to the Schuylkill Trust Company. Some Pottsville stores took advantage of the store closing by advertising on it. Hummel's (a furniture store) and Malarkey's (a music store) are among the advertisers.

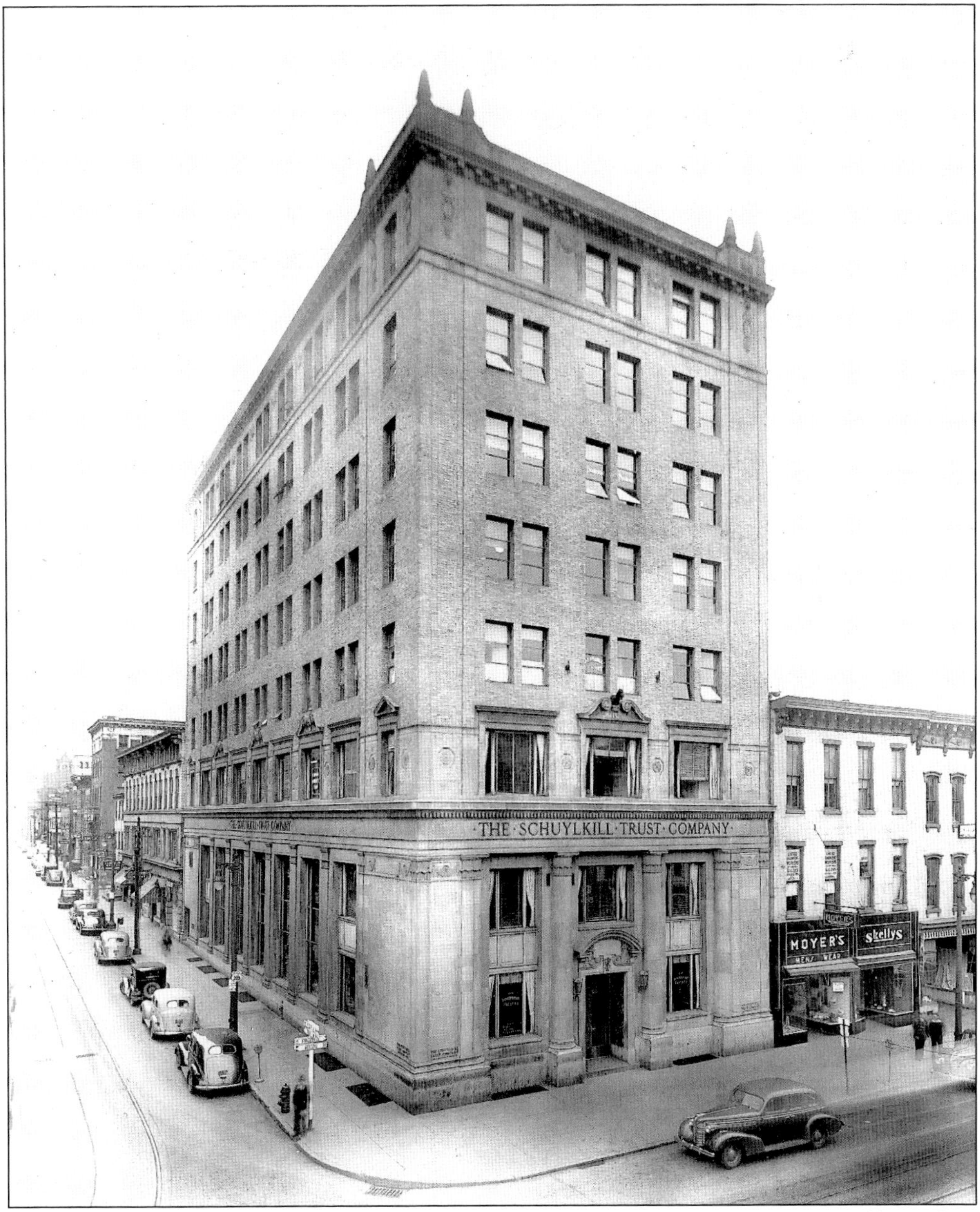

The Schuylkill Trust Company joined the Thompson Building as one of Pottsville's tallest buildings in 1924. Moyer's and Skelly's have been torn down, and the First Union Bank uses that space for its drive-through window.

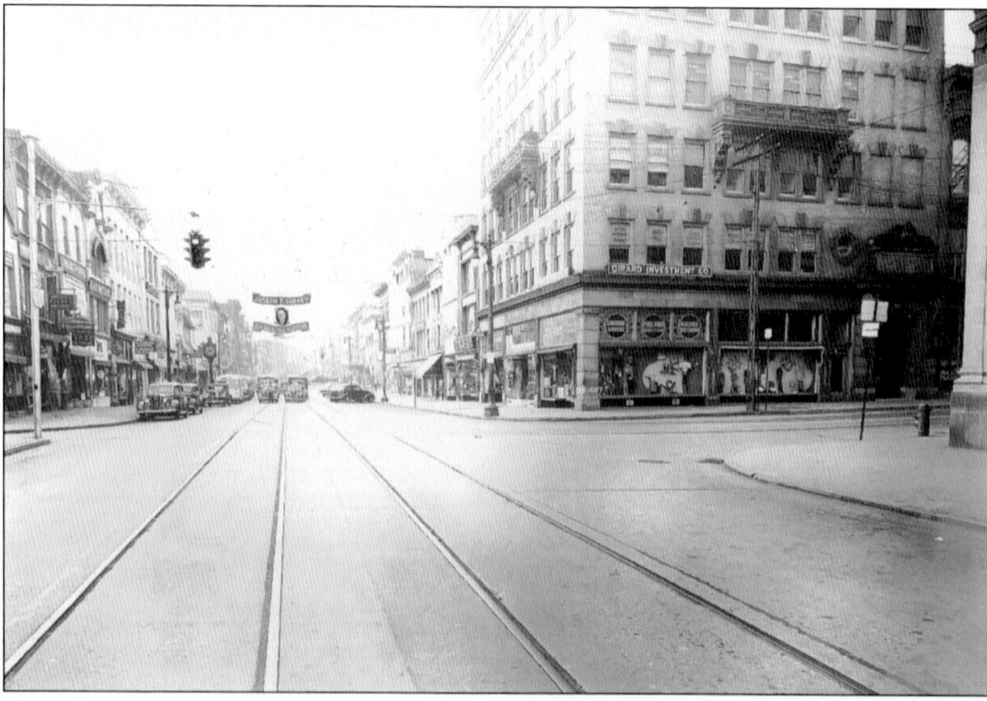

This 1940 view looks south on Centre Street near the corner of West Market Street. The Thompson Building is on the right. The trolley tracks are still on Centre Street even though the trolley was shut down in 1932.

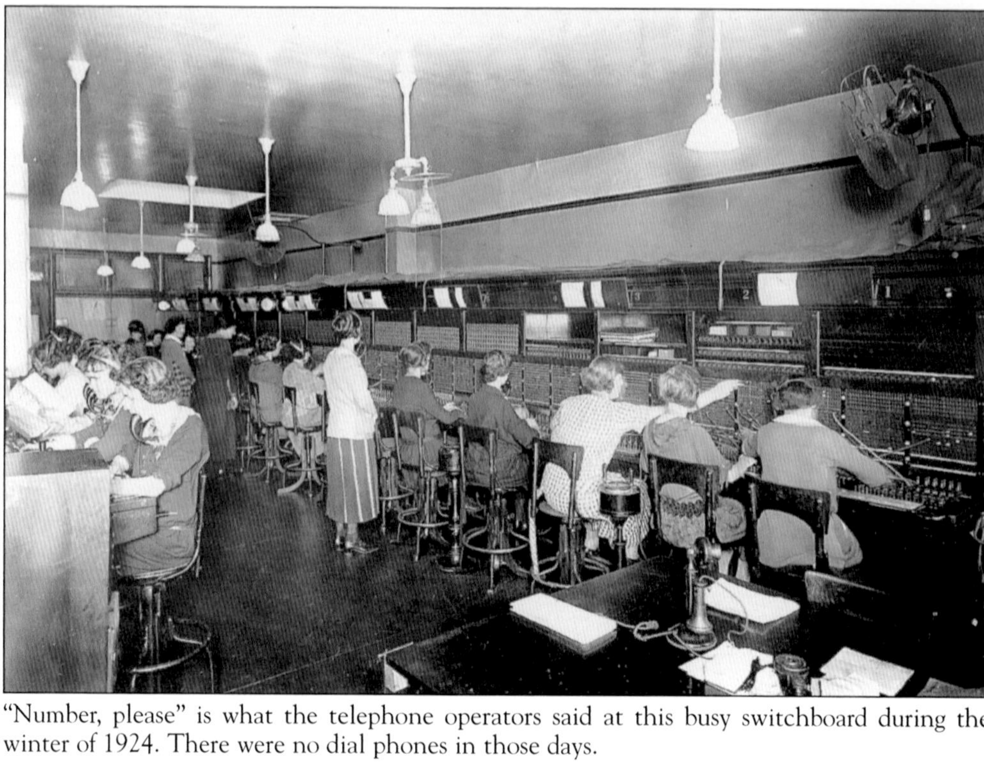

"Number, please" is what the telephone operators said at this busy switchboard during the winter of 1924. There were no dial phones in those days.

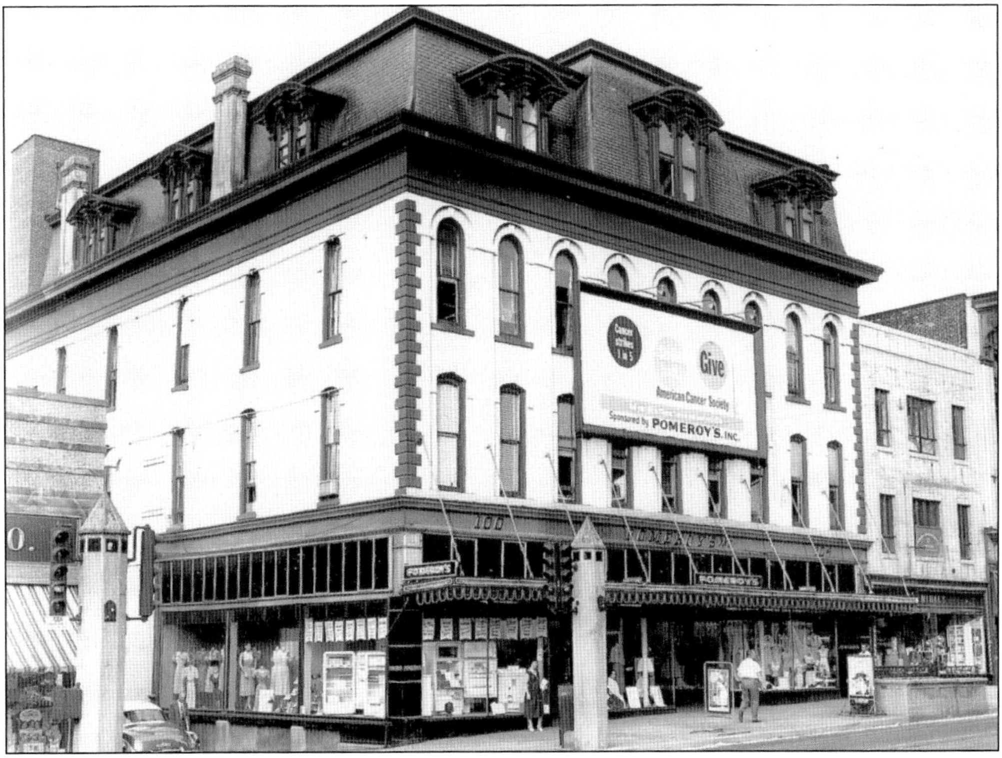

Pomeroy's, at 100 South Centre Street, was the major store in Pottsville for all the shoppers in Schuylkill County. Both Pomeroy's and Sears moved to the Schuylkill Mall near Frackville in the 1980s.

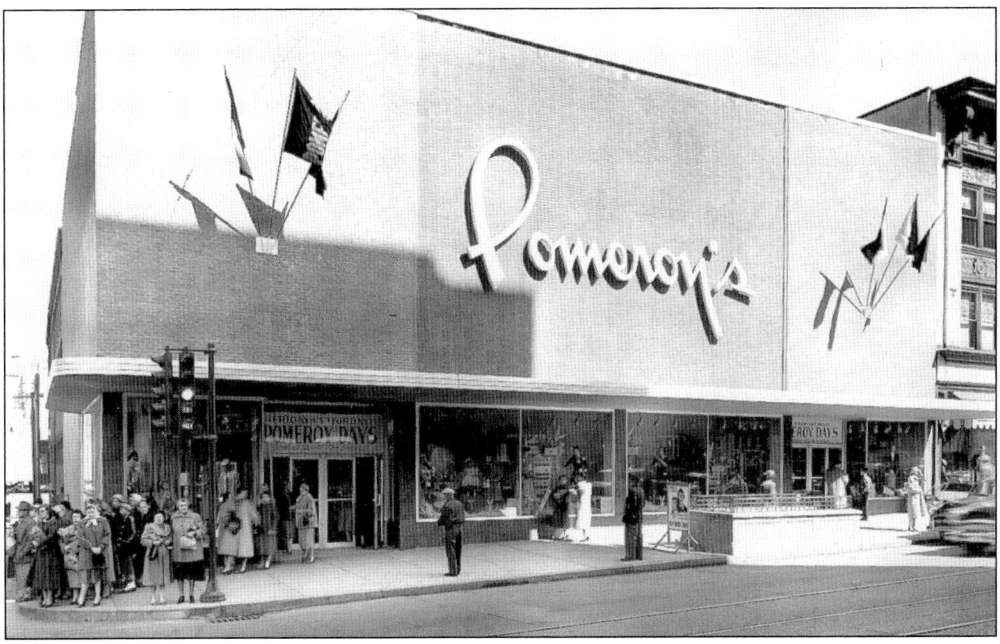

Pomeroy's changed the front of its store during the 1960s. The sign above the doors reads, "Pomeroy Days." After the store moved to the mall, the building was converted into a hotel.

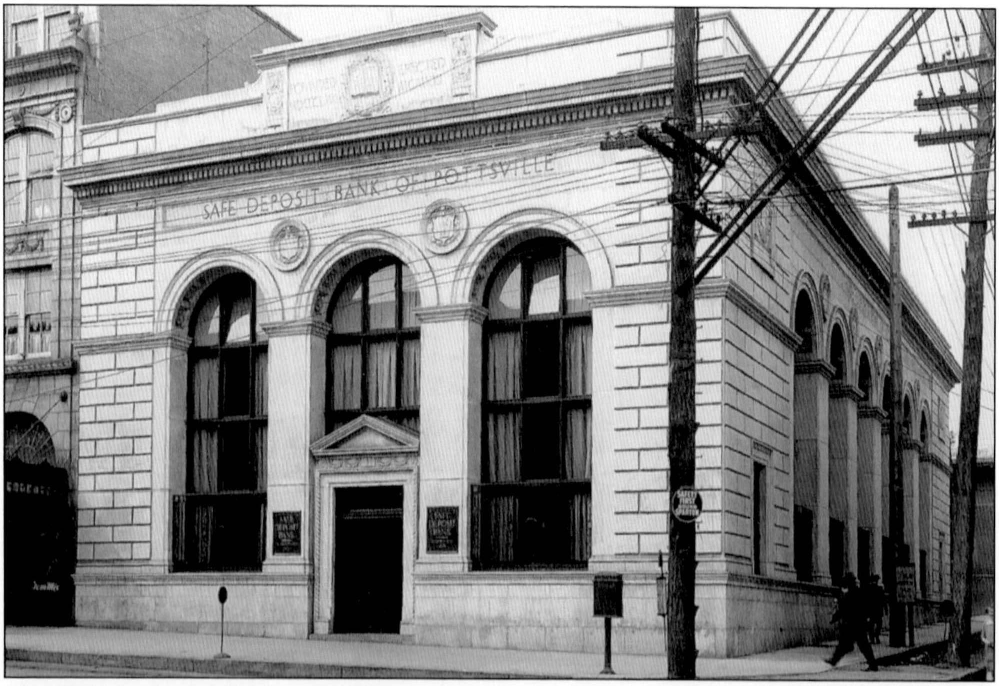

The Safe Deposit Bank of Pottsville was located at the southwest corner of Centre and Norwegian Streets after the Great Pottsville Fire on December 17, 1914. Miehle's department store had been at that location for many years but was destroyed by the fire.

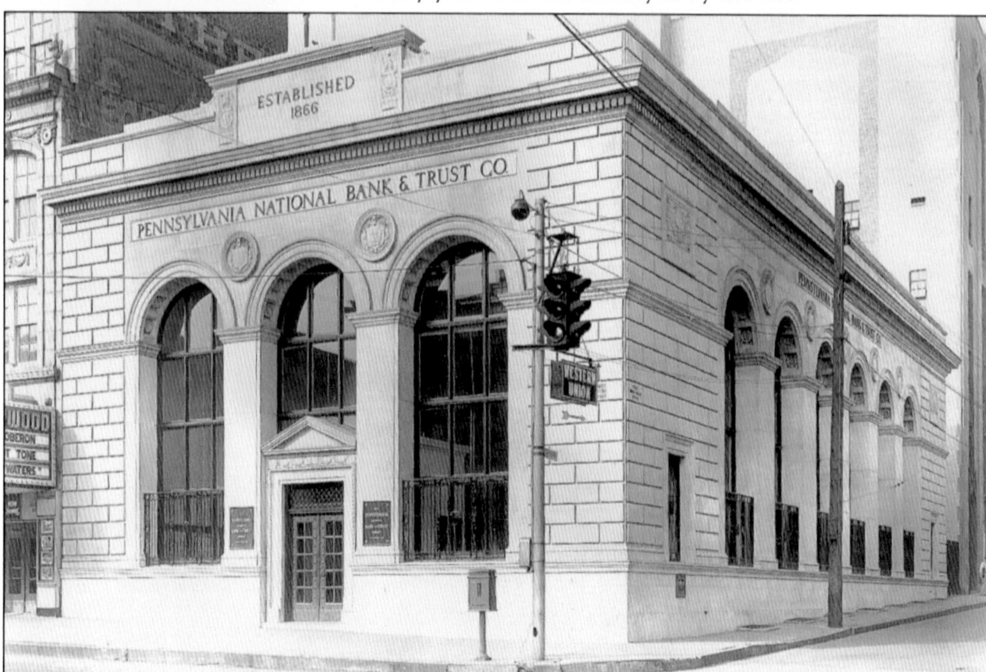

The Pennsylvania National Bank was in the middle of the block on South Centre Street before and after the 1914 fire. When the bank purchased the Safe Deposit Bank, it moved its headquarters to the corner location.

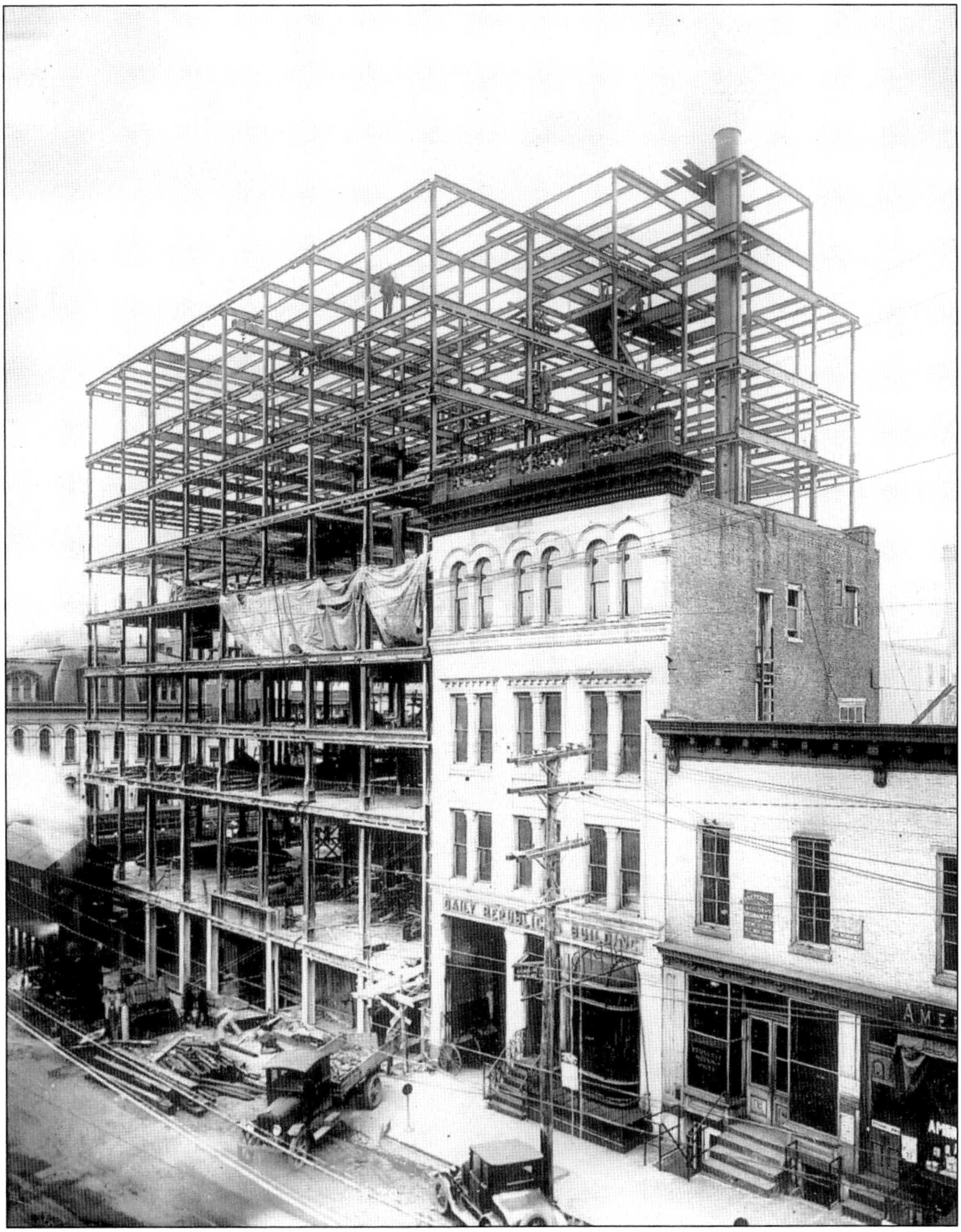

The Necho Allen Hotel was constructed in 1927. In this image, the steel girders are being erected. The Daily Republican Building is next to the hotel. The hotel closed during the 1980s, and the ballroom is now the press room of the newspaper.

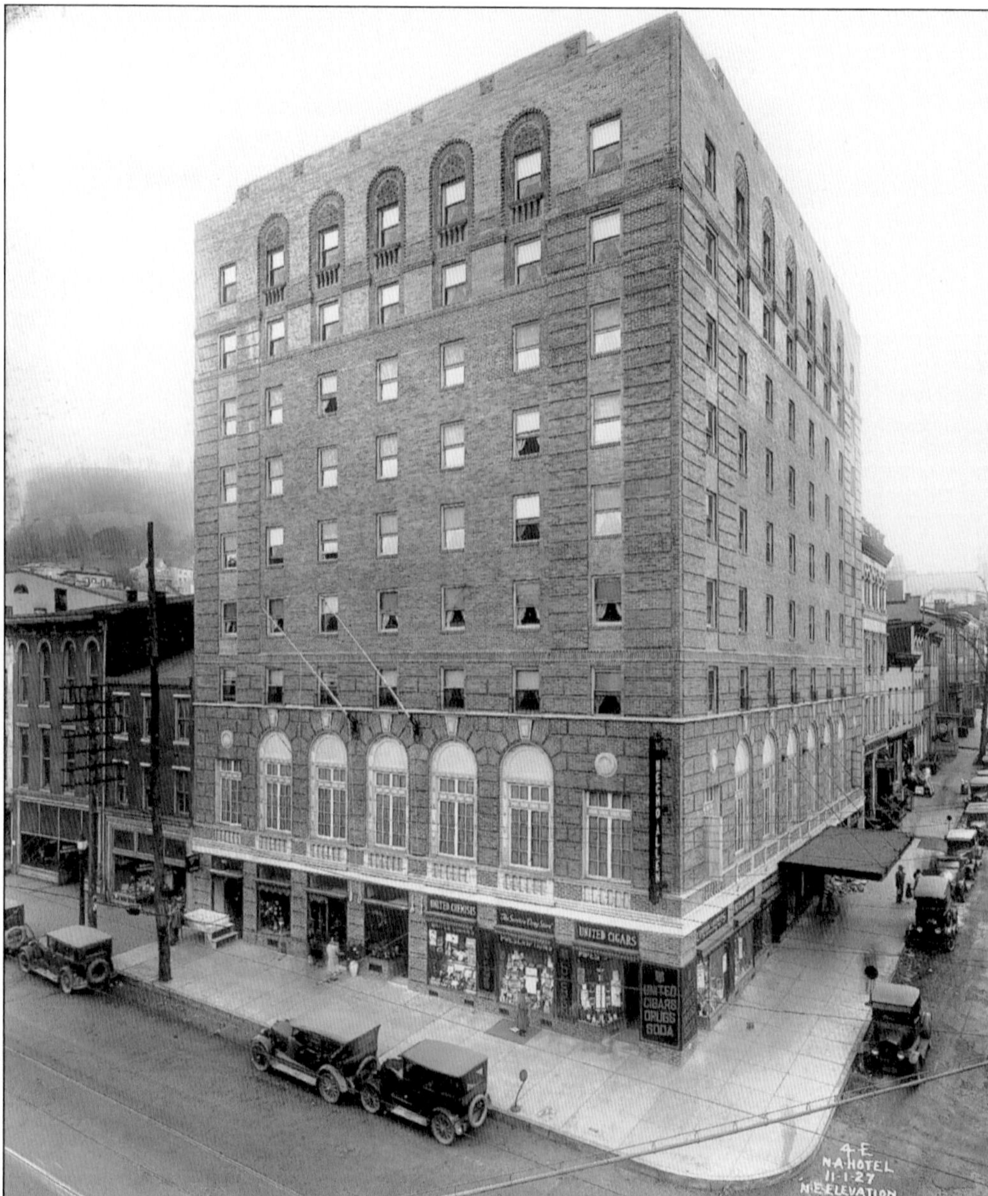

The main entrance to the Necho Allen Hotel faced Mahantongo Street. It was the community center of social activities until it closed. It was named for the legendary Necho Allen, who made the first discovery of anthracite in the county in 1790.

The Alco Restaurant was closed after World War II. It was the most popular restaurant in Pottsville during its heyday and was a favorite place for a cup of coffee before people went home for the night. The Grace Shop bought it and doubled the size of the store.

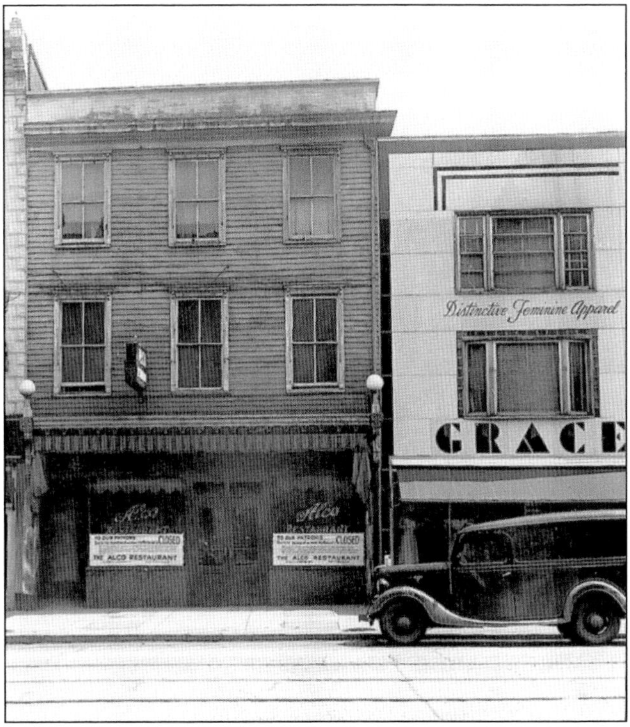

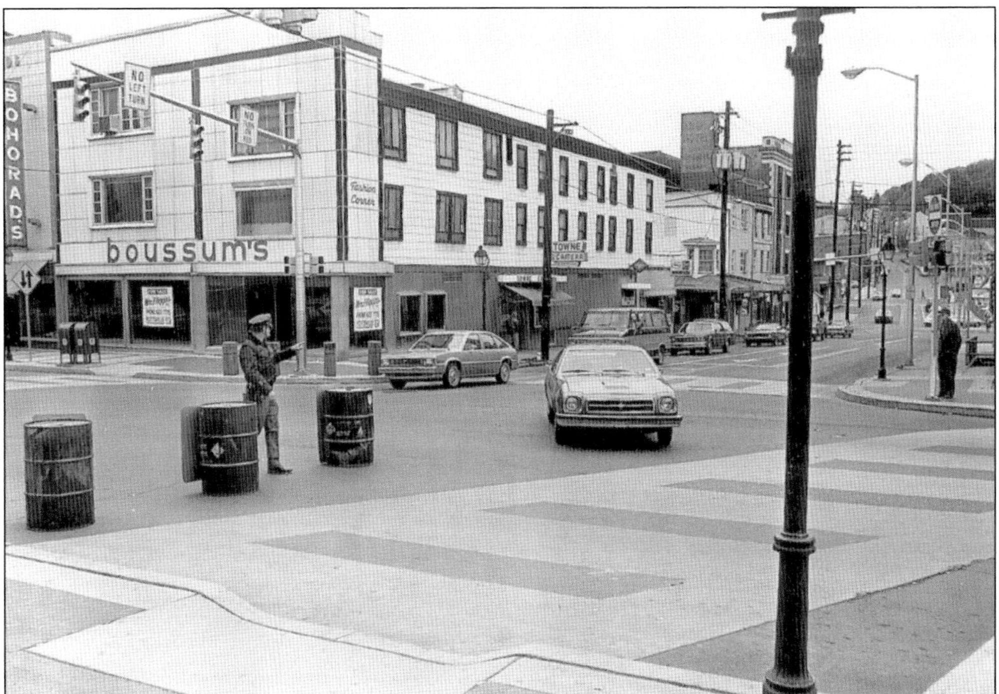

When the Grace Shop closed, Boussum's men's store purchased the building. Notice that Towne Camera was in the basement on the East Norwegian Street side of the building. The police officer is directing traffic coming on to Centre Street from East Norwegian Street.

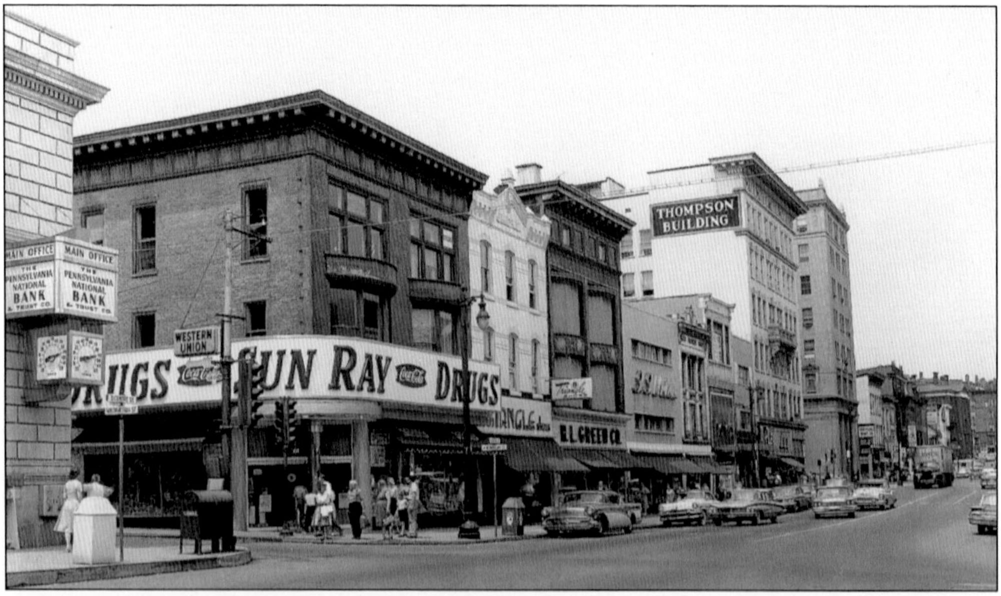

It looks like the two floors above the Sun Ray drugstore are empty in this image. The Triangle shoe store and the H.L. Green Company five-and-dime store were nearby. The Community Bank is situated today where the three stores were during the 1960s.

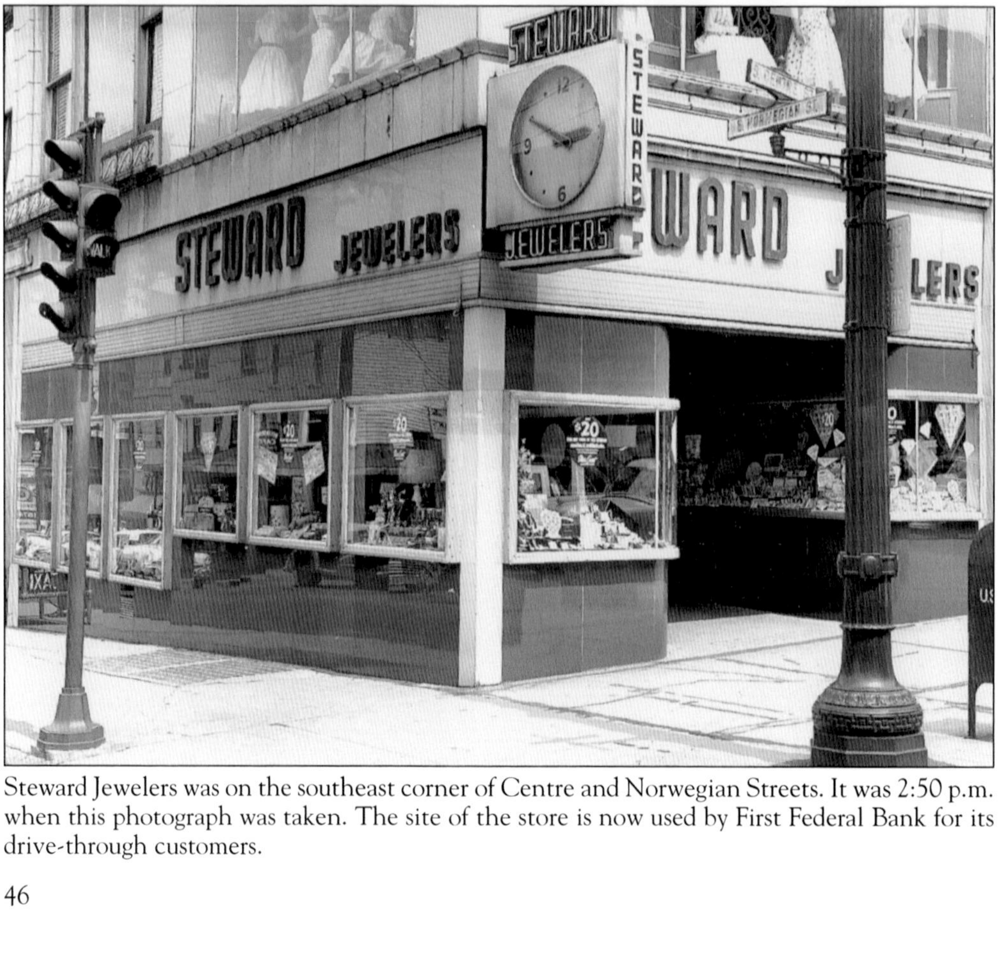

Steward Jewelers was on the southeast corner of Centre and Norwegian Streets. It was 2:50 p.m. when this photograph was taken. The site of the store is now used by First Federal Bank for its drive-through customers.

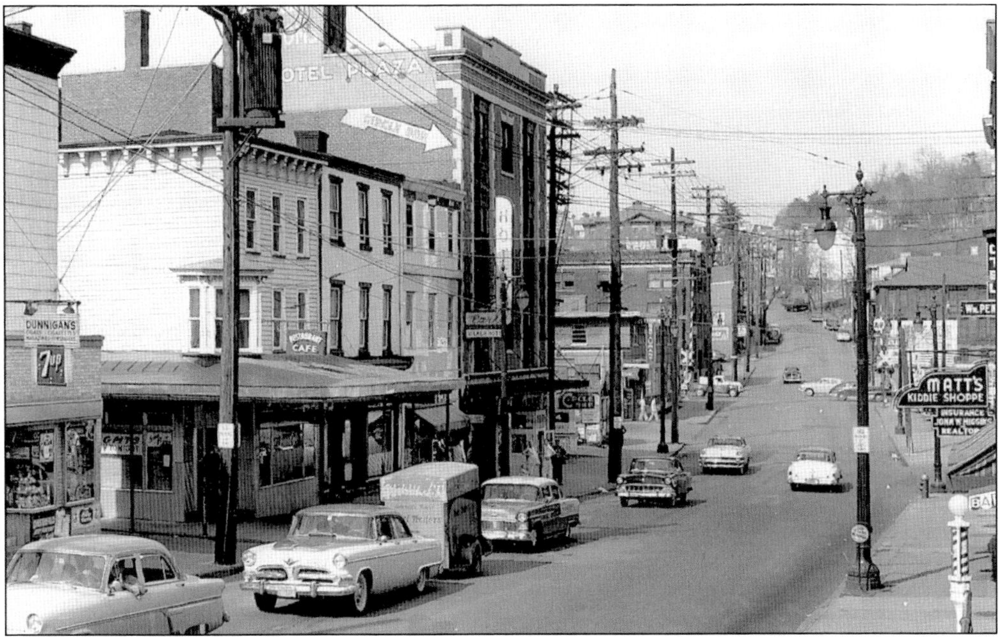

Dunnigan's newsstand and Joyce's Restaurant and Café were located on East Norwegian Street during the 1960s. An arrow on the Milner Hotel points to the Circle Bar, one of Pottsville's liveliest bars in the early 1950s.

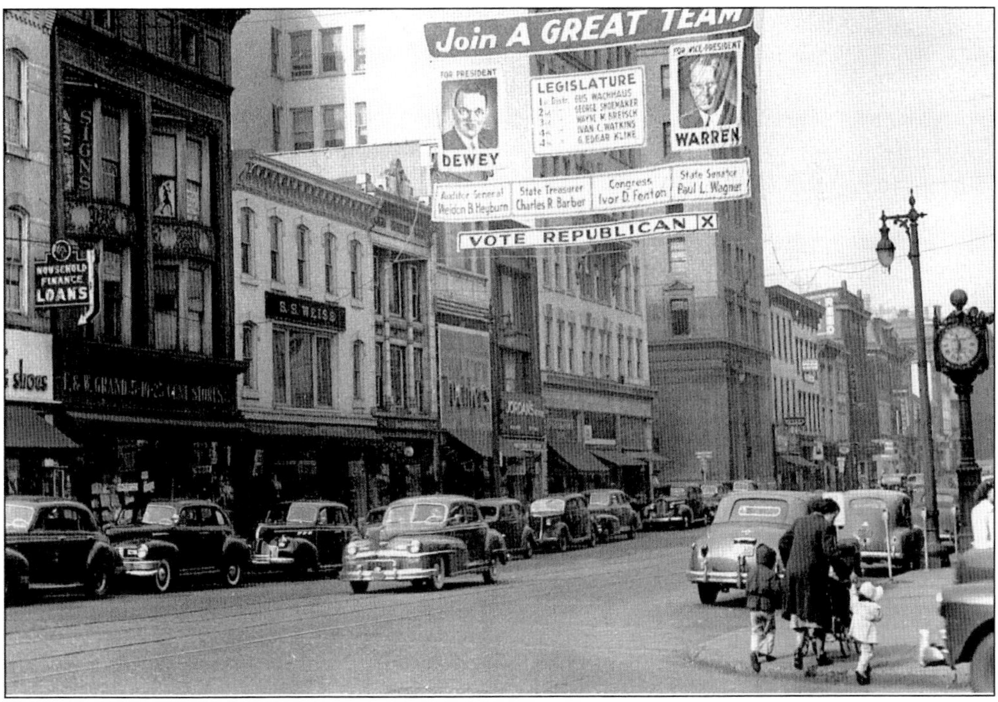

A huge banner hangs across Centre Street for Republican presidential candidate Thomas E. Dewey during the 1948 election campaign. That election became famous when some newspapers proclaimed Dewey the winner over Harry Truman, but Truman won a close election.

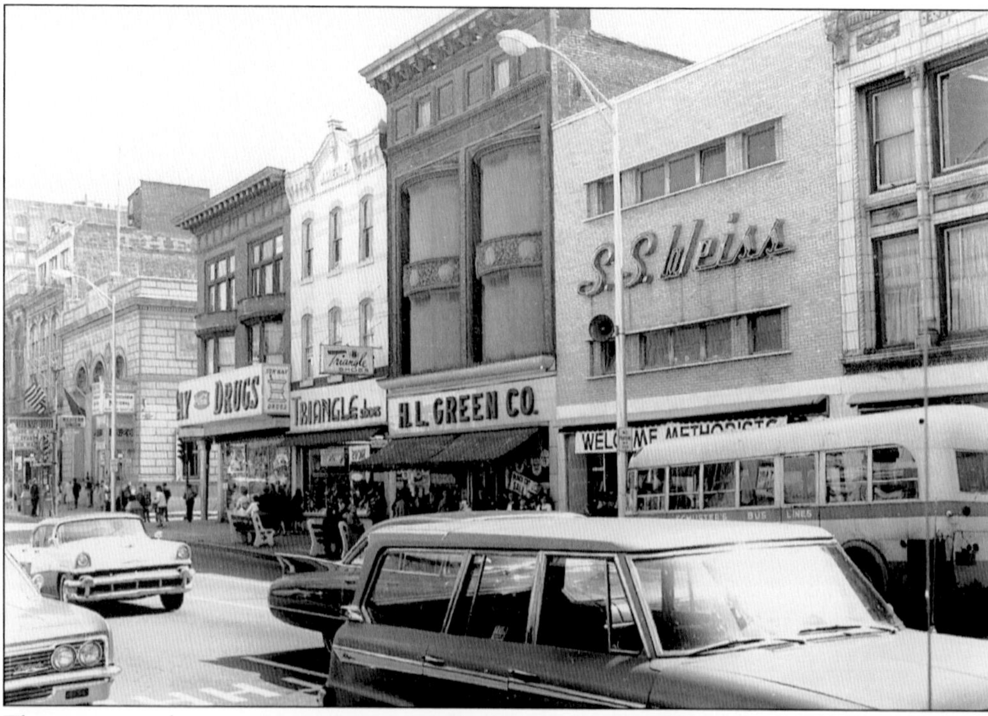

The sign over the entrance welcomes Methodists to the S.S. Weiss department store in this image. Schuster's bus is making a stop to unload shoppers near the store.

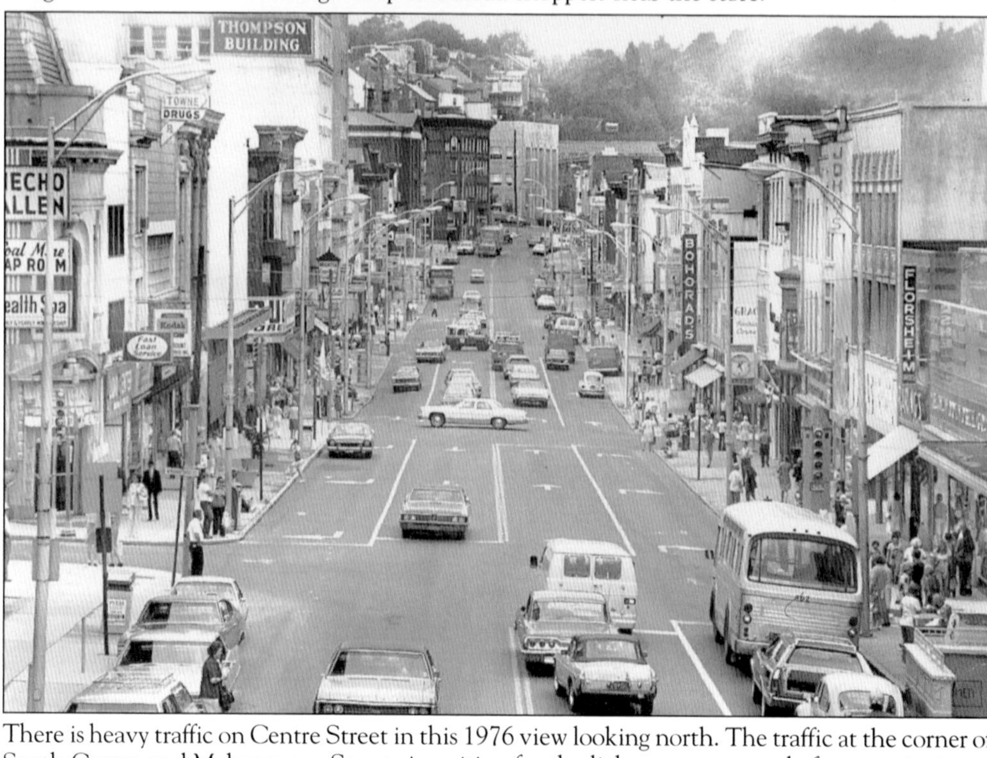

There is heavy traffic on Centre Street in this 1976 view looking north. The traffic at the corner of South Centre and Mahantongo Streets is waiting for the light to turn green before continuing.

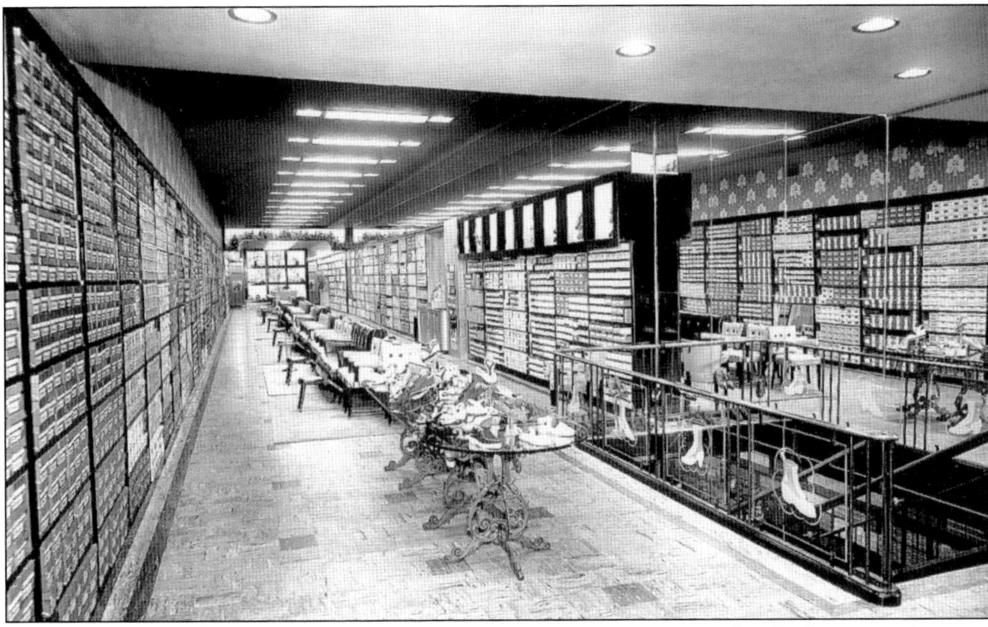

John Raring's shoe store was one of the most popular shoe stores in Schuylkill County for many years. This is a view of the ladies' shoe department. Men's shoes were in the basement. When shopping malls arrived in the 1970s, all of the shoe stores on Centre Street disappeared.

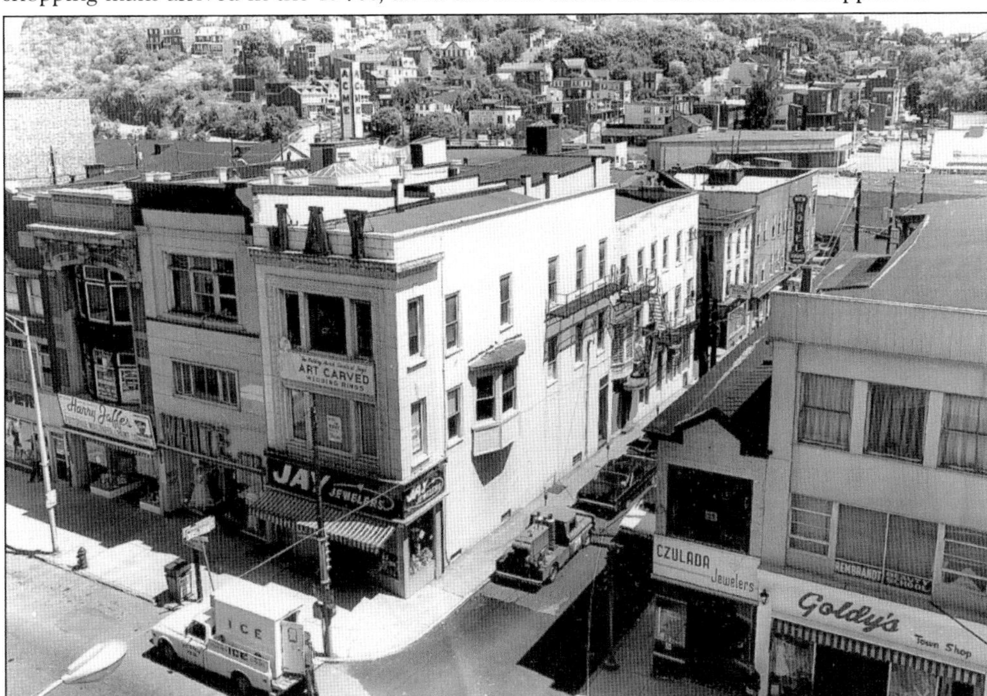

This photograph of North Centre and East Market Streets was taken from the Thompson Building. All of these stores have gone out of business. The three stores on the left were recently hit by a fire. The two buildings at the end of East Market Street have been torn down to make way for a parking lot.

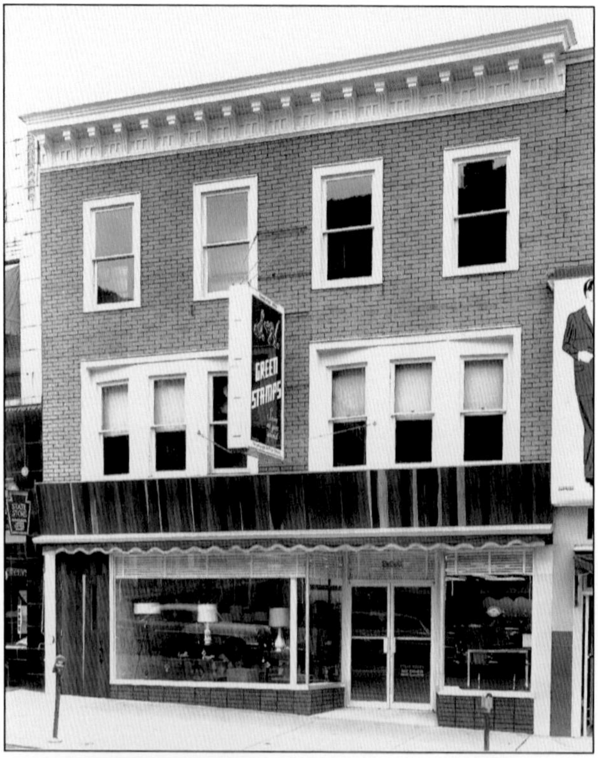

S & H Green Stamps were given to shoppers who collected and saved them to get premiums from this store on North Centre Street. The store was opposite the Female Grammar School, which is now the headquarters of the Historical Society of Schuylkill County.

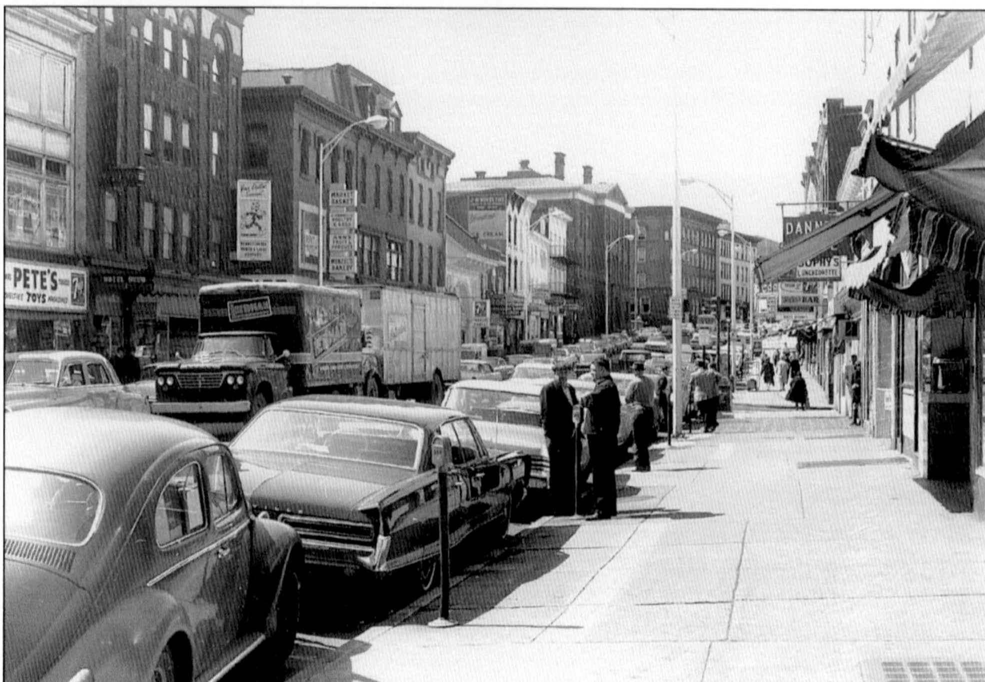

Centre Street traffic was heavy when this 1960s photograph was taken. Pete's and the Reed Hotel on the corner were torn down to make way for a parking lot for the American Bank, which purchased the Schuylkill Trust Company.

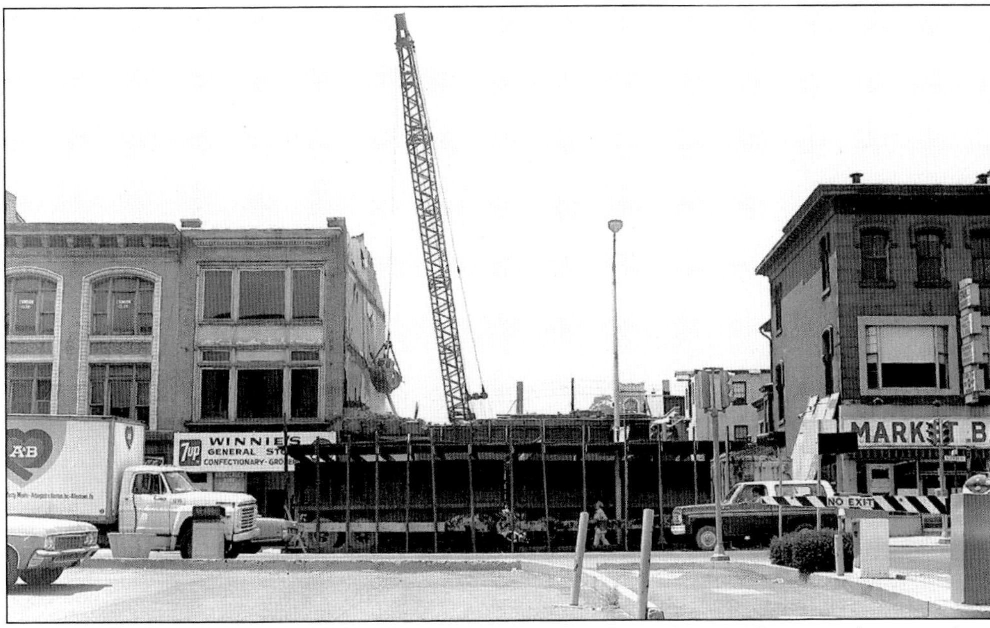

The Reed Hotel was torn down in 1976 by the American Bank to make room for its parking lot. Winnie's was razed after the hotel. All of the stores on Centre Street in this block were torn down for the parking lot.

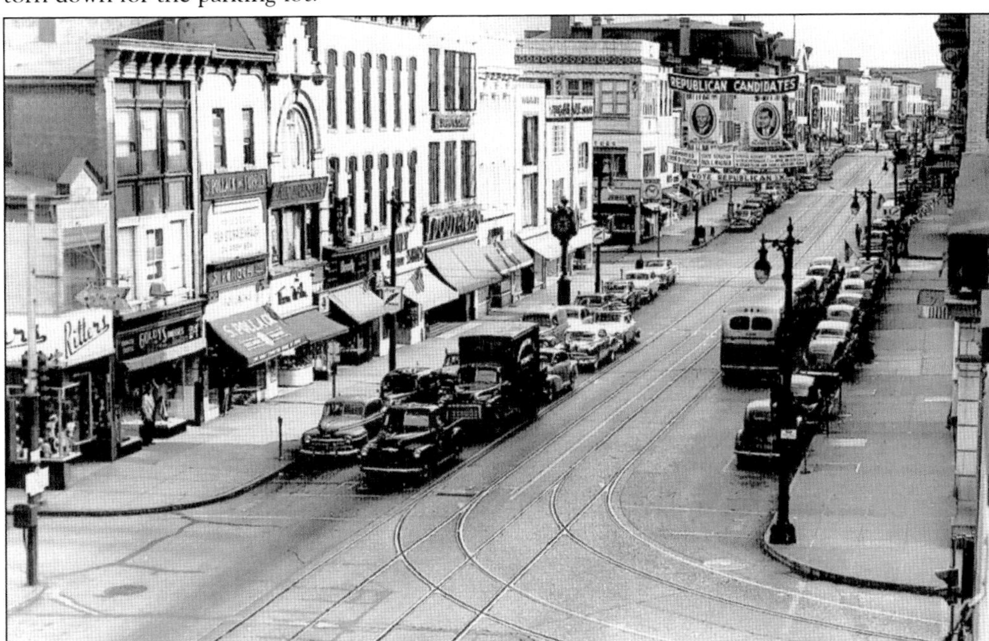

This Republican banner hung over Centre Street during the 1960 elections. Richard M. Nixon was running in the presidential campaign against John F. Kennedy. Ivor D. Fenton of Mahanoy City was running for a seat in the House of Representatives, and Paul Wagner of Tamaqua was running for state senator.

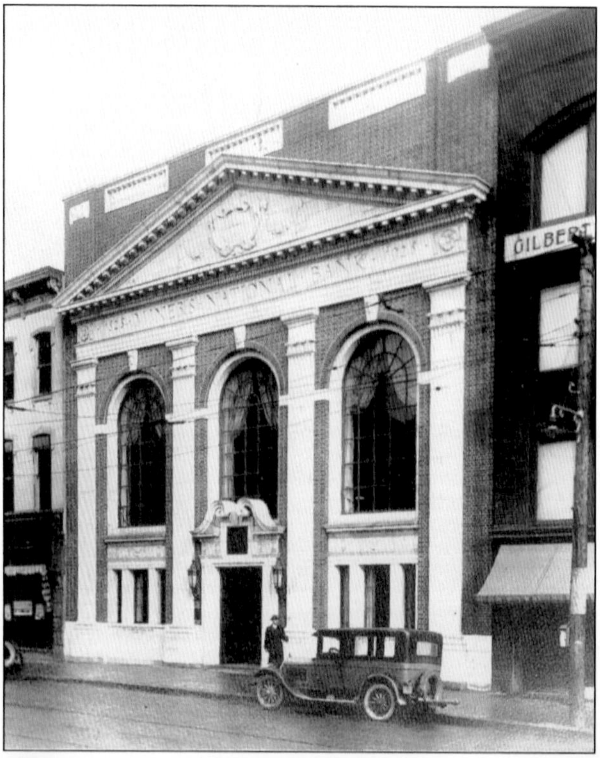

The Miners National Bank built its new headquarters in 1928. It was the oldest bank in Pottsville. Today, it is Sovereign Bank.

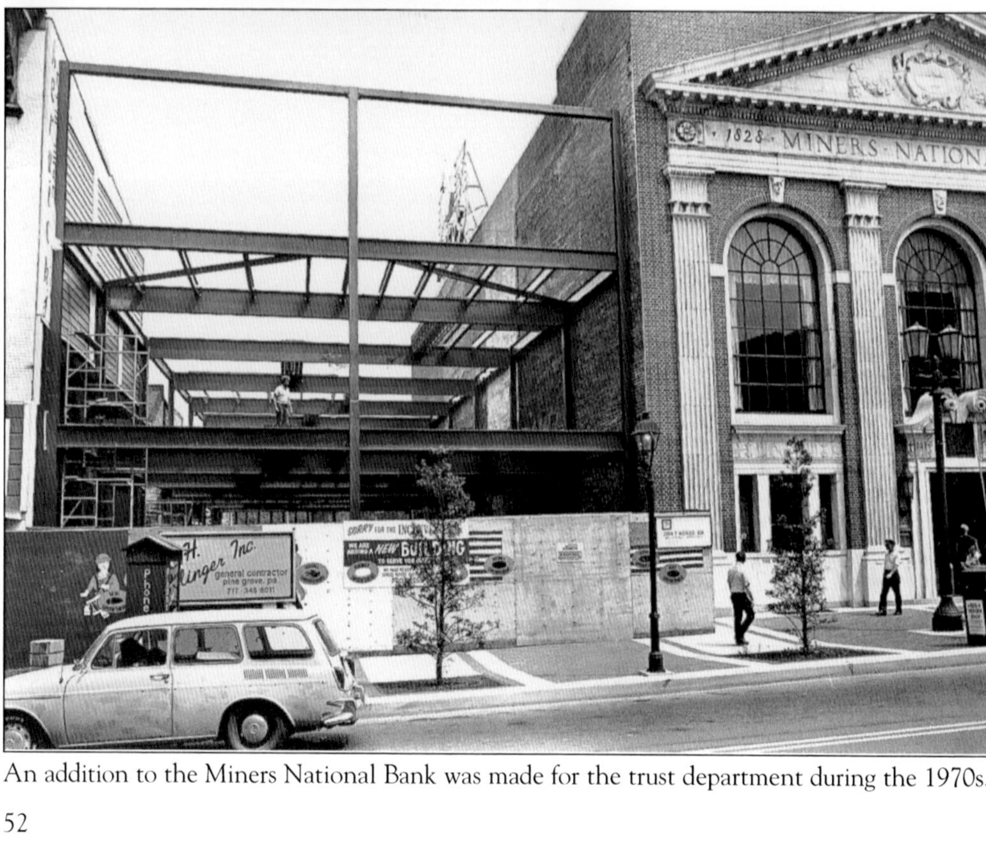

An addition to the Miners National Bank was made for the trust department during the 1970s.

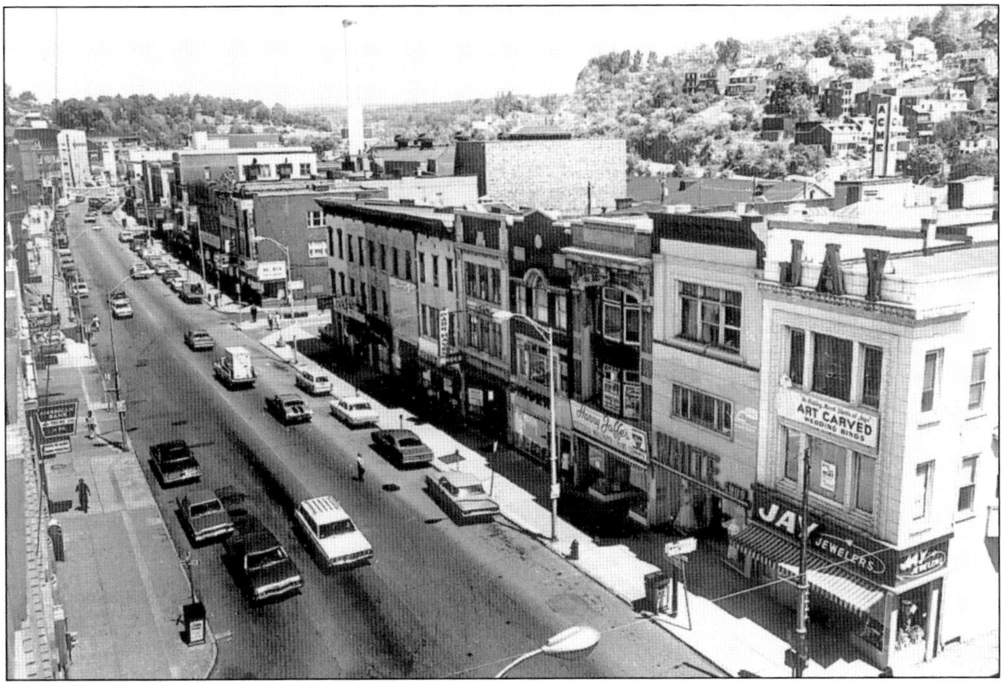

This view looks north from the Thompson Building up Centre Street. Notice the smokestack of the Pottsville Steam Heat Company.

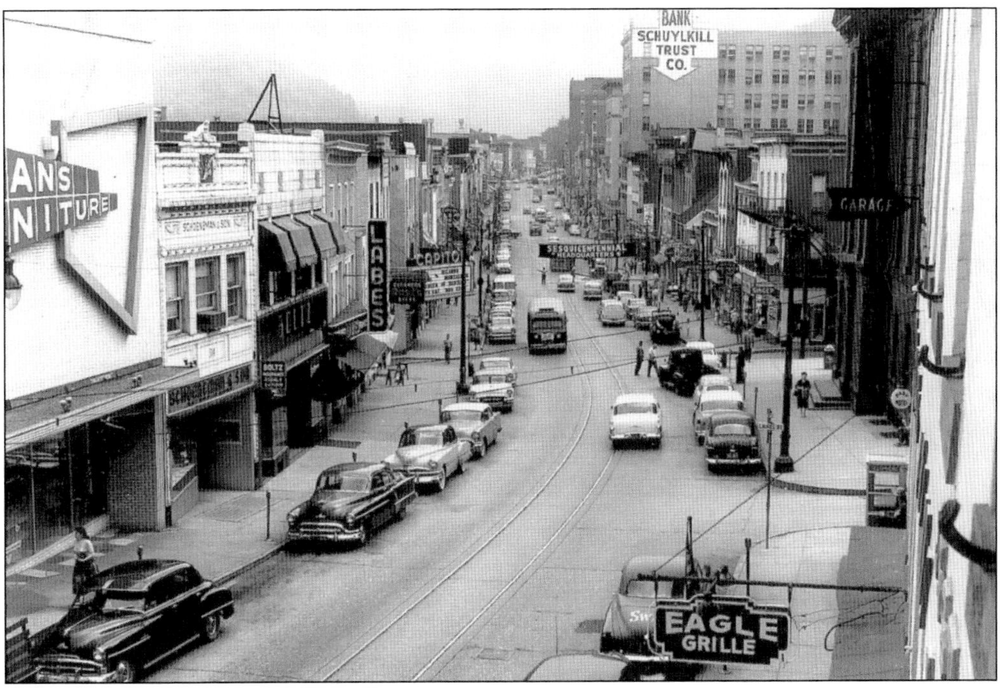

This 1956 view of Centre Street looks south from Minersville Street. A sign hanging near the Capitol Theater is pointing toward the headquarters of the sesquicentennial celebration.

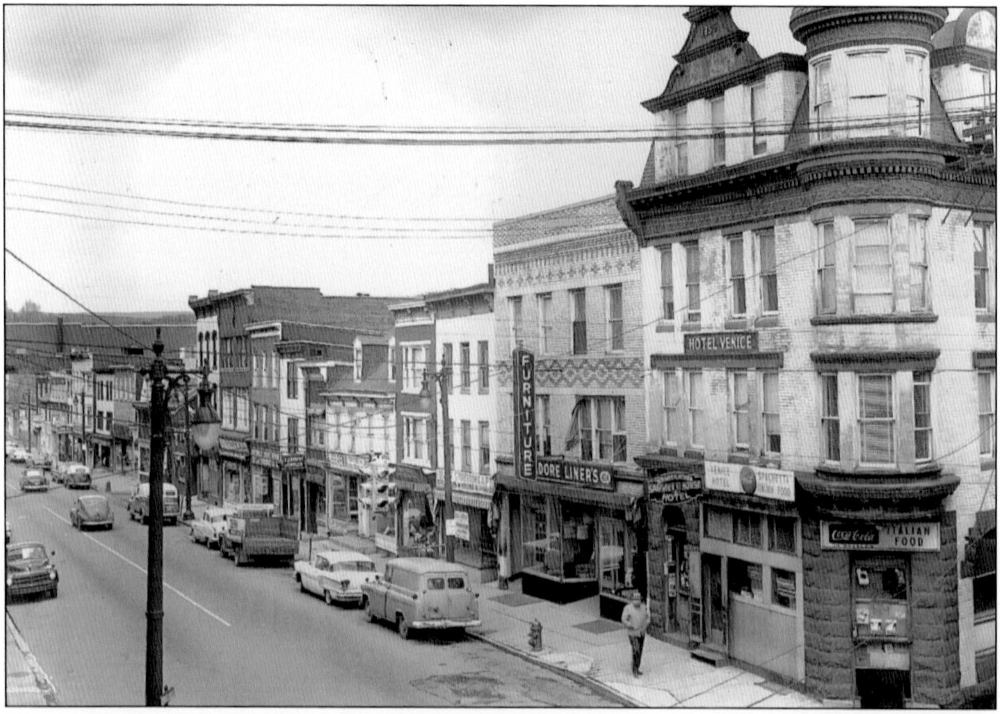

These buildings extending from East Minersville Street north to a point opposite the Charlton's Hall building were doomed for destruction under redevelopment plans for North Centre Street. The plan was never completed, and today, the county has its human resources offices on the corner, while the Pottsville post office stands next to the county offices.

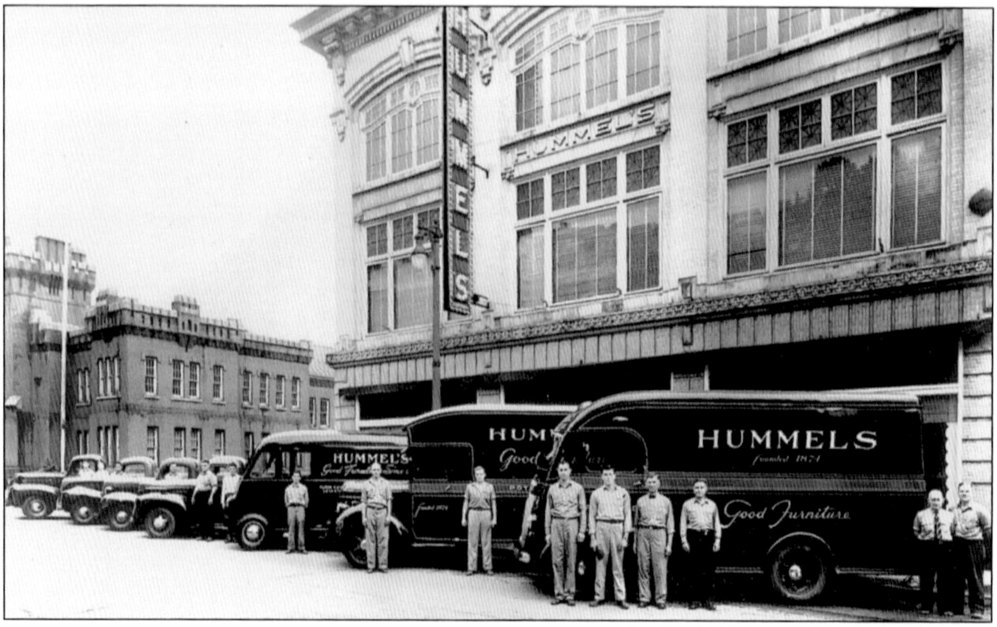

Hummel's, a furniture store, was farther north on Centre Street. The Pottsville Armory is the building on the left. This 1948 image has all of the store's trucks and employees lined up on Centre Street.

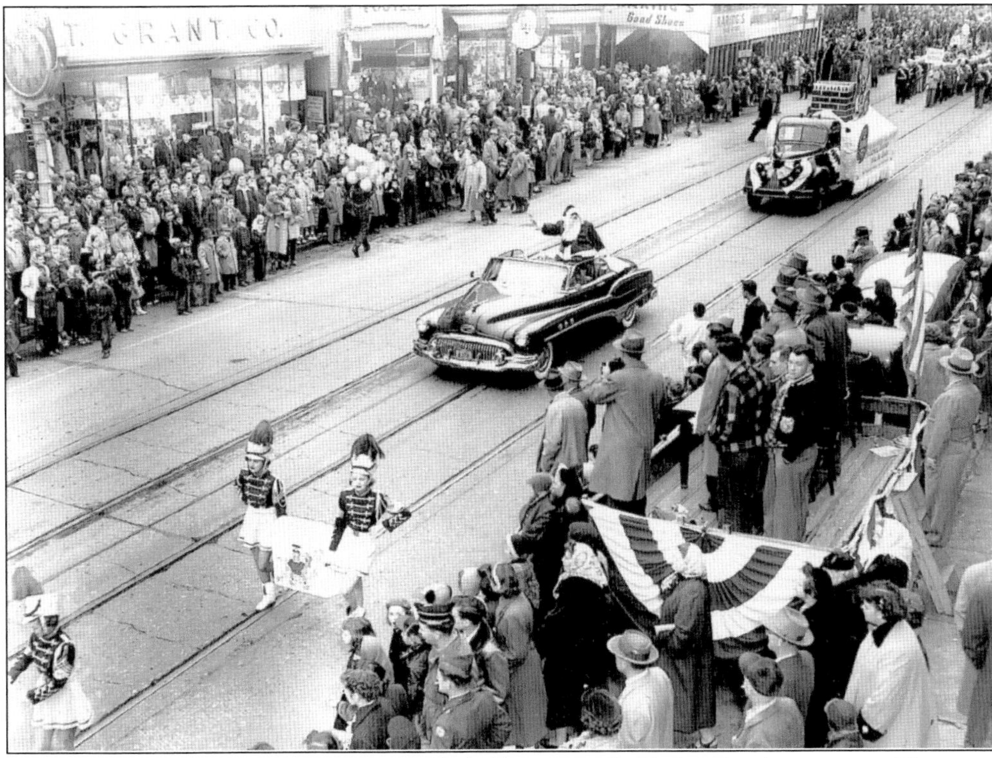

Santa Claus is shown riding in a convertible led by Pottsville High School majorettes. There was a large crowd on Centre Street to greet the man from the North Pole when he arrived in 1951.

The Pottsville Steam Heat Company was organized on June 25, 1888, to provide heat to downtown buildings. The plant was located at East Minersville and Railroad Streets. When the plant was closed in the 1980s, the smokestack was torn down.

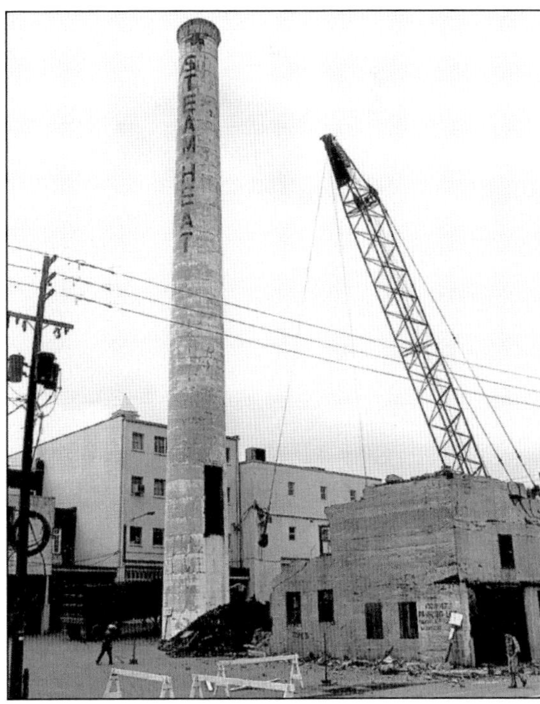

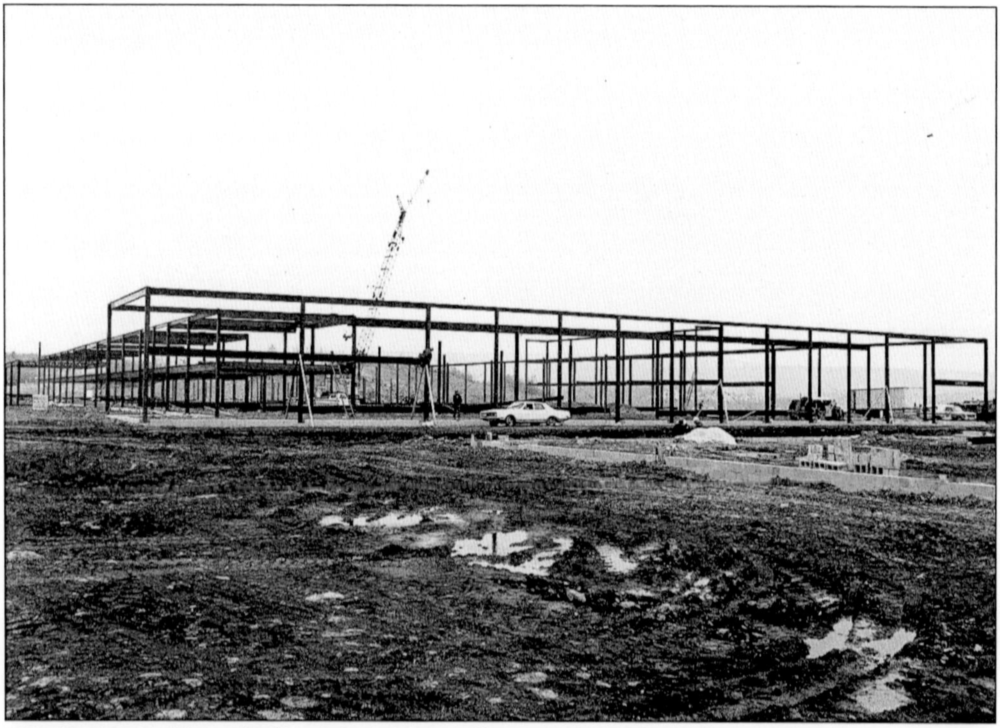

The Fairlane Village Mall came to Pottsville in 1974. When the mall opened, Pottsville shoppers rushed to see all of the new stores. Merchants who had stores on Centre Street could not compete with the stores in the mall.

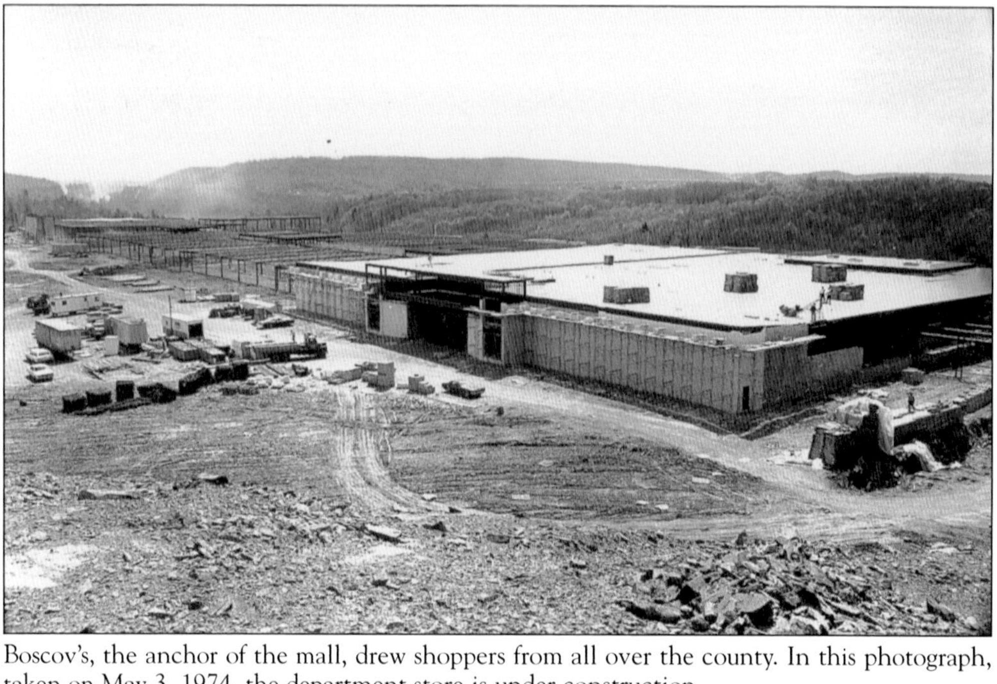

Boscov's, the anchor of the mall, drew shoppers from all over the county. In this photograph, taken on May 3, 1974, the department store is under construction.

Three

GOVERNMENT AND ORGANIZATIONS

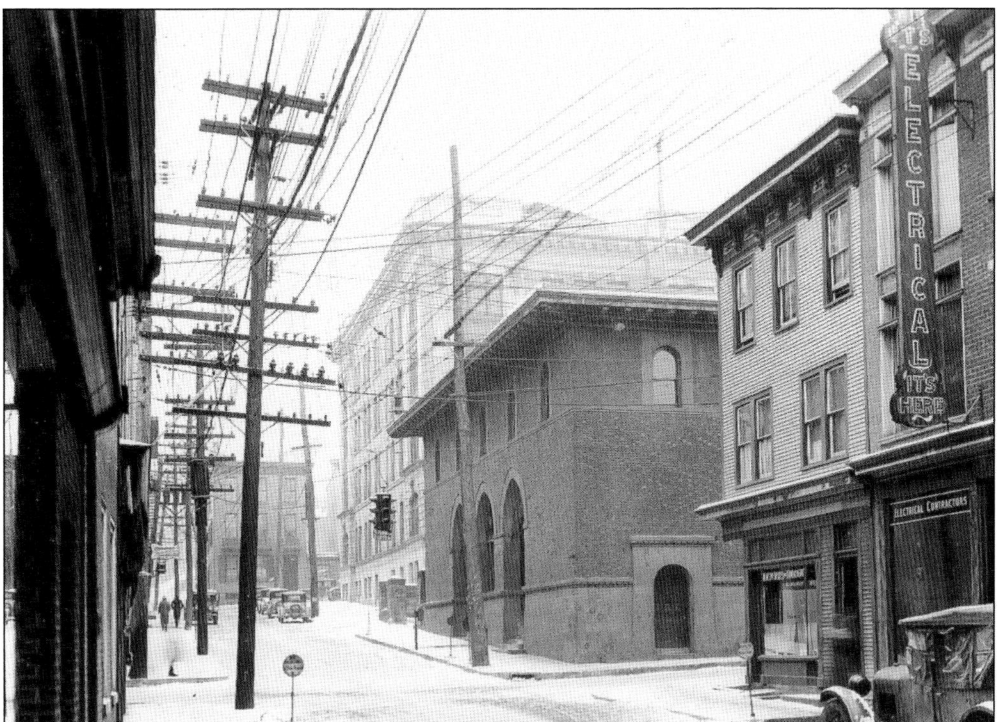

In 1895, there were 23 clerks and carriers, including 5 railway clerks, on the payroll at the post office. A larger building was needed, and this site at Second and West Norwegian Streets was selected on September 3, 1895. By 1935, mail service had increased to such a degree that a larger building was again needed.

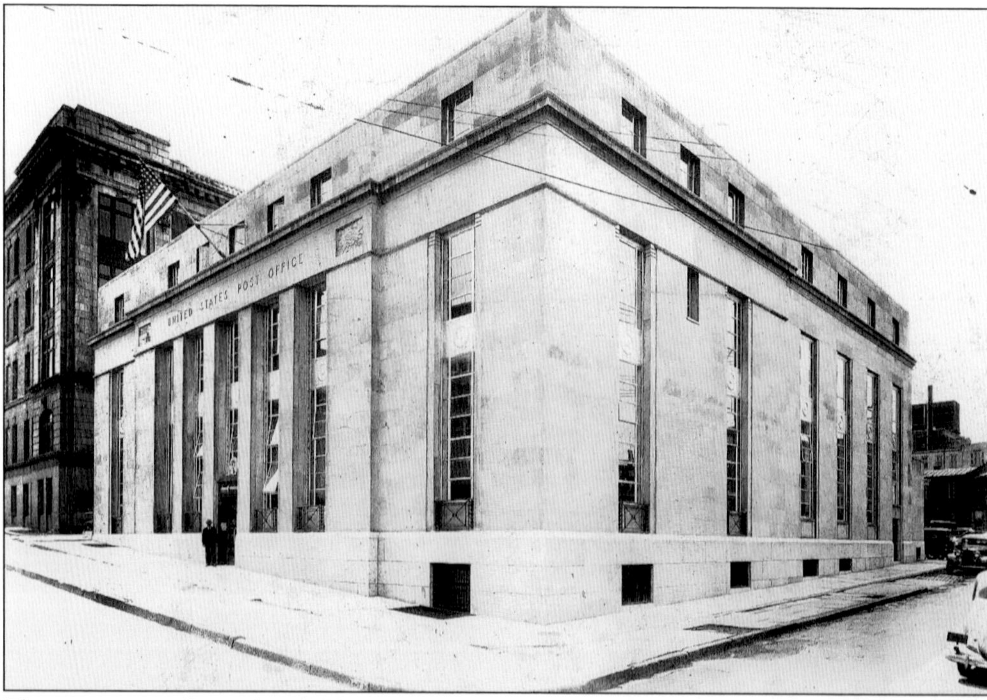

The same site at Second and West Norwegian was chosen for the post office that was built in 1936. The American flag waves briskly over the main entrance in this image. This building has been used as an office building since a larger post office was built on North Centre Street in 1968.

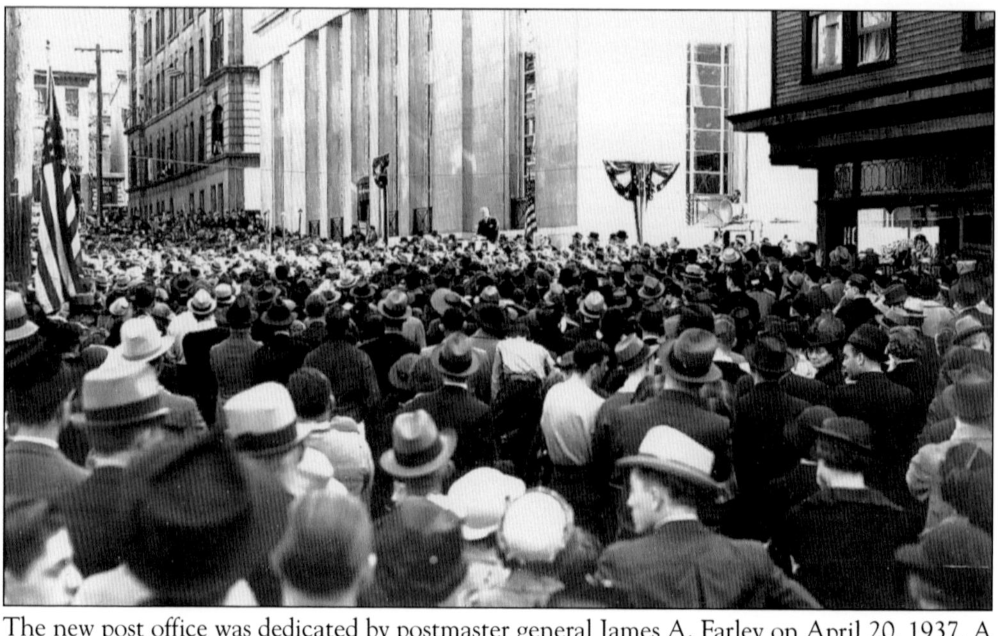

The new post office was dedicated by postmaster general James A. Farley on April 20, 1937. A large crowd was in attendance for the ceremonies at the corner of Second and West Norwegian Streets. A dinner was held in the Necho Allen Hotel, where turkey was served and there were no speeches.

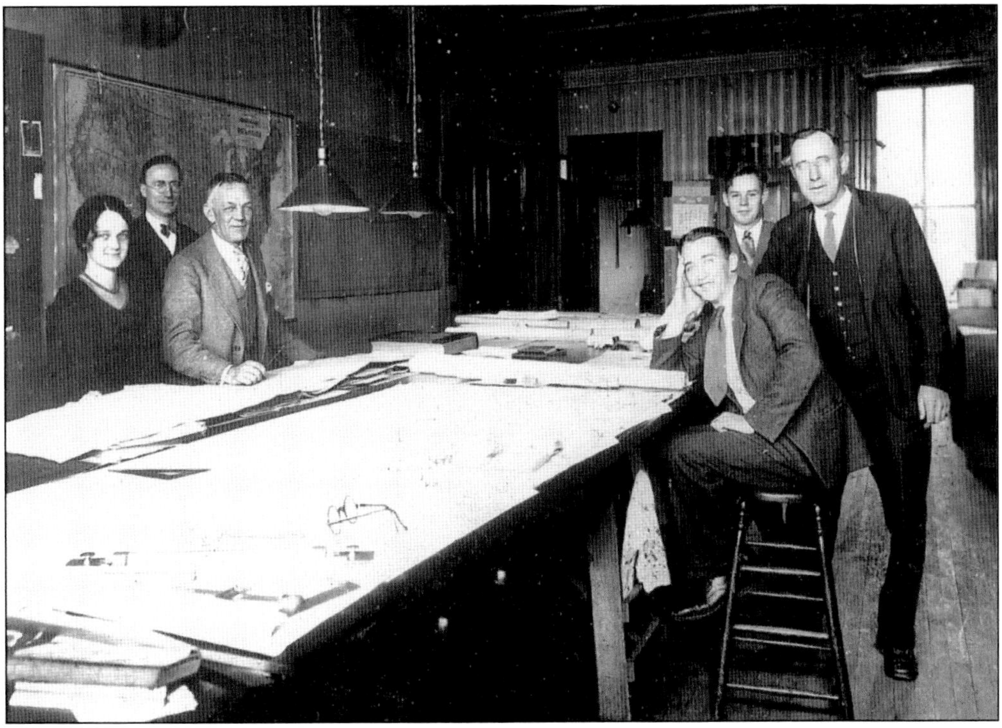

City engineer George Steidle and his staff are shown in his office on October 18, 1929. From left to right are Gertrude Brixius, R.R. McCoffrey, George Steidle, John Lynaugh, K.W. Falls, and I.E. Fery.

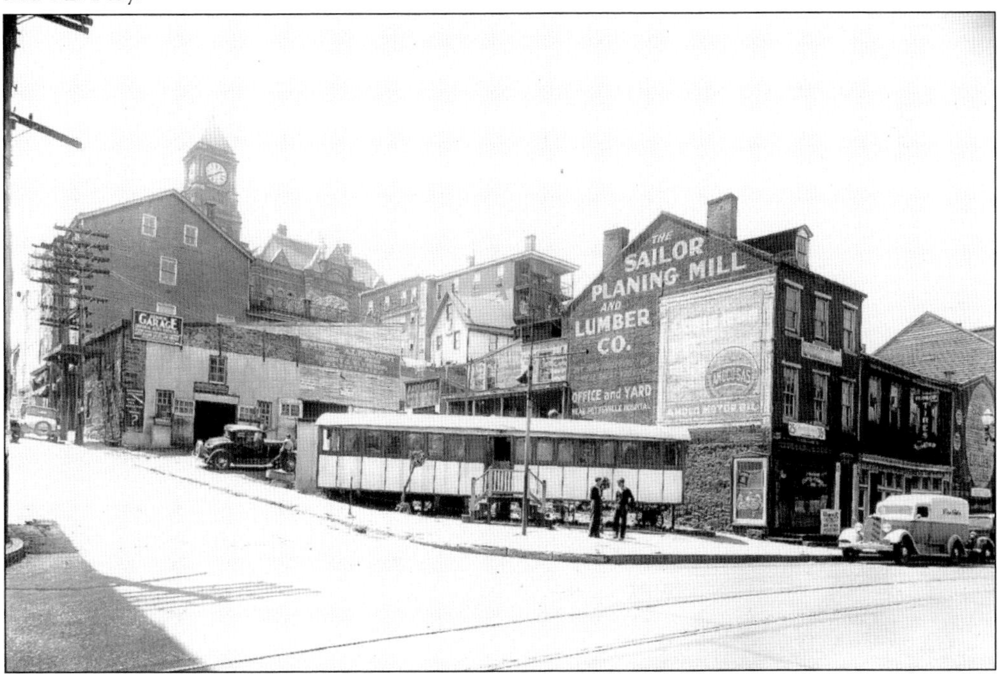

The city selected this site at the corner of Centre and Minersville Streets to build the new city hall in 1936. The diner was removed to make way for city hall.

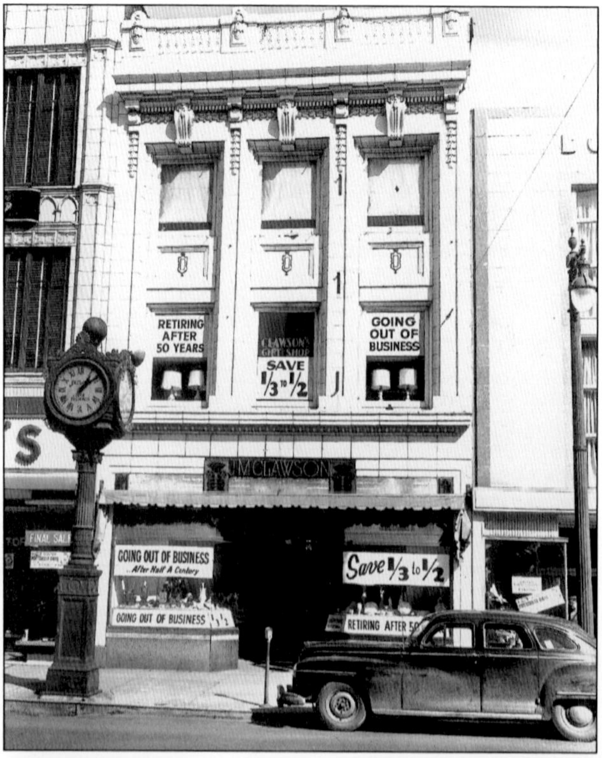

Jake Clawson's shop is shown during its going-out-of-business sale in 1959. The clock shown here is also visible in front of city hall in the next photograph. The clock is no longer in front of city hall, and no one knows what happened to it.

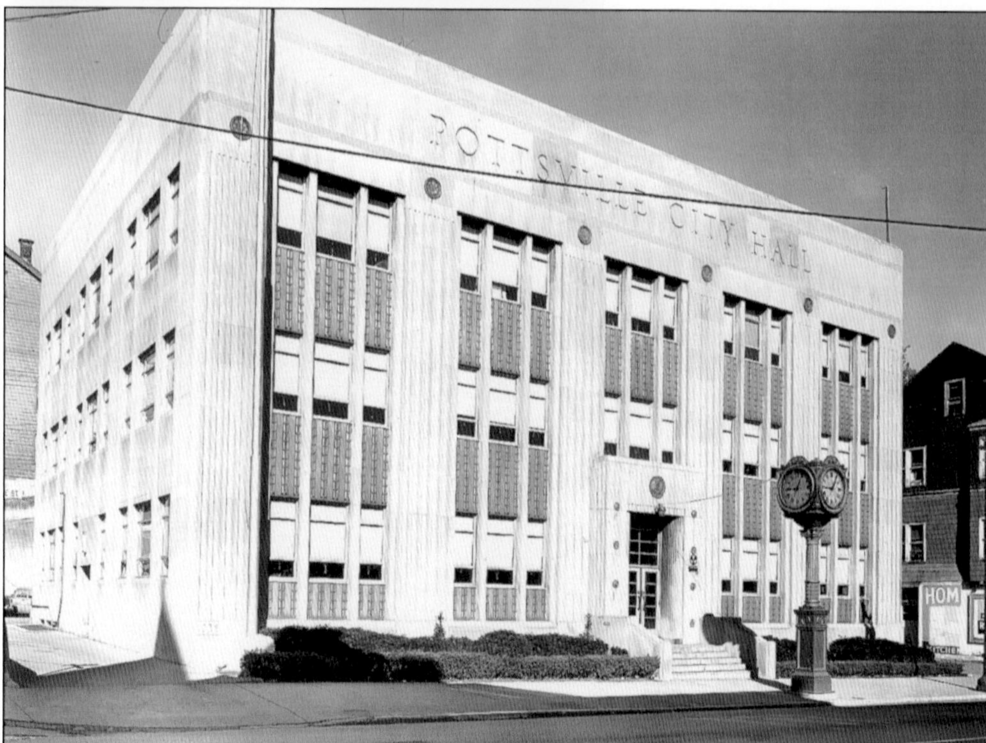

The city hall was designed by architect Philip Knobloch.

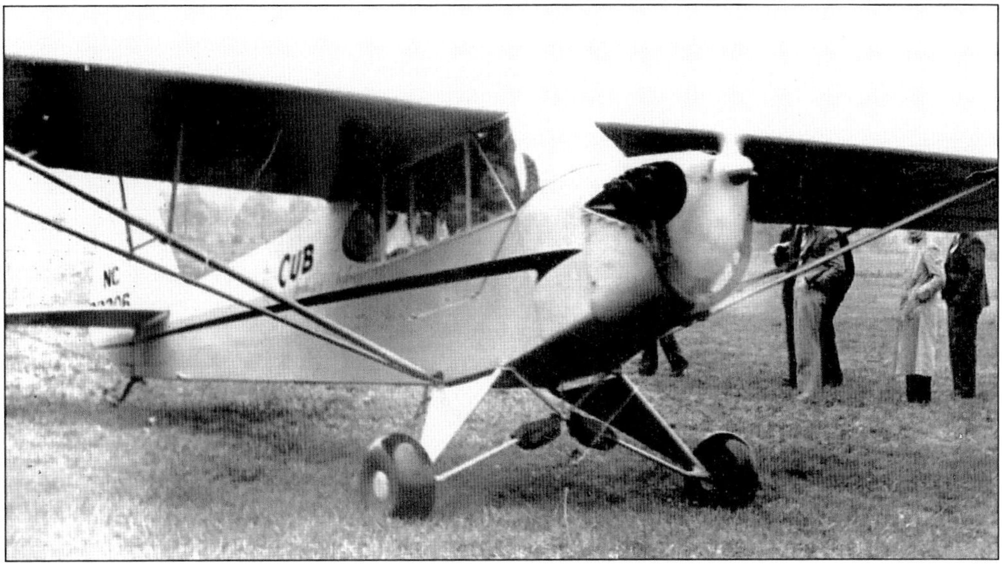

The first airplane flight of mail in Schuylkill County was carried by this airplane from the Deer Lake airfield on May 19, 1938. The plane carried two pouches of mail and flew to the Allentown airfield, where it was dispatched to its destinations.

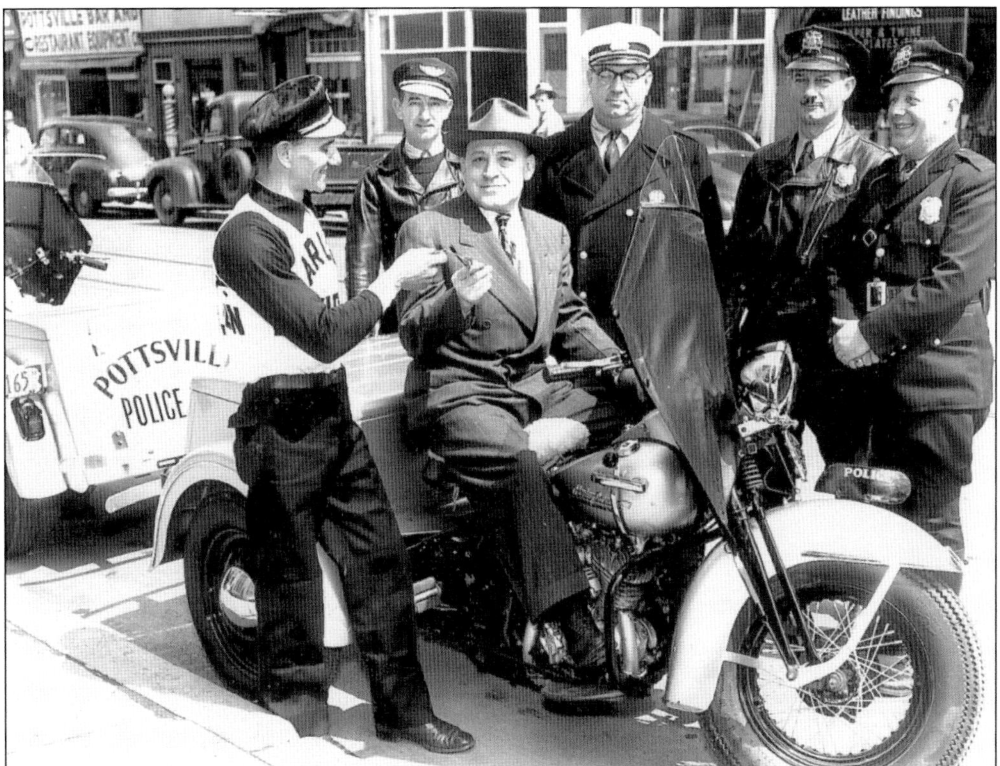

Mayor George Heffner is ready to take the first ride on the city's new motorcycle. The police officers watching the mayor are, from left to right, A.J. Downey, Ernest Ehlers, and Wally Berger.

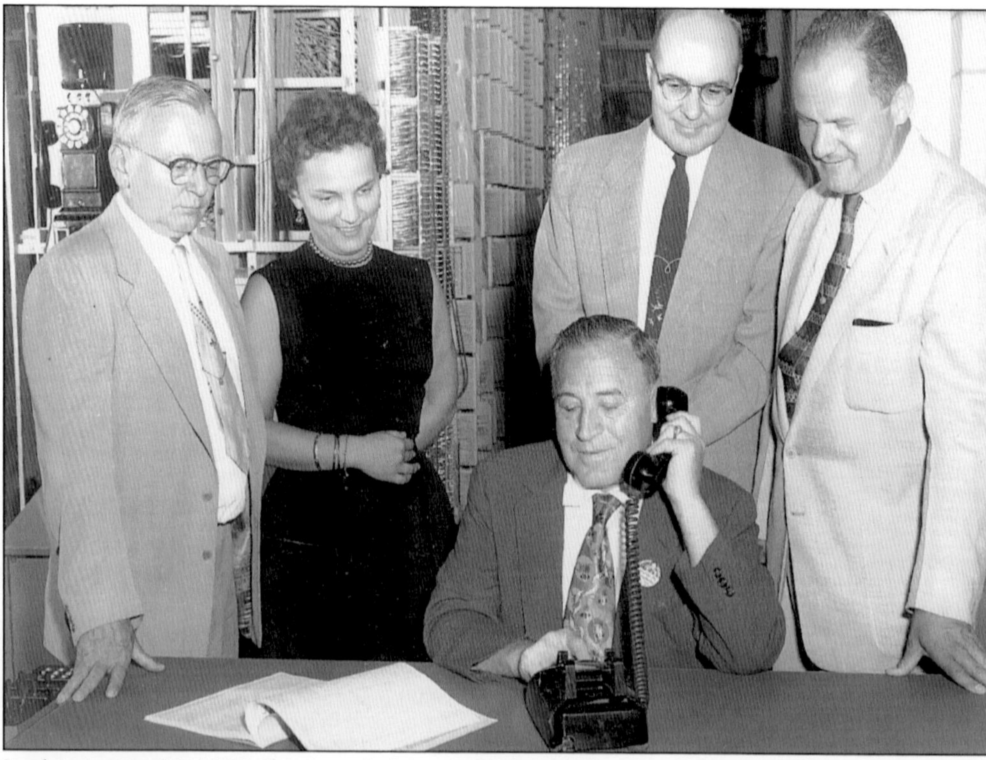

In this August 30, 1956 photograph, Mayor George Heffner is placing the first dial-phone call in Pottsville. The observers are unidentified, but the woman is the chief telephone operator in Pottsville, and the man standing behind the mayor is the manager of the Pottsville Bell Telephone office.

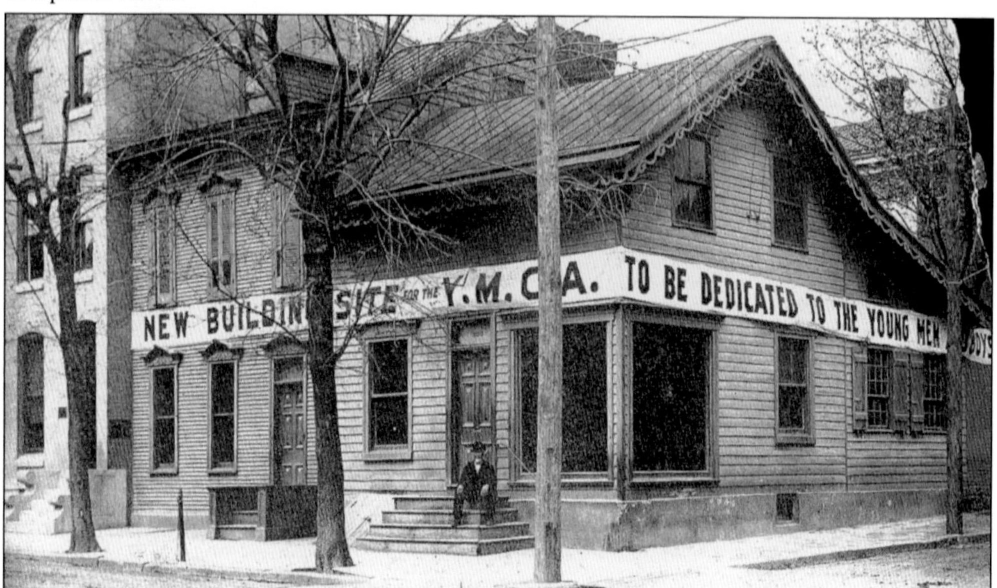

The new YMCA was built at the corner of West Market and Second Streets. The YMCA was a popular place until it was torn down in 1972.

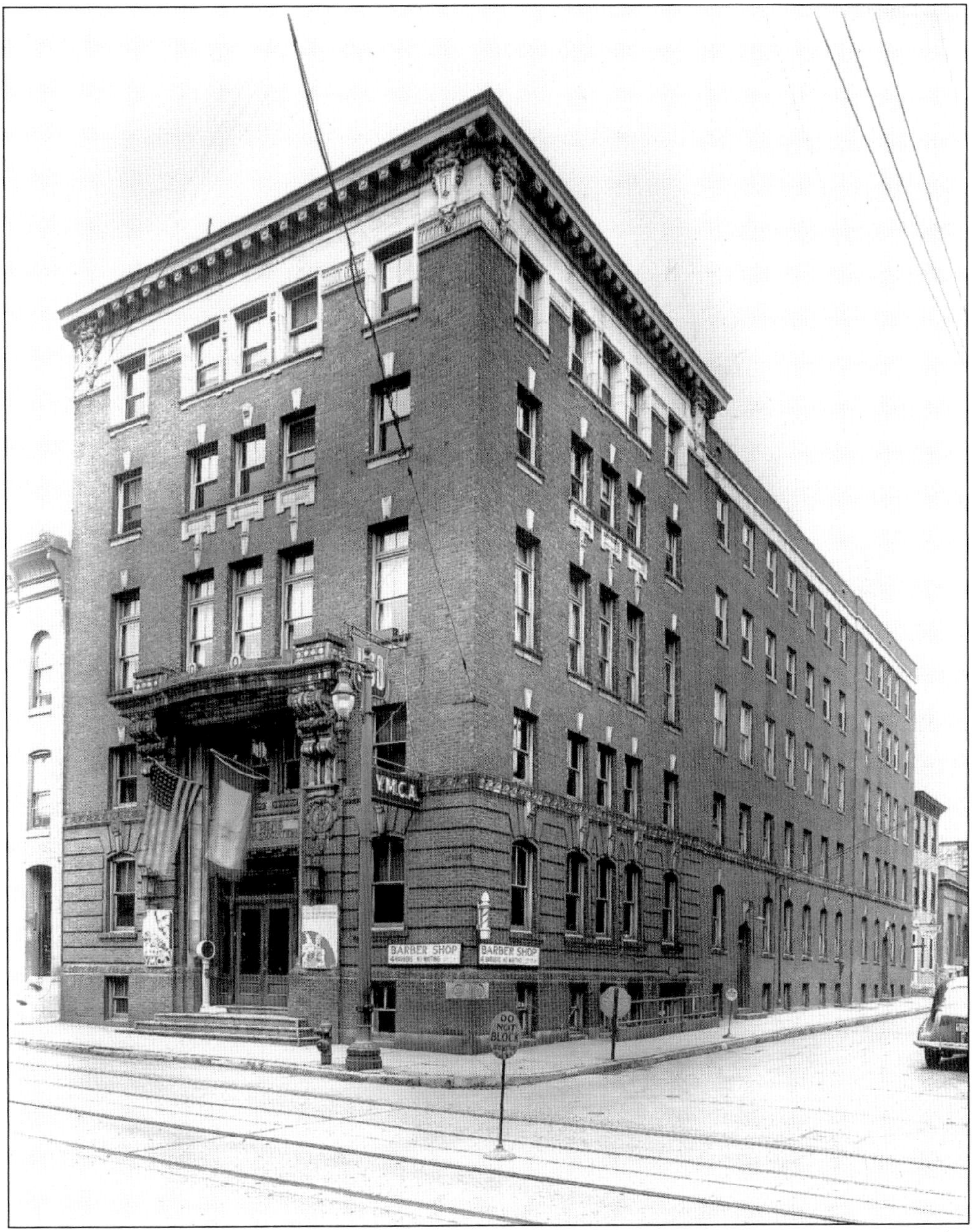

Flags are hanging over the front doors of the YMCA during World War II. Notice the barbershop in the basement on the corner and the penny scale on the front steps.

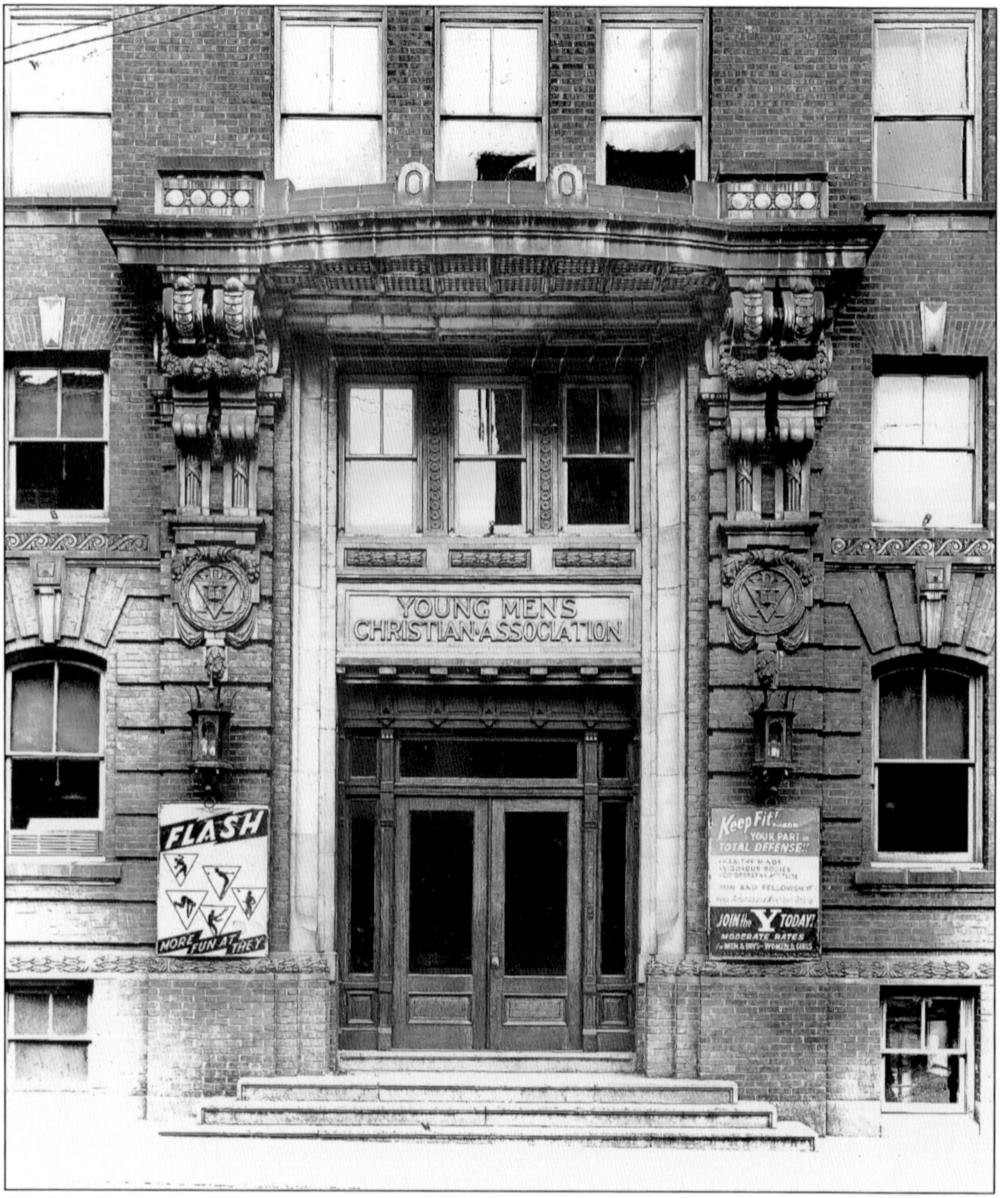

The YMCA had very ornate doors, through which thousands of boys and young men passed for various activities, such as boxing, swimming, basketball, wrestling, gymnastics, checkers, and other sports.

The boys' entrance was on Second Street, and the boys' department was on the second floor. The YMCA conducted classes in hobbies, and there were clubs for the boys. There was much competition between the boys clubs when they played touch football and basketball.

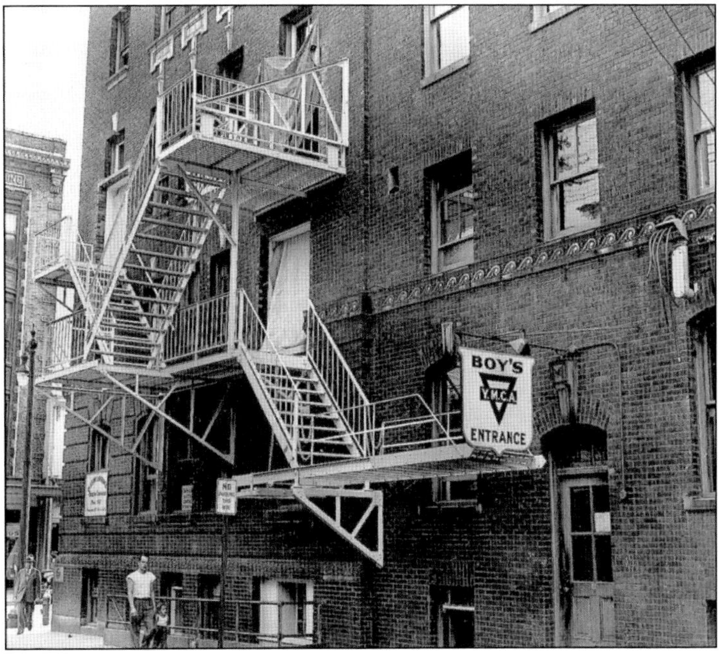

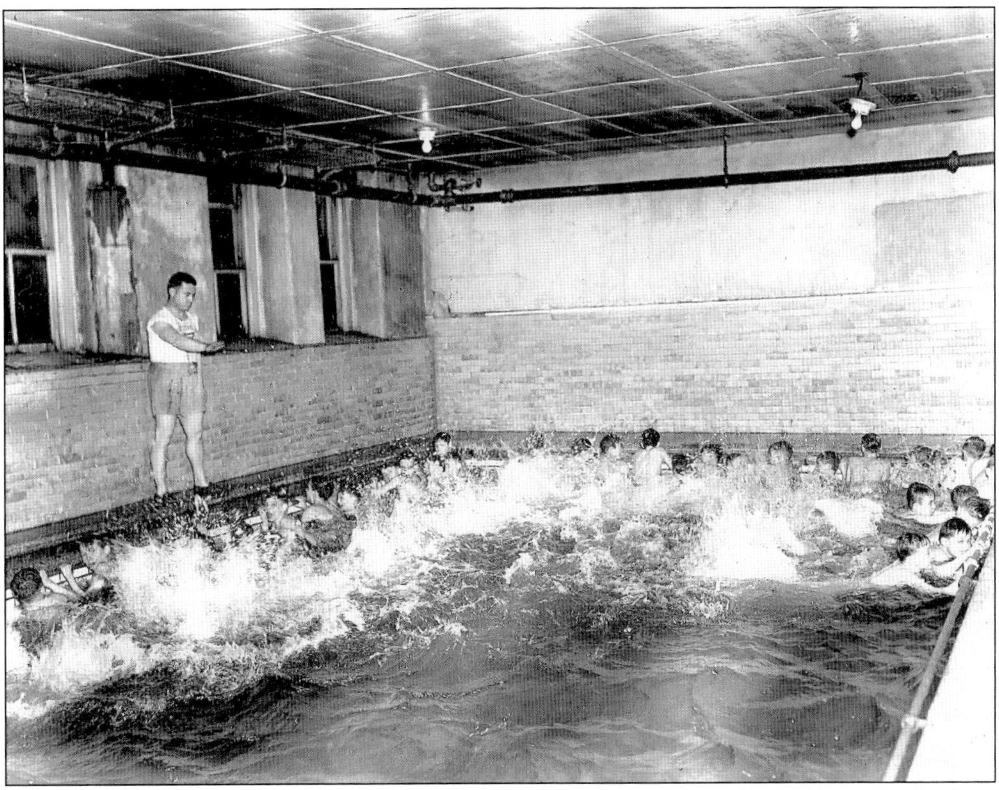

Physical education director Blandford Jones is teaching a swimming class to boys. As the boys advanced in their swimming skills, they were given emblems to sew on their bathing suits. However, suits were not used at the YMCA; it was all skinny dipping.

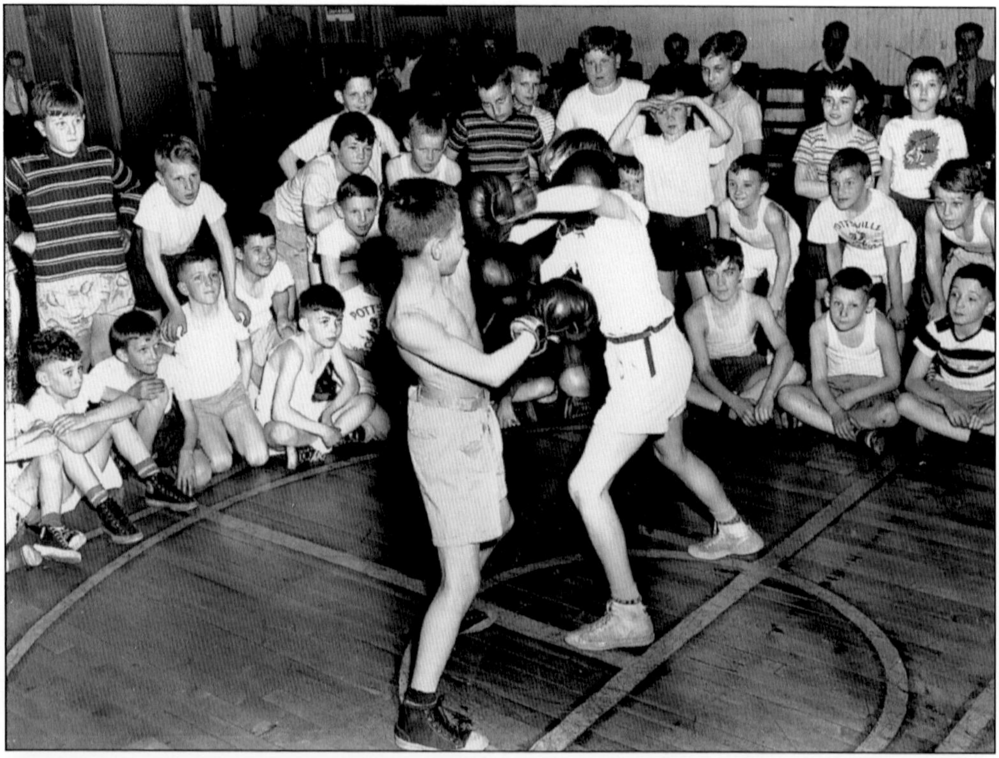

The boys are having a boxing lesson in this image. Notice how closely all of the boys are watching the action. The gloves were big and soft so that the boys would not get hurt.

The Pottsville Free Public Library was built at the corner of West Market and Third Streets in 1921 with the help of a large contribution from industrialist Andrew Carnegie. Thousands of people passed through the main entrance on North Third Street in search of the books that they wanted to read.

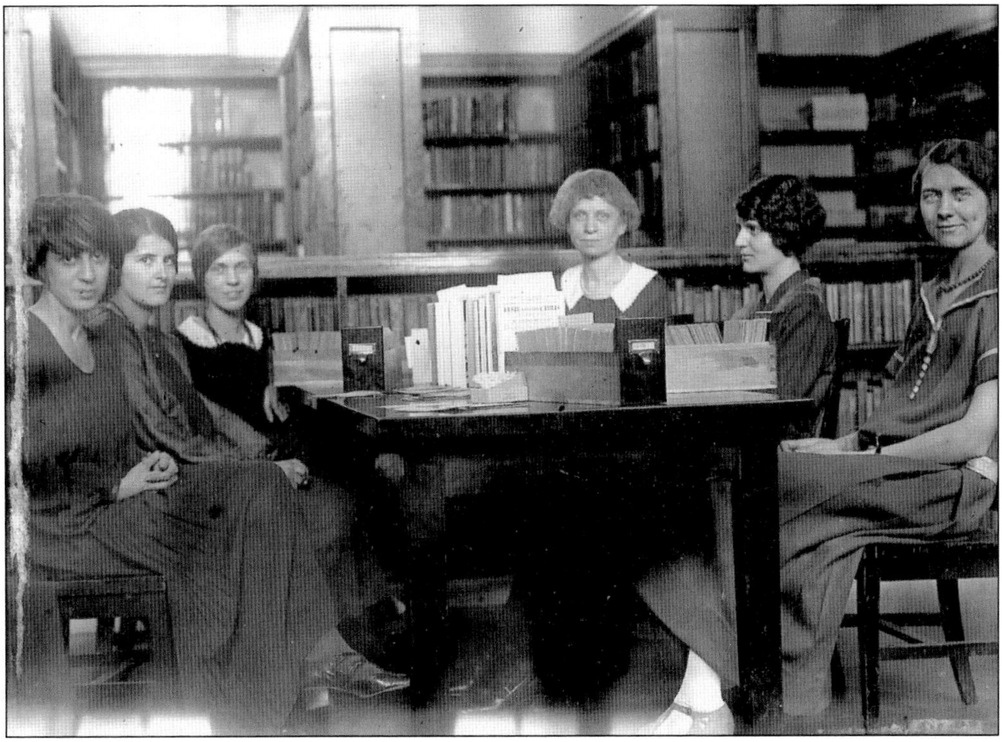

Edith Patterson was the director of the library for many years. In this 1924 image, she is seen with her staff. From left to right are Hazel Leddy, Euyer Schnerring, Mary Beddall, Edith Patterson, Ruth Roehring, and Lorraine Patterson. The library doubled its size in 1999 with a major addition to the building.

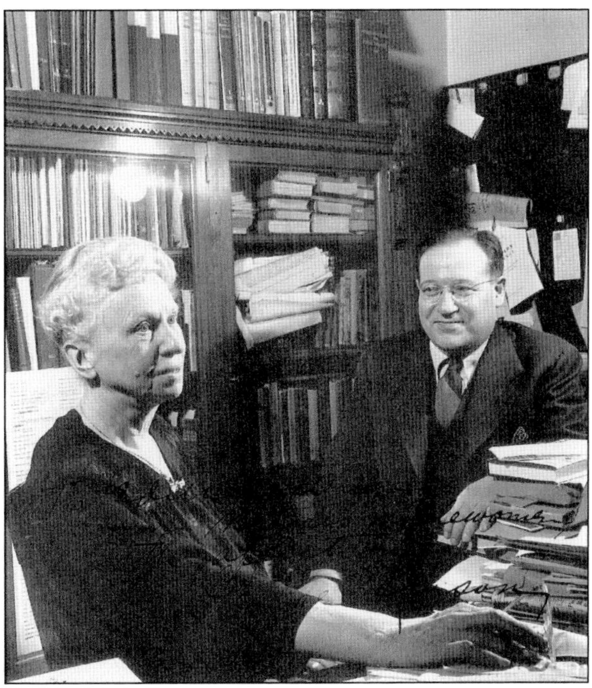

Edith Patterson meets with author George Korson. She encouraged him to write about miners' ballads and poetry before they were gone and forgotten. He signed the photograph, "To Edith Patterson, One of Nature's noblewomen, With Affection, Korson."

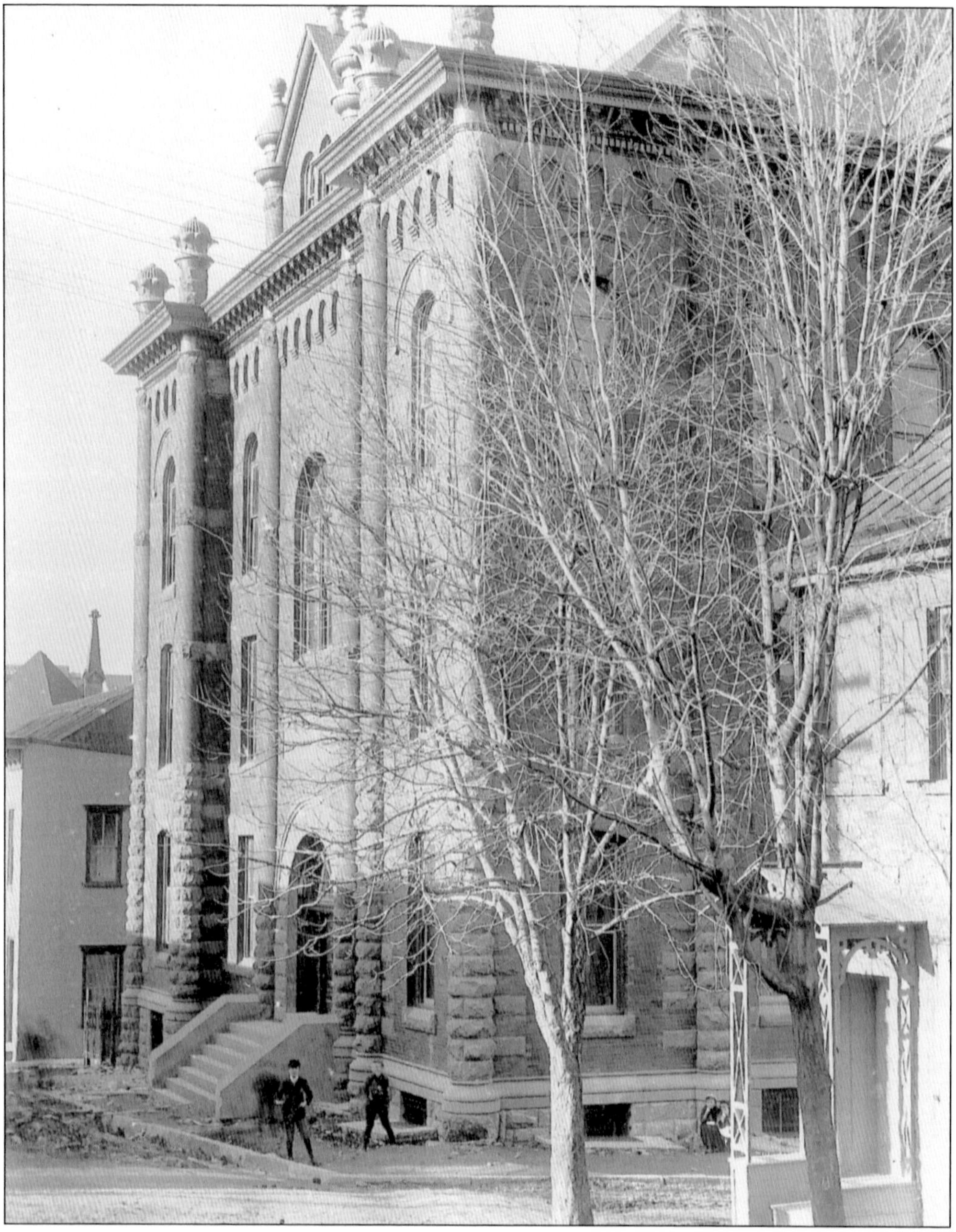

The Garfield School was erected in 1894 and served the town as an elementary and high school until the Patterson Building was constructed in 1916. In the 1950s and 1960s, the business office of the Pottsville School District had its headquarters in the Garfield School building, which was recently razed.

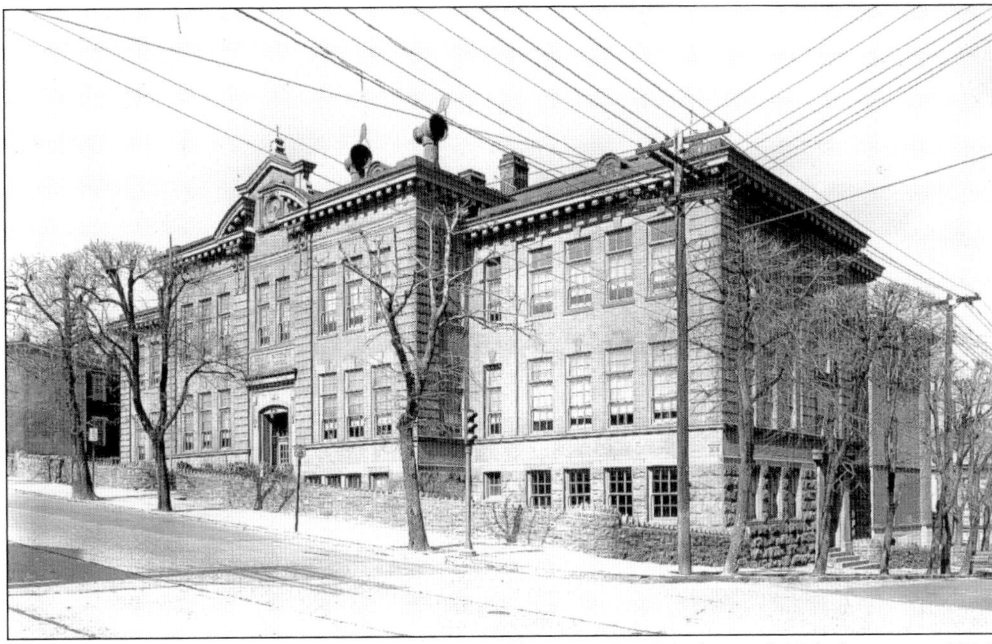

The high school was moved to the Patterson Building, at West Market and 12th Streets, in 1916. When the new high school was built in 1933, the Patterson Building was used as the junior high school. The Patterson Building was razed, and the site is now used for low-cost housing.

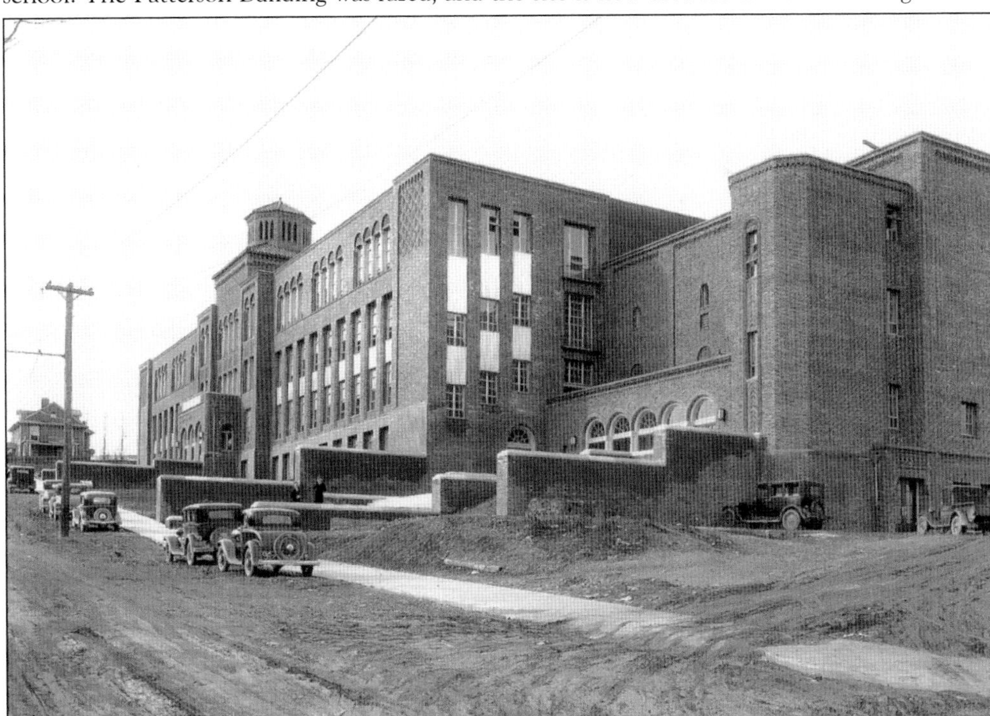

The imposing Pottsville High School was built at 16th Street and Elk Avenue in 1933. Many young men and women have spent their high school years in the "Castle on the Hill," and it appears that it will stand for many more years to come.

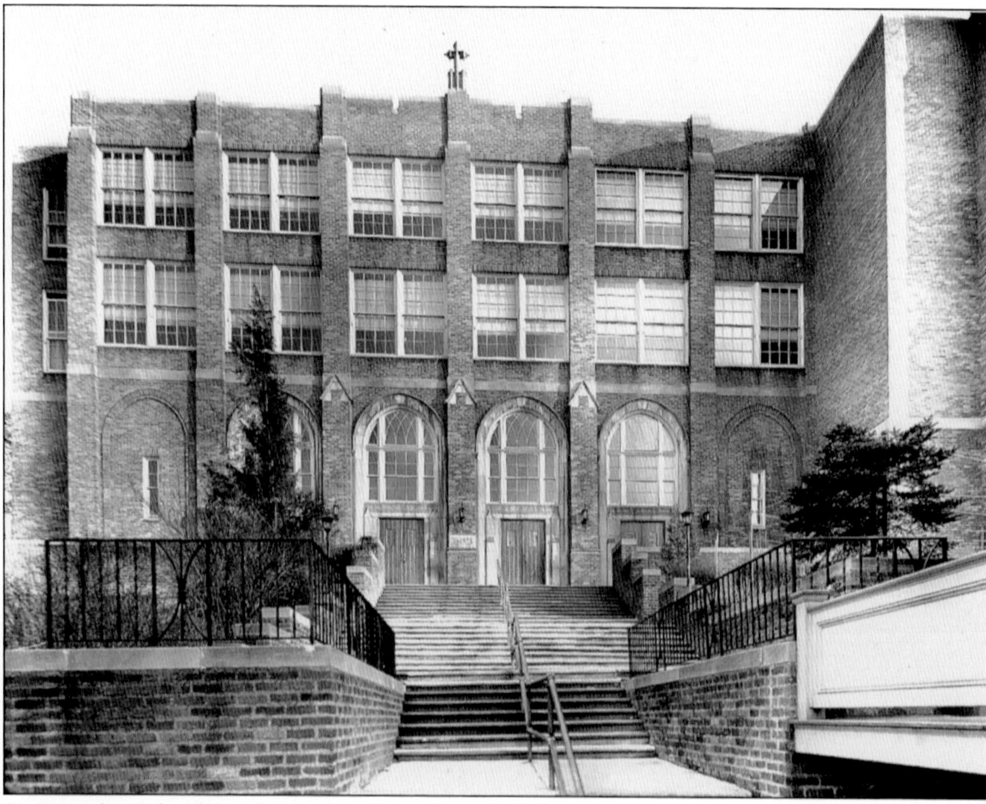

St. Patrick's School was located at Seventh and Mahantongo Streets for the benefit of families who wanted to send their children to a parochial school. Today, it is All Saints School and is used for the elementary grades.

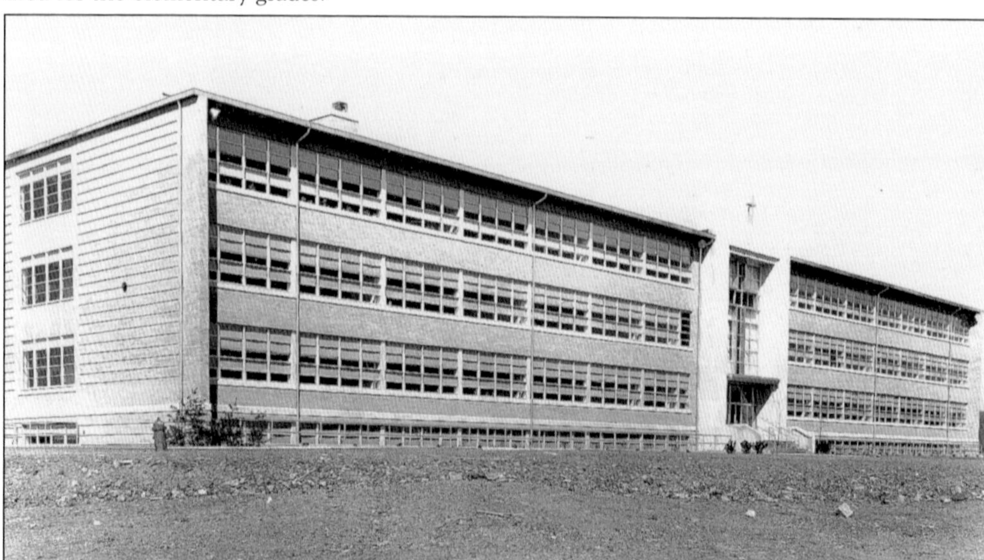

Nativity B.V.M. High School was built on the top of Lawton's Hill in 1955, when the bishop decided that each parish was unable to support its own high school. Today, it serves as a central high school for Catholic families in the Pottsville area.

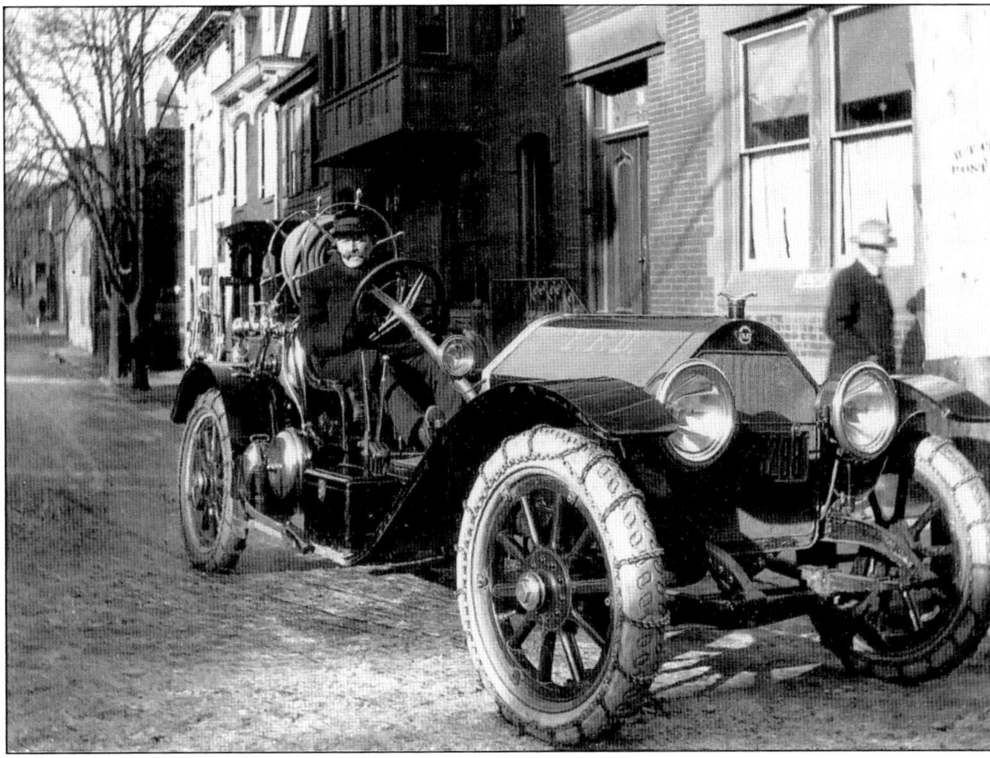

Fire chief Bill Stevenson is ready for a fire to occur anywhere in Pottsville as he sits in his car on North Third Street in 1917. The fancy car had chains on both the front and back wheels. Borough hall was at 14 North Third Street in 1917. In 1937, the Historical Society of Schuylkill County made the building its headquarters.

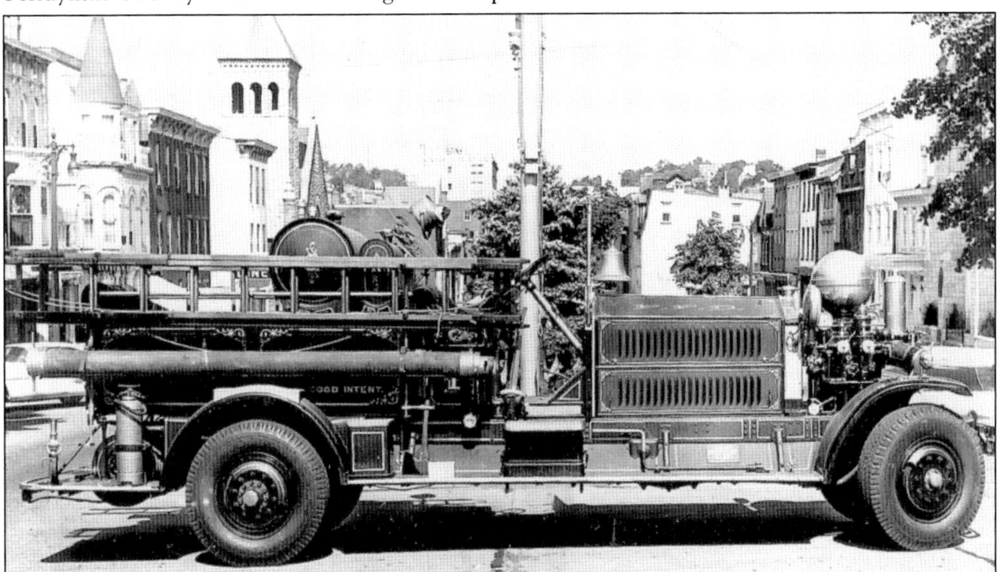

The Good Intent Fire Company has its truck parked near the Soldiers and Sailors Monument in Garfield Square on a sunny summer day. The fire company's hose house was at North Second Street, only a few blocks away.

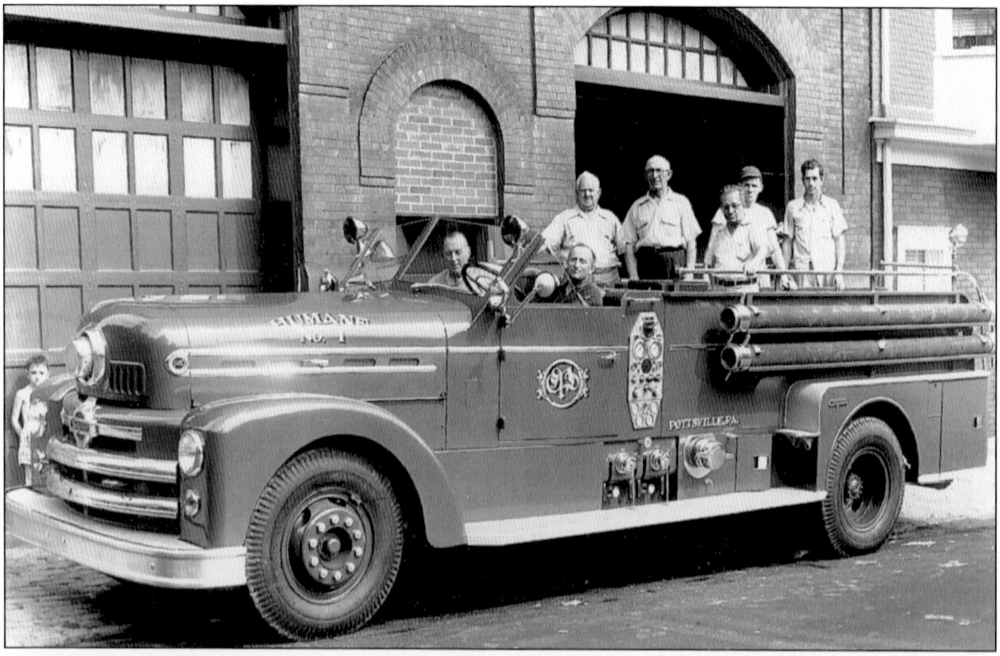

Members of the Humane Fire Company show off their new truck at the firehouse, located at North Third and Laurel Streets, probably *c.* 1950. The company was organized on October 3, 1821. In 1859, its charter was amended so that the name was Humane Hose Company No. 1.

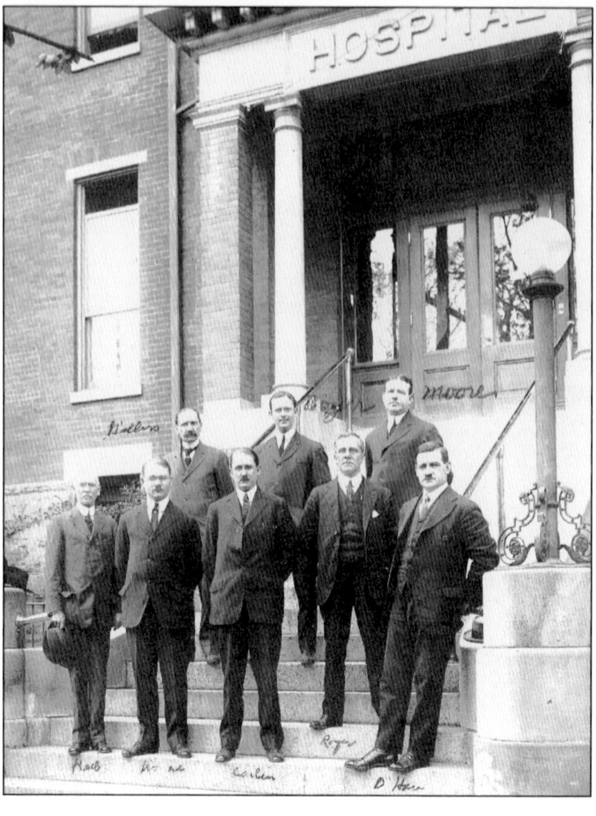

The doctors on the medical staff of the Pottsville Hospital are standing at the front door of the hospital. From left to right are the following: (front row) Halberstadt, Warne, Carling, Rogers, and O'Hara; (back row) Gillars, Boyer, and Moore.

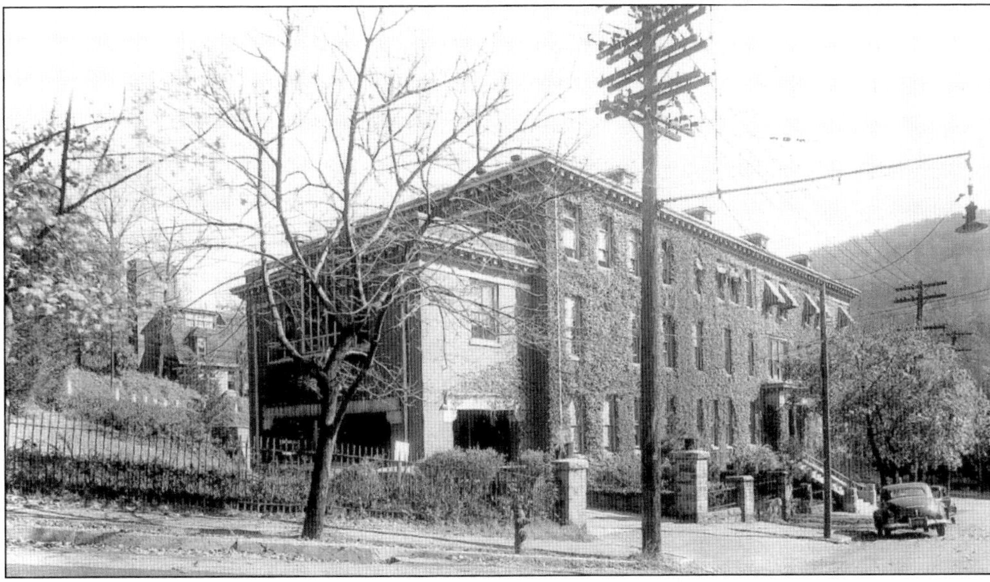

The Pottsville Hospital was organized in 1895 after an epidemic struck Pottsville. The ivy on its brick walls gives the hospital a very comforting feeling, as seen in this 1930s image. It is still at its original location at Mauch Chunk and Jackson Streets.

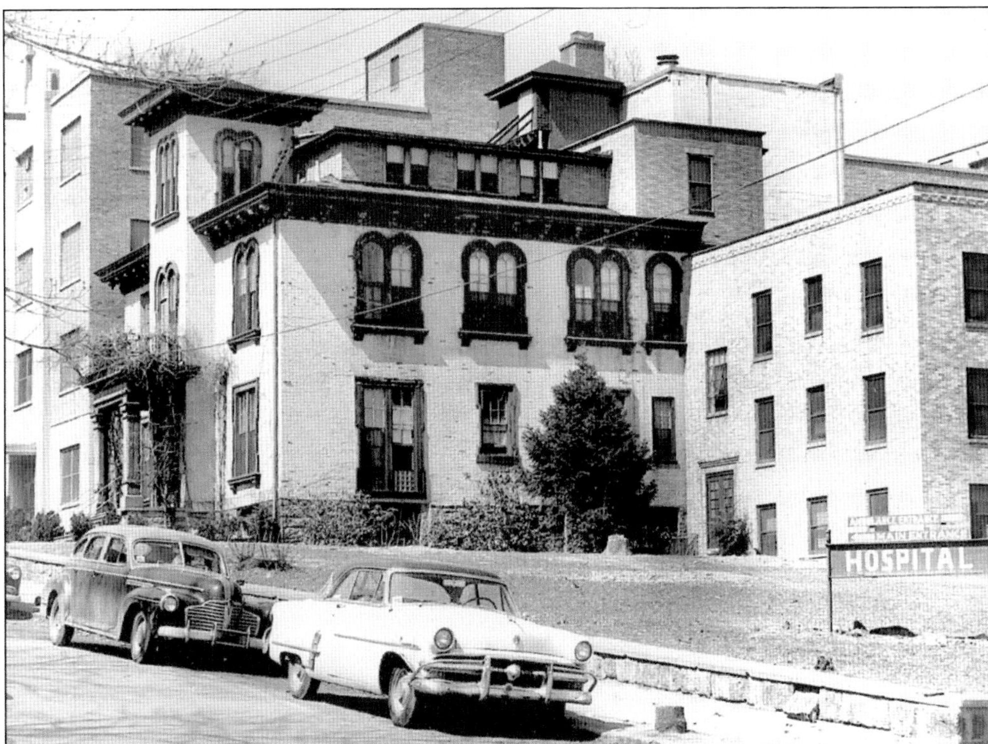

The Good Samaritan Hospital was built on the grounds of the mansion of lawyer Francis Hughes at East Norwegian and Tremont Streets. The hospital was built around the mansion, which was used as the emergency room in the 1930s and 1940s. Eventually, the mansion disappeared.

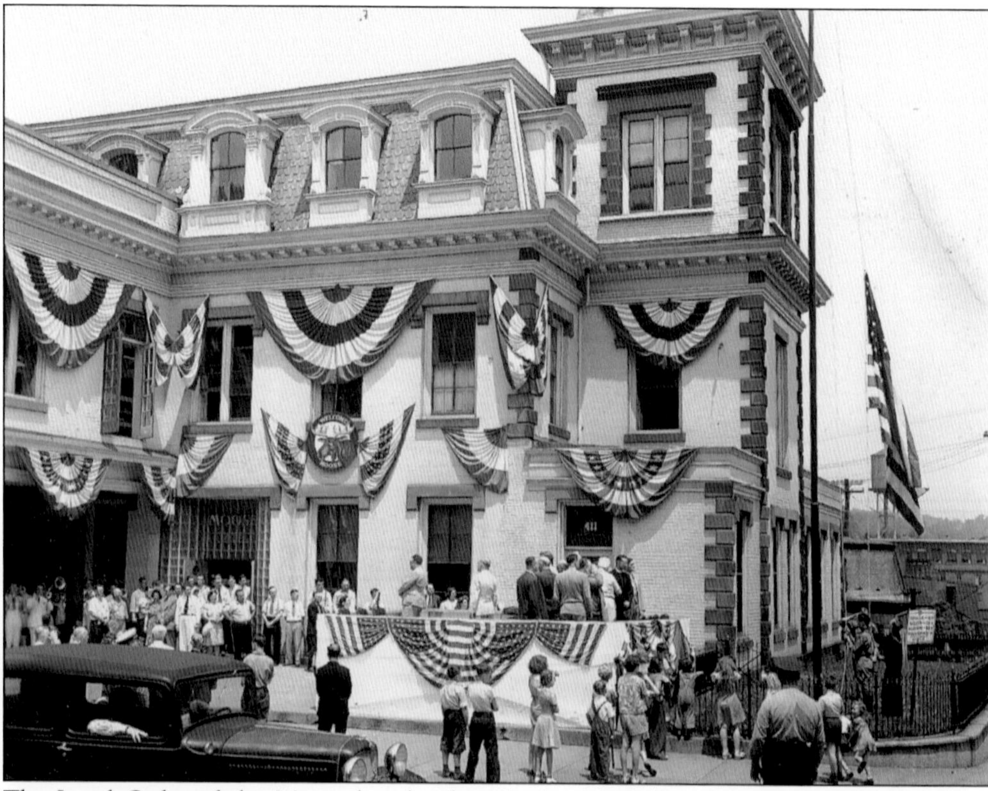

The Loyal Order of the Moose bought the Charles M. Atkins mansion, at South Centre and Mauch Chunk Streets, in 1917. There is a big celebration going on in this 1942 image. The lodge had a peak of 2,400 members on its rolls and was the most active organization in Pottsville.

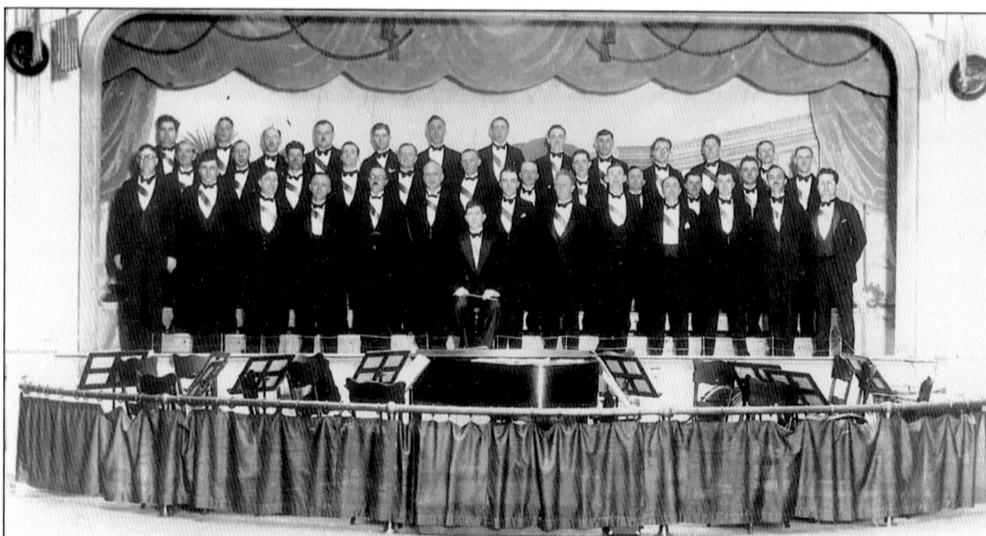

The Pottsville Elks Famous Forty was a male chorus that held forth in Pottsville during the 1920s and 1930s. Edgar D. Brown was its originator, promoter, and conductor. Lee Berger, a talented young pianist, was the accompanist and star soloist.

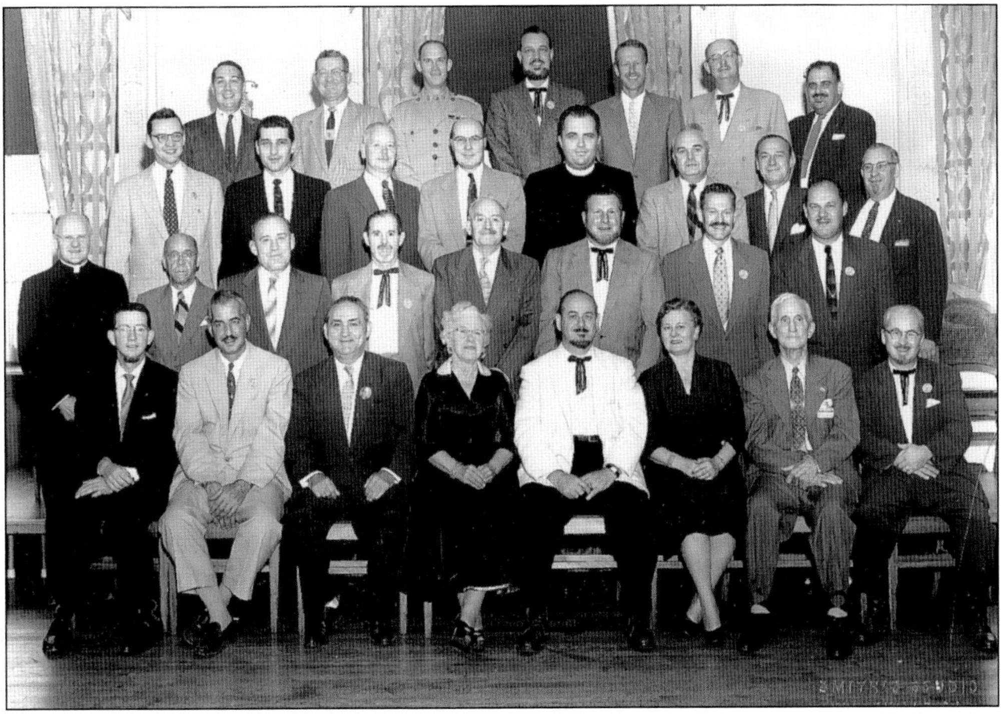

Pottsville celebrated its sesquicentennial in 1956. The board of directors assembled in the Necho Allen Hotel for this image.

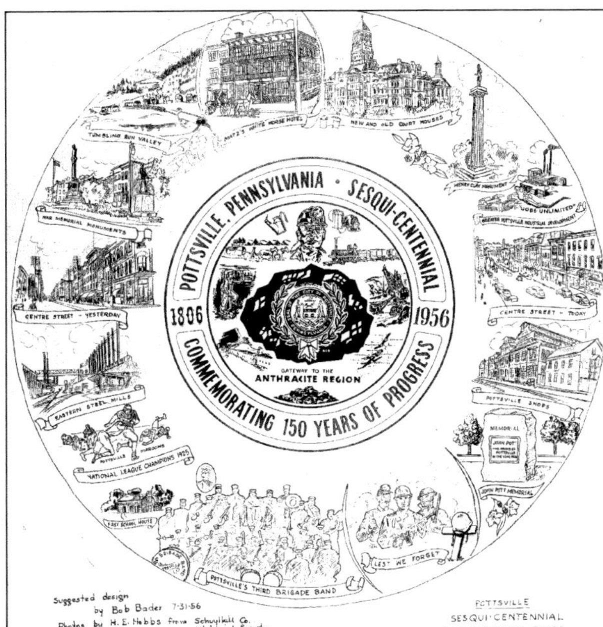

Bob Bader designed this commemorative plate as a souvenir for the sesquicentennial celebration of 1956. The artist drew various scenes of Pottsville on the plate.

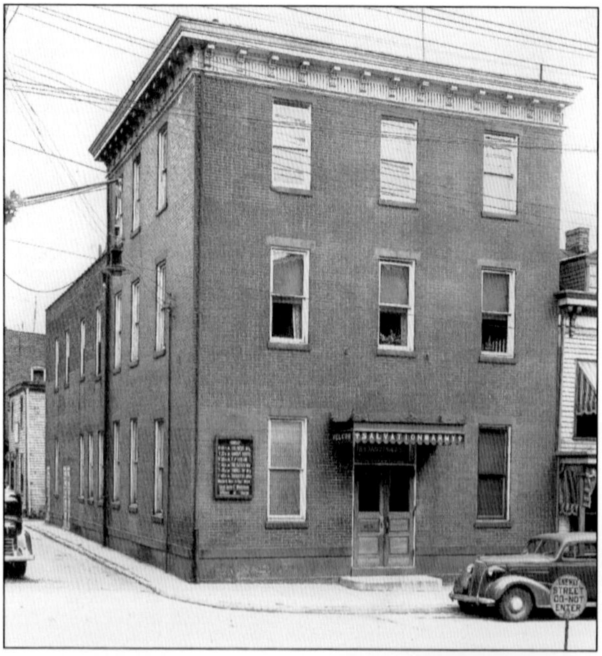

The Salvation Army has been quietly serving Pottsville for many years. It was located at the southeast corner of North Second and West Race Streets, as seen in this 1940s image. It helped feed the poor during the holidays.

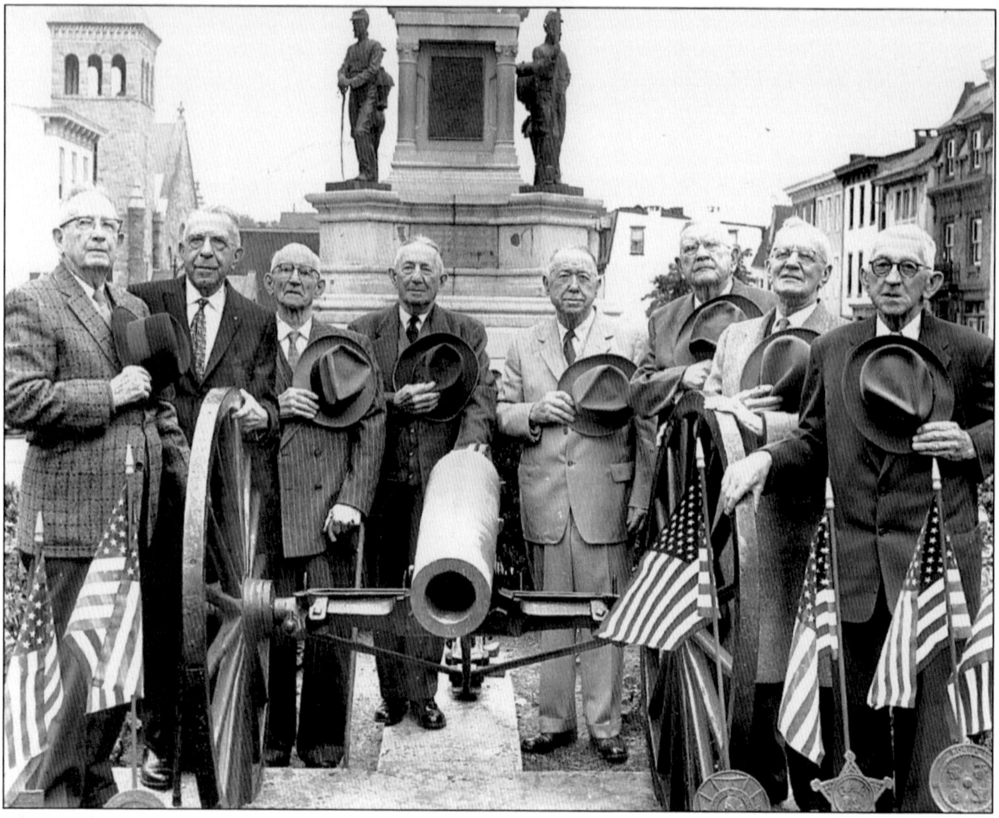

The ranks of the veterans of the Spanish-American War are thinning in this image of the survivors, who are in Garfield Square to commemorate Memorial Day in 1960.

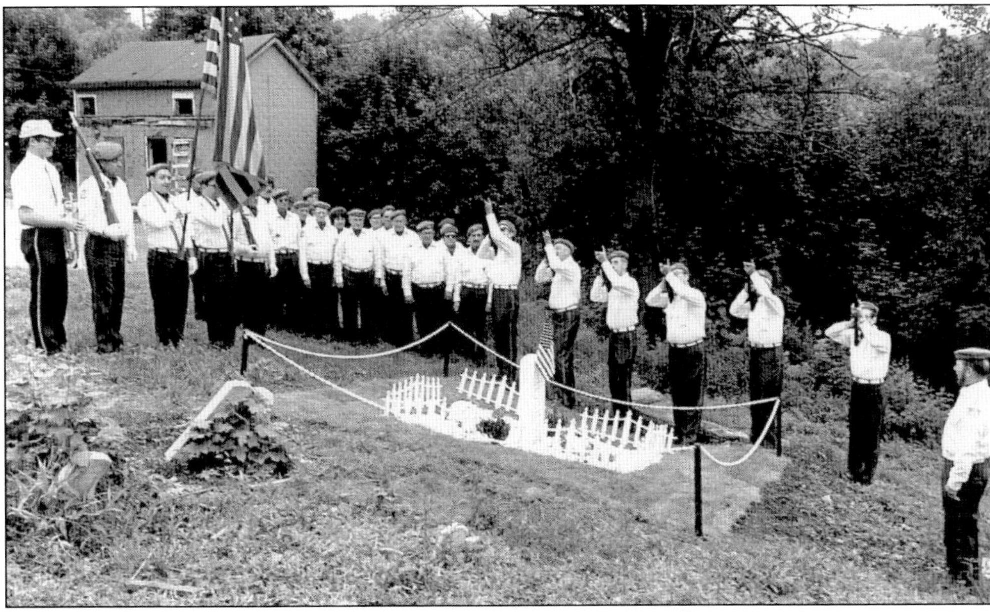

The color guard, drill team, and firing squad of Walter Griffiths AMVETS Post 180 are conducting services over the grave of Nicholas Biddle. Biddle, an African American, was the first man to shed blood in the Civil War when he marched through the streets of Baltimore on April 18, 1861.

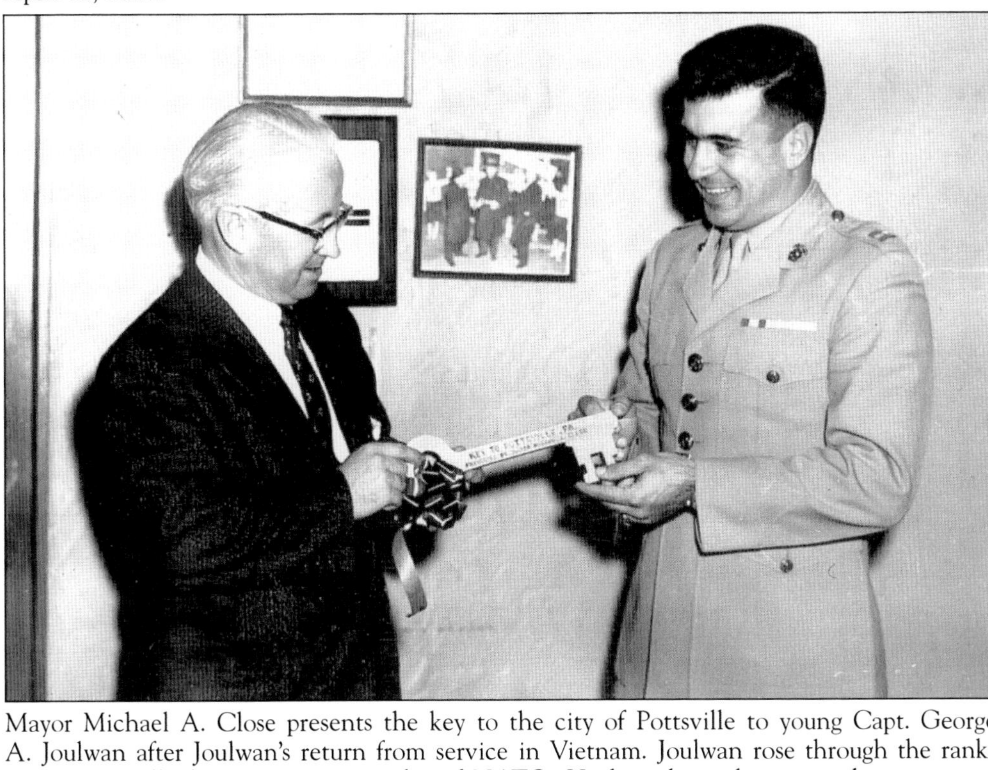

Mayor Michael A. Close presents the key to the city of Pottsville to young Capt. George A. Joulwan after Joulwan's return from service in Vietnam. Joulwan rose through the ranks to become Allied supreme commander of NATO. He has always been proud to represent Pottsville during his military career.

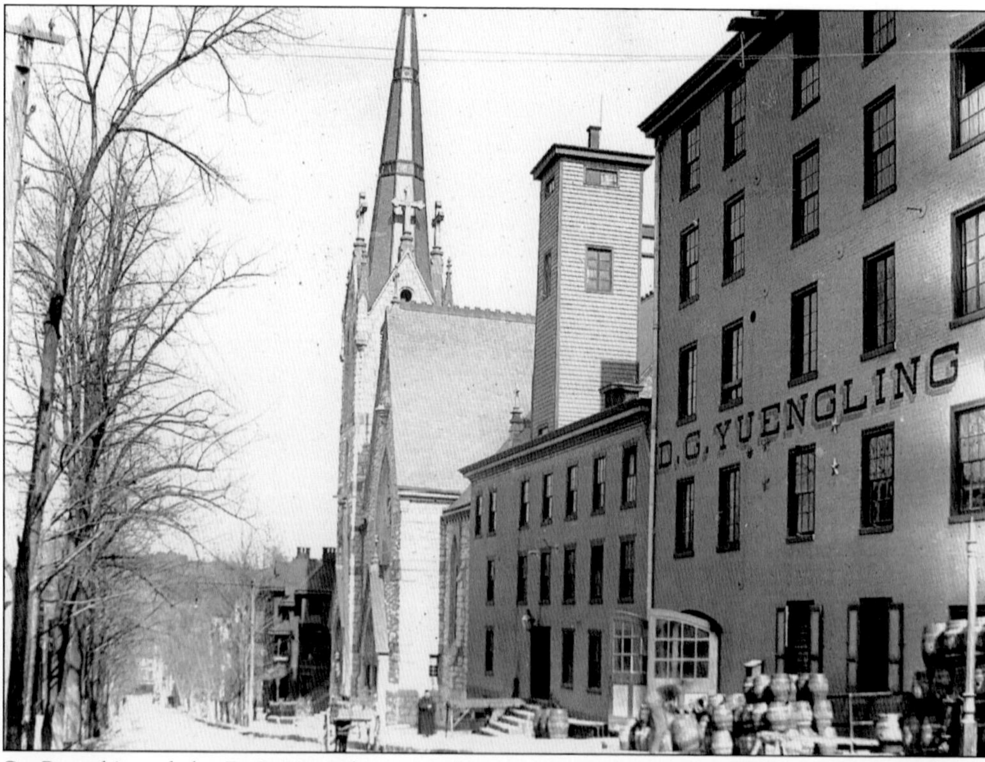

St. Patrick's and the D.G. Yuengling and Son Brewery have been neighbors since 1829. The church settled on its site at Mahantongo and Fourth Streets in 1825. D.G. Yuengling located his brewery here since he could tunnel into Sharp Mountain and store his beer to keep it cold.

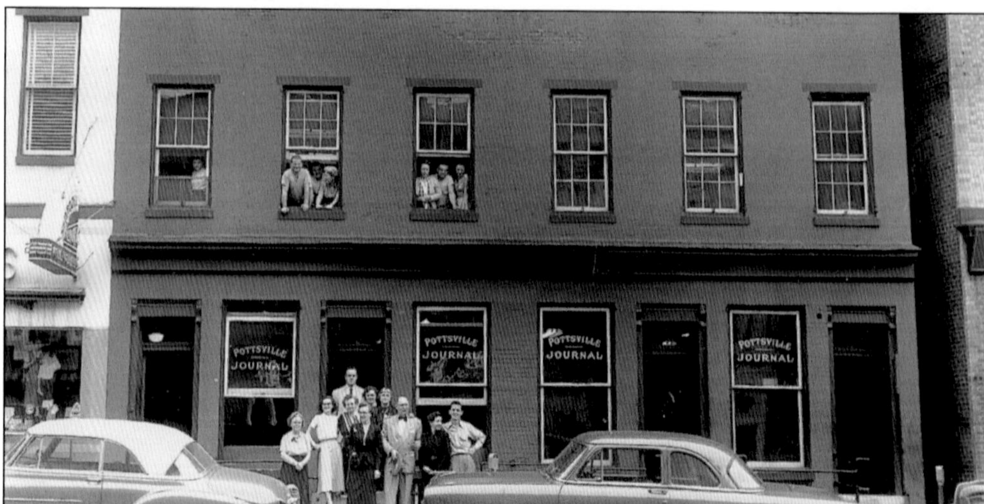

September 15, 1953, was the last day for the *Pottsville Journal* at its headquarters on South Centre Street. The newspaper served the county for 128 years. The last of the employees pose for this picture on closing day. The *Pottsville Republican* purchased the newspaper, and some of the journal employees began working for that newspaper the next day.

Four

RECREATION

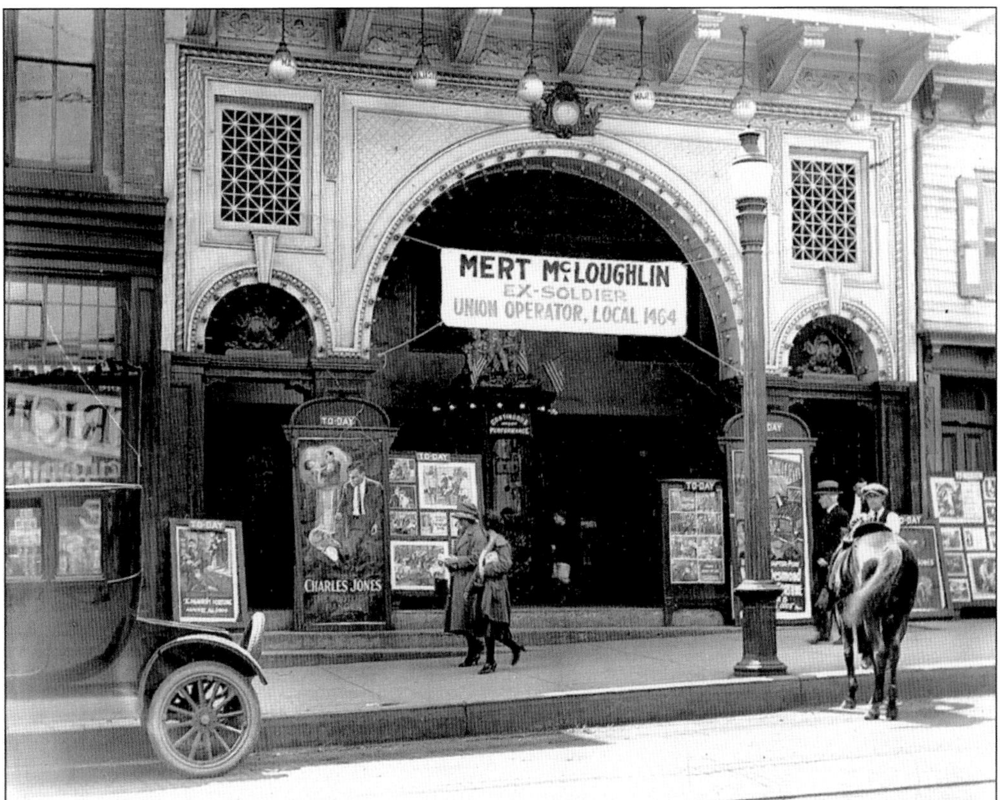

The Majestic Theatre opened its doors in 1910 as a silent movie house at 209–211 North Centre Street. The theater enjoyed popularity for nearly two decades, but the competition from motion picture houses forced the Majestic to close its doors early in 1930. Today, the Majestic Theatre Association is working toward renovating and reopening the theater.

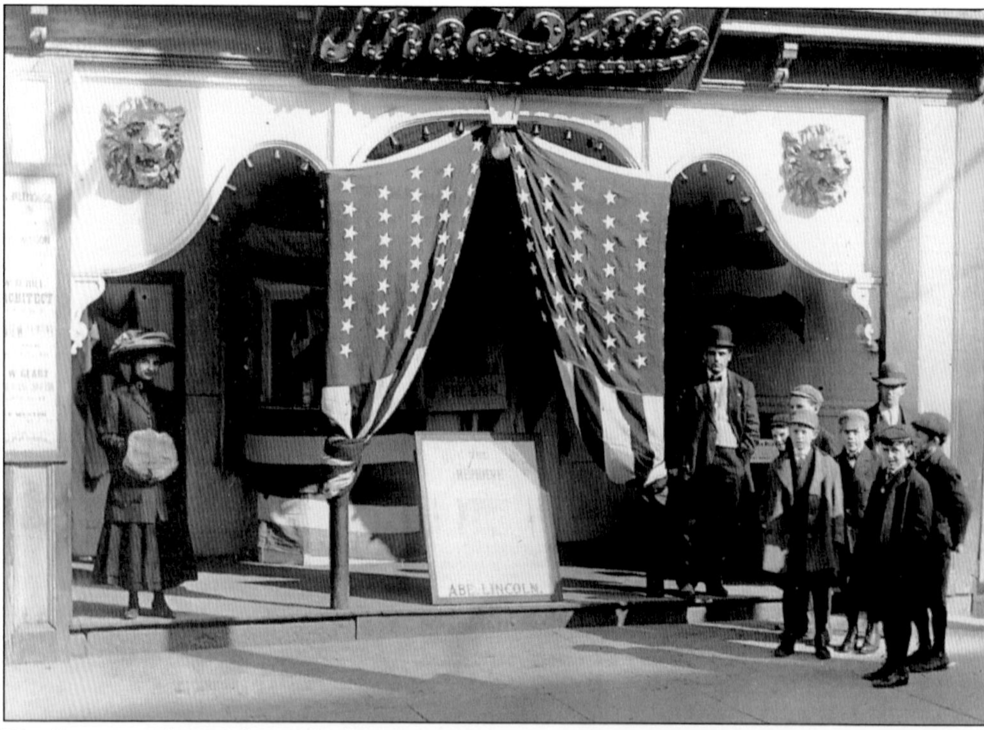

The Lion, another of the early downtown theaters, operated between 1909 and 1917. It was located on the northeast corner of Centre and Mahantongo Streets at the present doctors' offices and former Woolworth building. In this c. 1909 image, the stars and stripes adorn the entrance for *Abe Lincoln*.

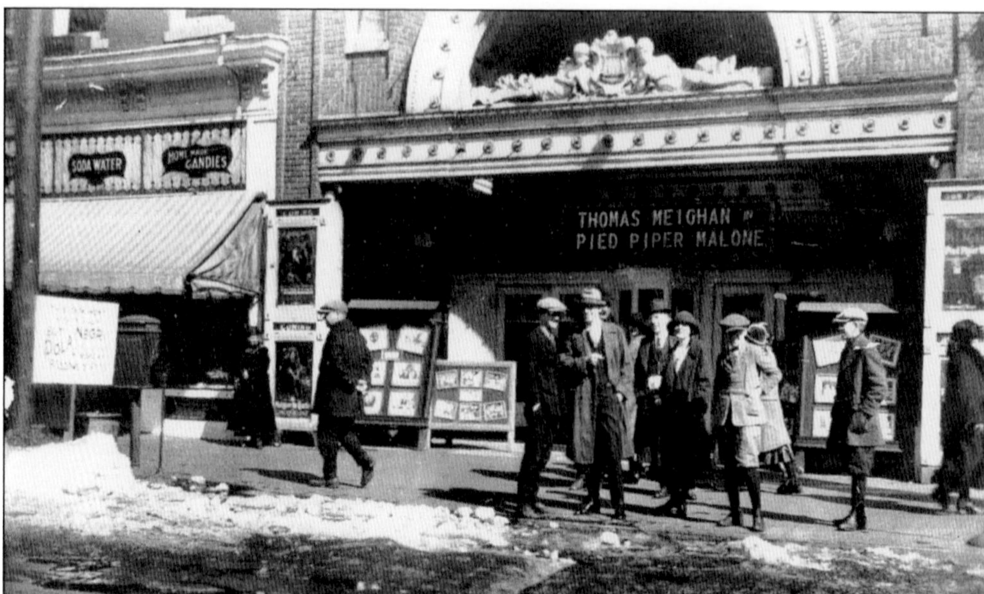

This 1924 image shows a crowd outside the Garden Theatre, located at 14 North Centre Street. The theater opened in the first decade of the 20th century and operated until May 1926, when it closed permanently.

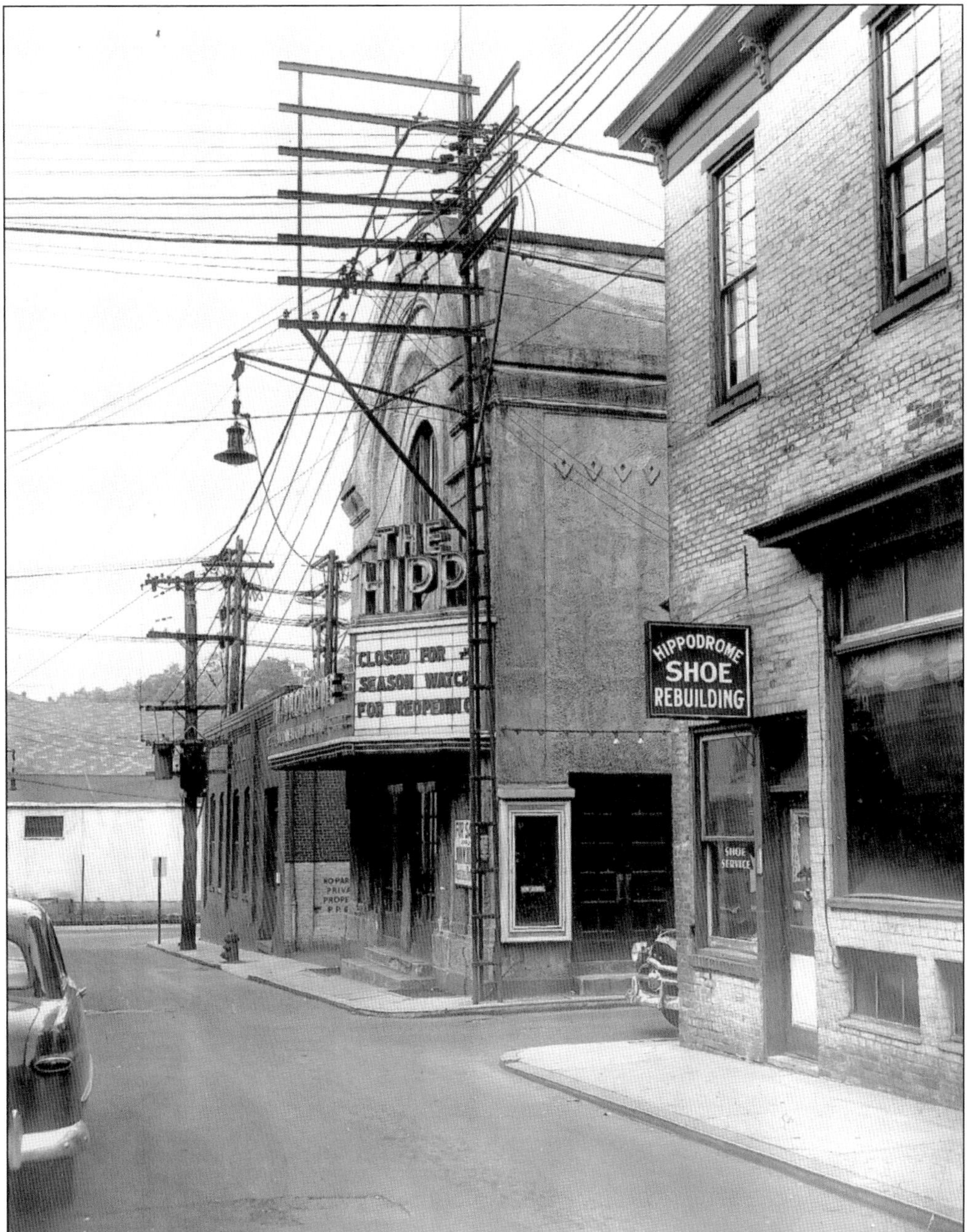

The Hippodrome Theatre opened in November 1913 and operated until the mid-1950s, when an aging facility and an economic recession forced its closing. The Braun School of Music often used the theater for commencement ceremonies. "The Hipp," as it was popularly known, was located at 111 East Market Street, now one of Pottsville's many parking lots.

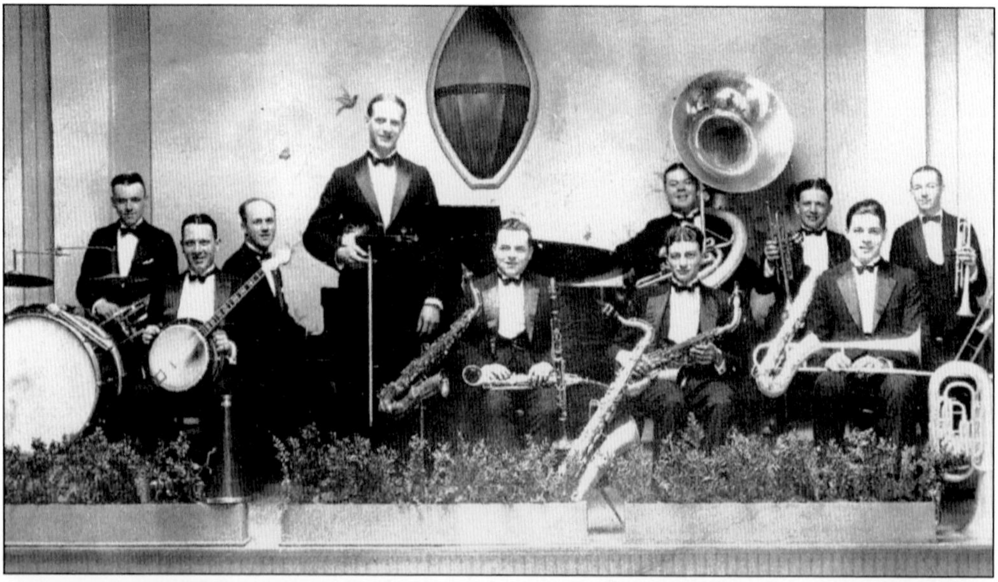

The popular Adelphia Players are pictured here at the Old Holly Roof atop the Hollywood Theatre. The band members are, from left to right, R.W. "Tommy" Knowles on drums, Carlton Simonds on banjo, Carpenter Purcell on piano, Clayton "Duke" Womer as violinist and group leader, Dave Witman on saxophone, Clay Reigle on bass horn (seated rear), Essenial Moyer on saxophone (in front of Reigle), "Bud" Baker on the trumpet (seated rear), Ed Brown on trombone (front), and "Chick" Confehr on trumpet.

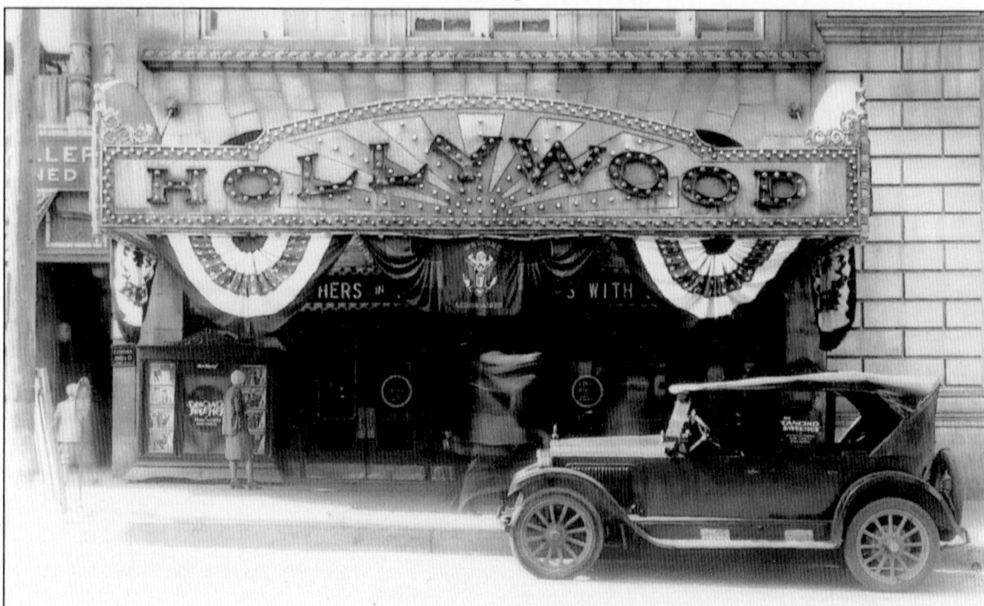

The American Theatre, at 7 South Centre Street, was purchased by William Shugars in August 1923 and was renamed the Hollywood. The Hollywood quickly became a popular movie theater and operated until 1969. The Pennsylvania National Bank acquired the building that housed the Hollywood, and now the M & T Bank features a meeting space named after the popular motion picture venue.

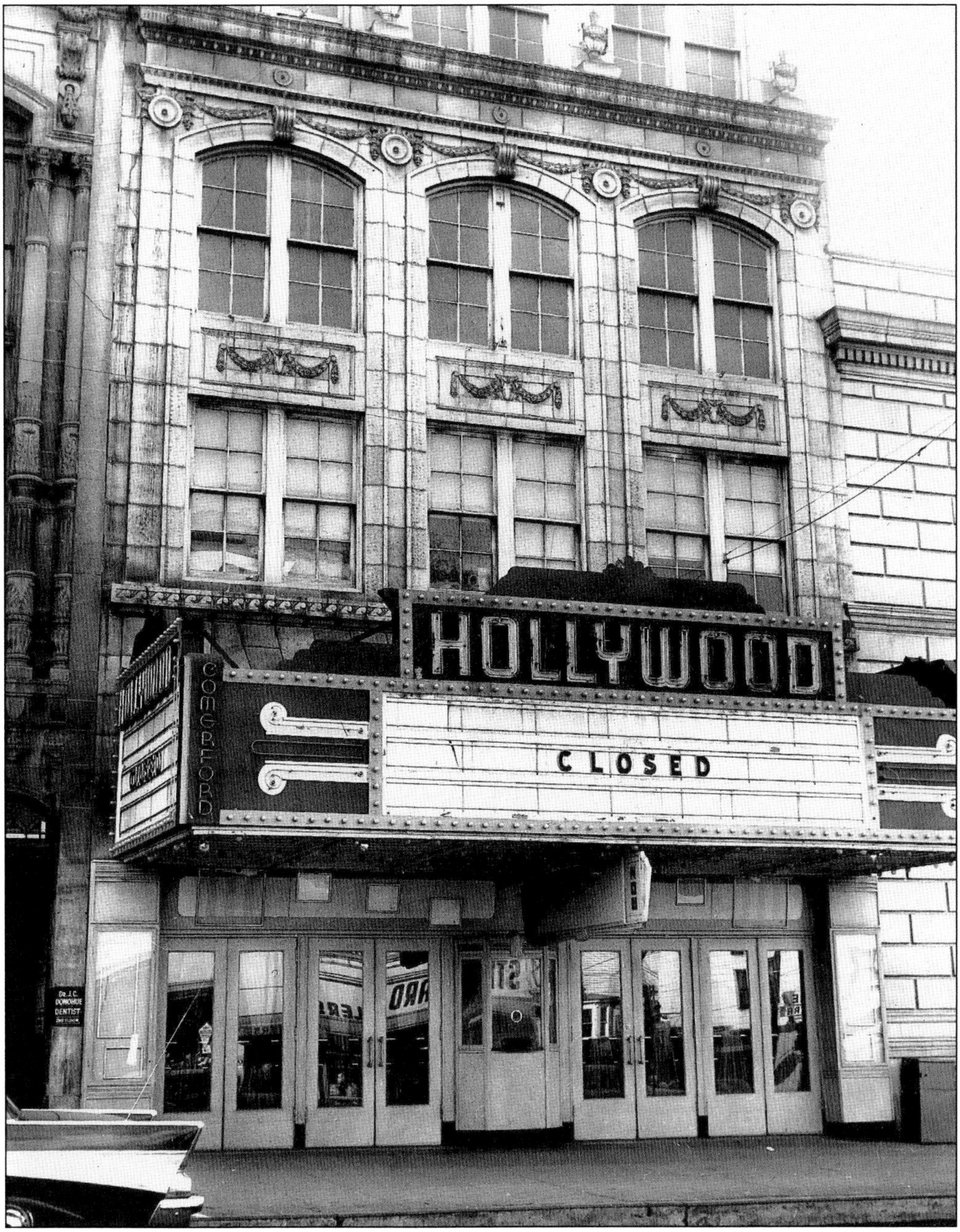

In this *c.* 1969 photograph, a more modern looking Hollywood announces the end of a more than 45-year run. Another clue to the passage of time is the automobiles parked out front, with the running board variety replaced by flashy chrome fins.

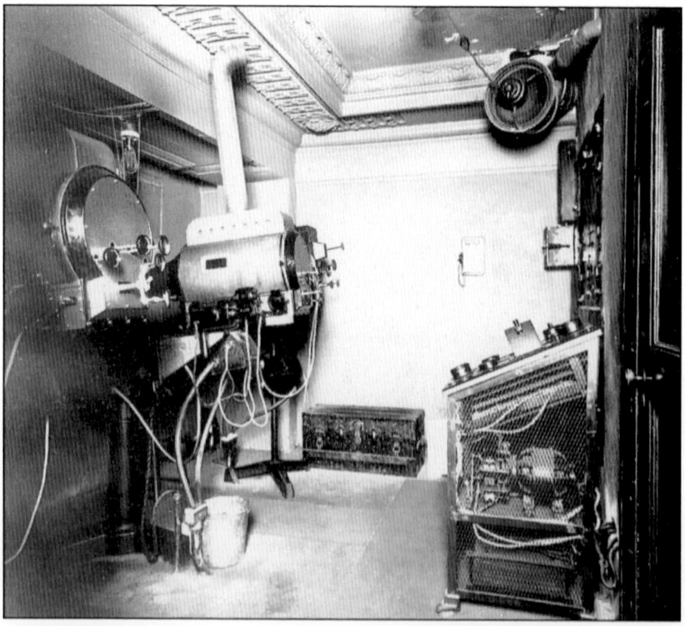

The projection room of the Hollywood is seen *c.* 1927. An early projectionist was Forrest A. Mosser, whose family donated this image to the historical society in 1985.

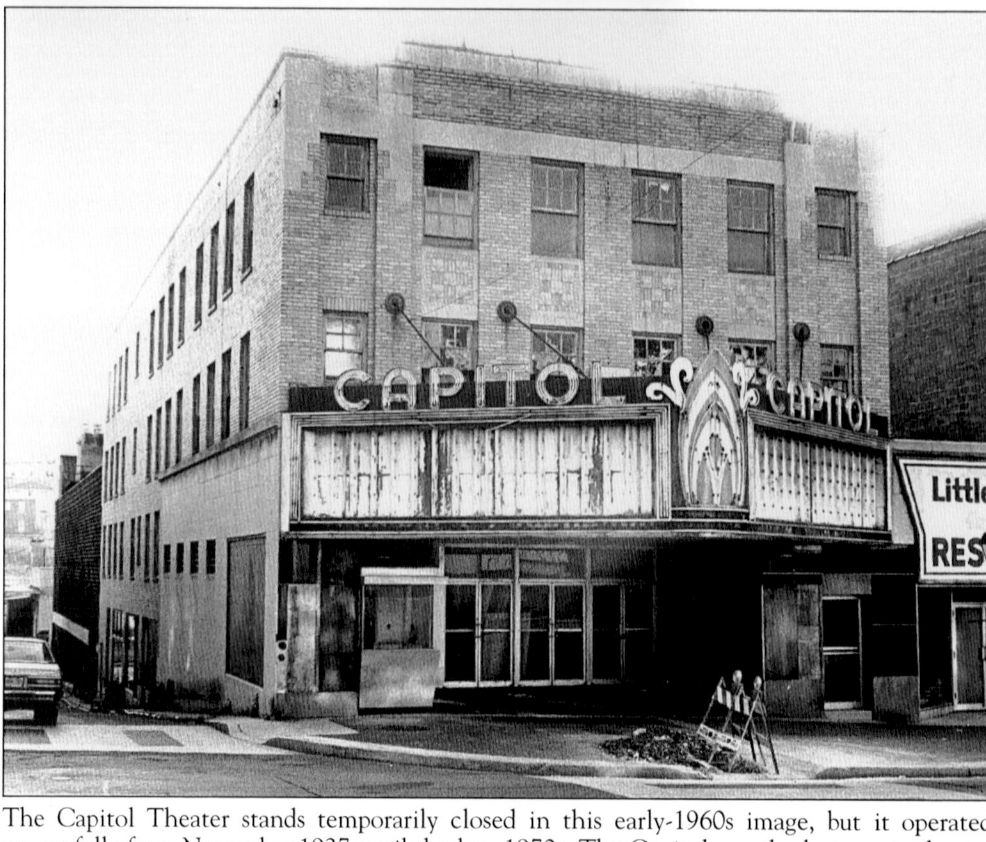

The Capitol Theater stands temporarily closed in this early-1960s image, but it operated successfully from November 1927 until the late 1970s. The Capitol was the last movie theater to operate in downtown Pottsville. The original plans called for a six-story building at a cost of more than $1 million in 1926.

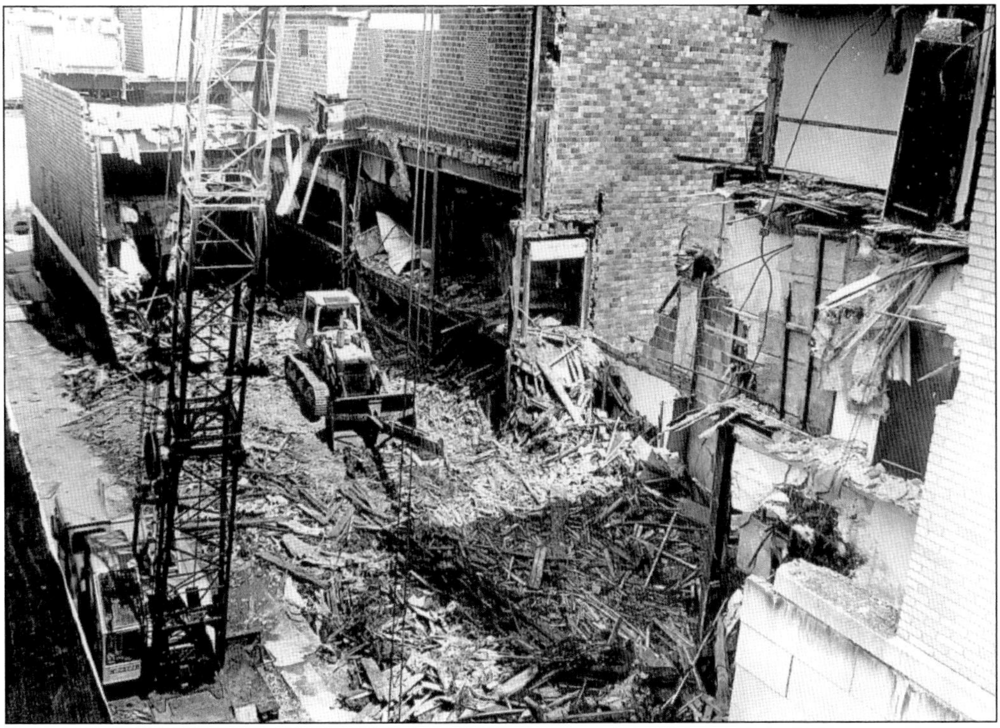

In this photograph, taken in the summer of 1982, the Capitol Theater is days away from demolition. The Capitol featured a seating capacity of 2,700 people, but it had been closed for several years when this picture was taken. More modern theater accommodations at nearby shopping malls took away the business from what was once called "the coolest spot in town" and "the pride of Pottsville."

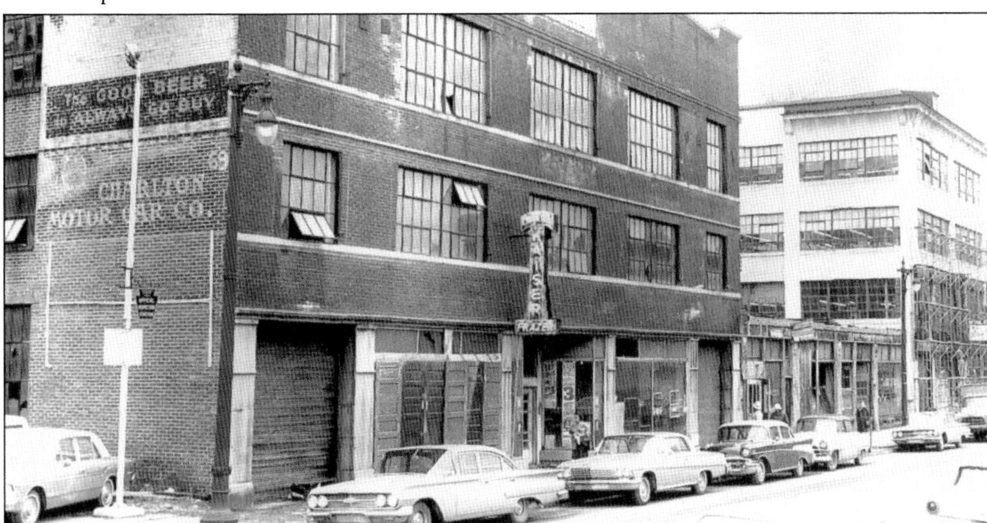

Charlton's Hall, located on North Centre Street just beyond the present 911 building, was a popular site for pugilistic encounters. The lettering on the wall makes note of the Charlton Motor Car Company. In the 1920s and 1930s, this was one of many sites for boxing matches, dances, and roller-skating in Schuylkill County.

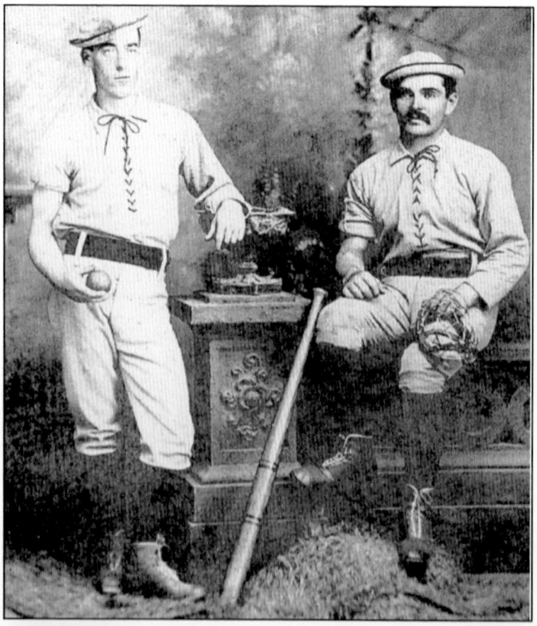

Another popular form of sporting recreation was the national pastime. In this 1880s image, pitcher Bernie McLaughlin and catcher Hugh Breslin are posing for the camera. McLaughlin and Breslin played semiprofessional baseball for one of Pottsville's early teams.

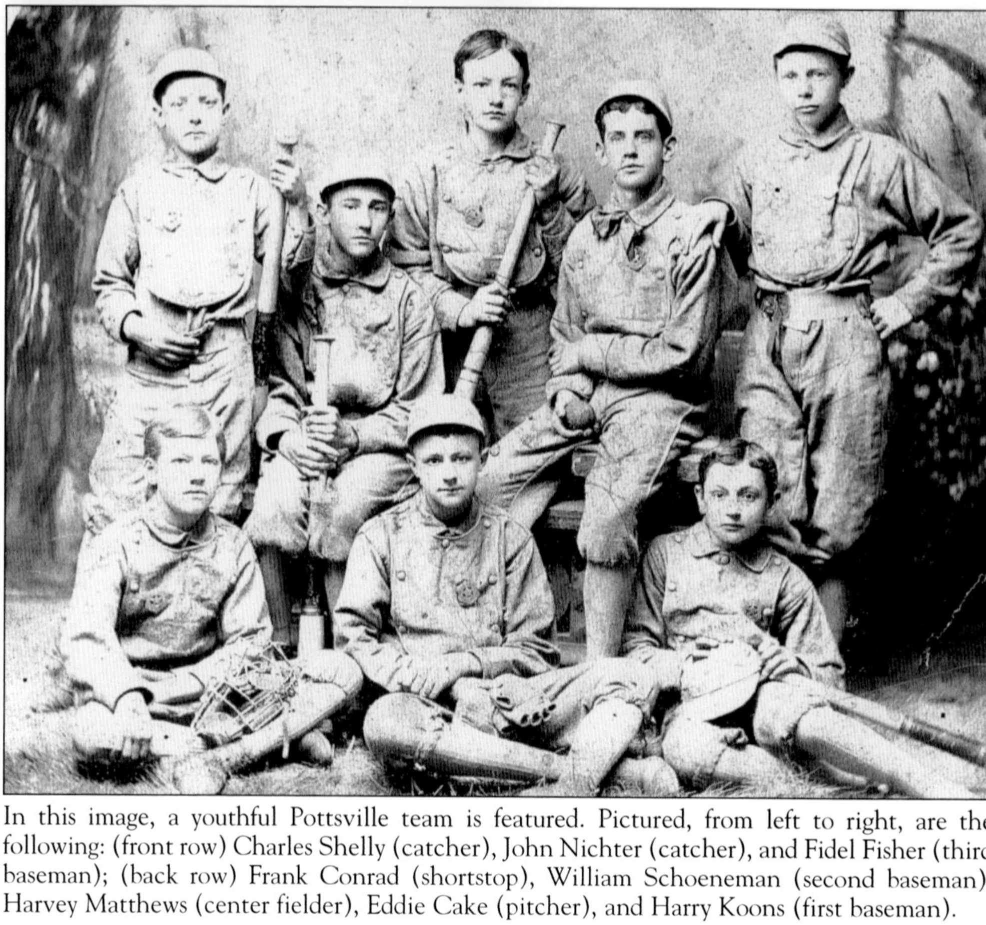

In this image, a youthful Pottsville team is featured. Pictured, from left to right, are the following: (front row) Charles Shelly (catcher), John Nichter (catcher), and Fidel Fisher (third baseman); (back row) Frank Conrad (shortstop), William Schoeneman (second baseman), Harvey Matthews (center fielder), Eddie Cake (pitcher), and Harry Koons (first baseman).

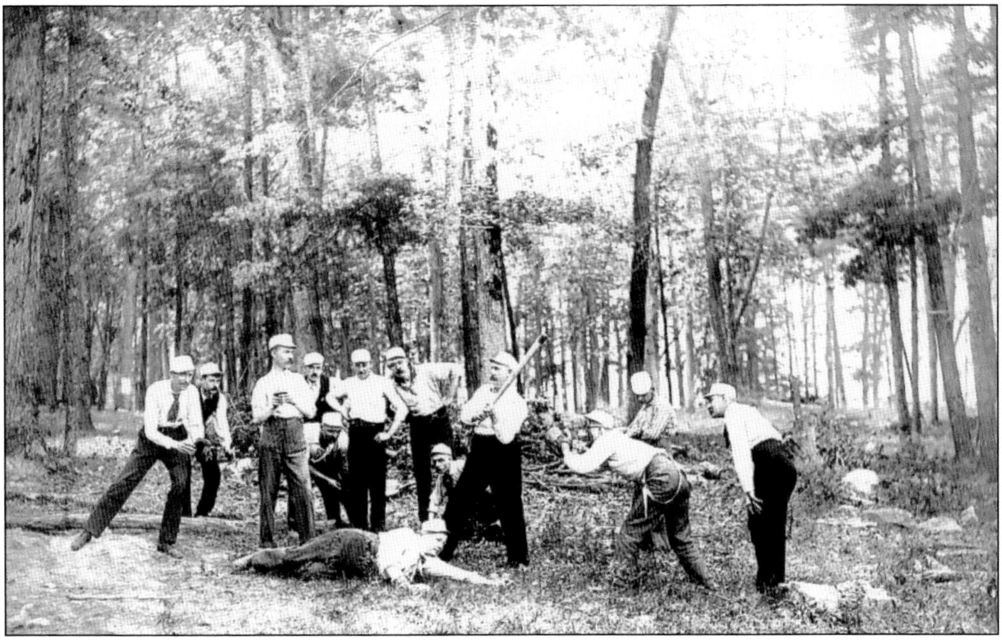

This late-19th-century George Bretz photograph features the boys from the Philadelphia & Reading shops during one of the annual company picnics. The peculiar posing of ballplayers is unrealistic, but the artist has captured the boys in a variety of game faces.

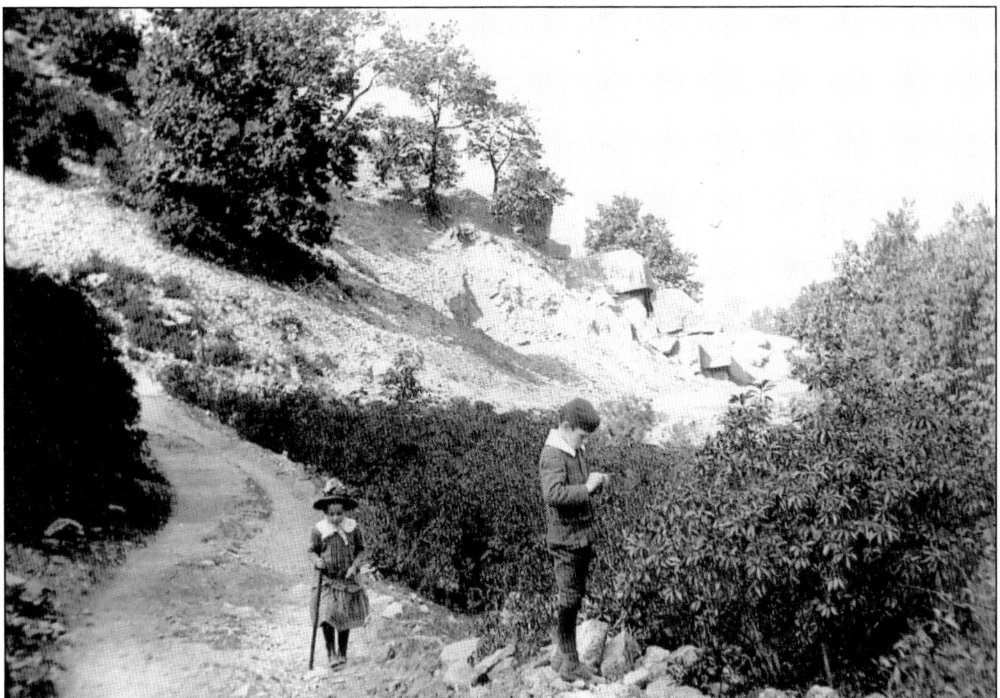

This Victorian-era image of a boy and his sister hiking on Sharp Mountain shows Pottsville in the distance, with a rugged trail winding up the slope of the hill. Hiking Pottsville's surrounding hills was a popular activity in the 19th and 20th centuries.

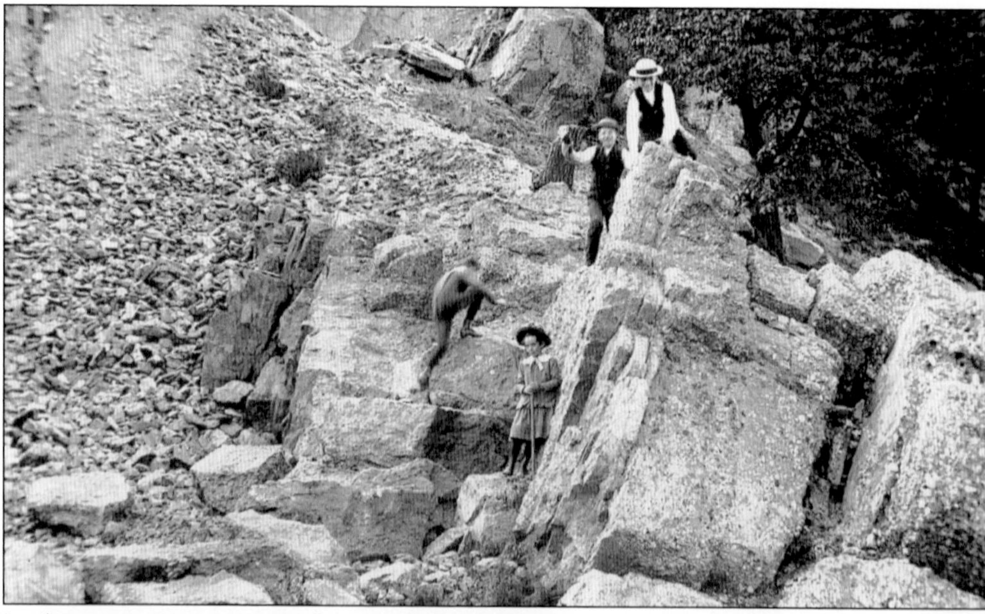

In this image, it appears as if more of the family are enjoying themselves as they scale the rock face on the eastern edge of Sharp Mountain. An outcropping of Pottsville conglomerate provides these climbers with a challenge. Today, much of this section of Sharp Mountain is covered with trees and brush.

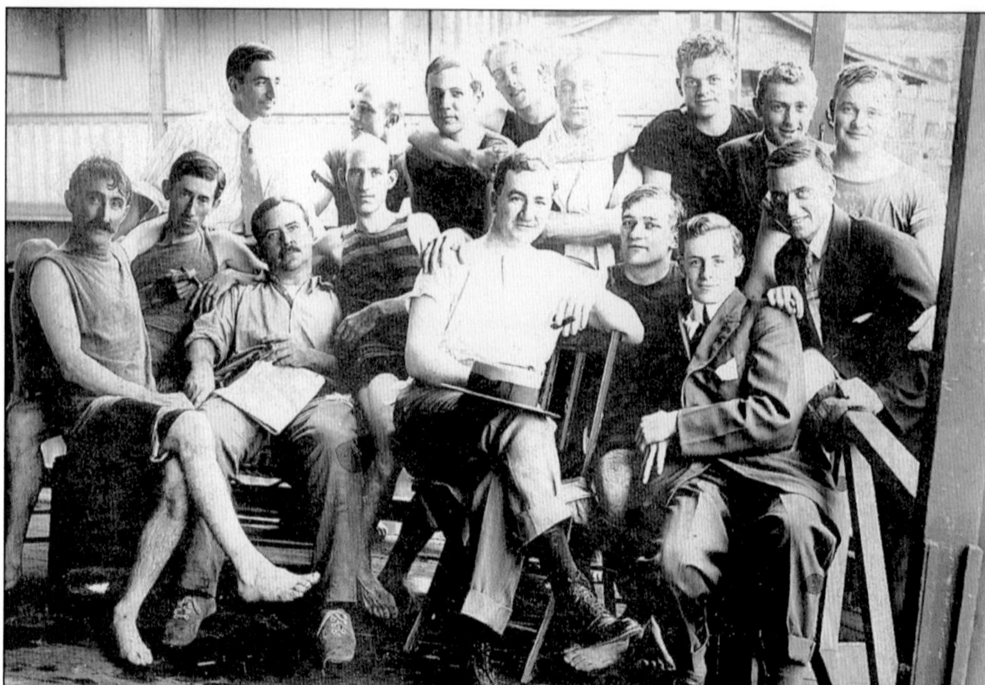

This group of men lounges around at one of the many boathouses lining Tumbling Run Reservoir outside of Pottsville. A number of Pottsville clubs and organizations maintained boathouses where their members and families could enjoy the recreational opportunities found at this popular 19th-century resort, located just south of Pottsville.

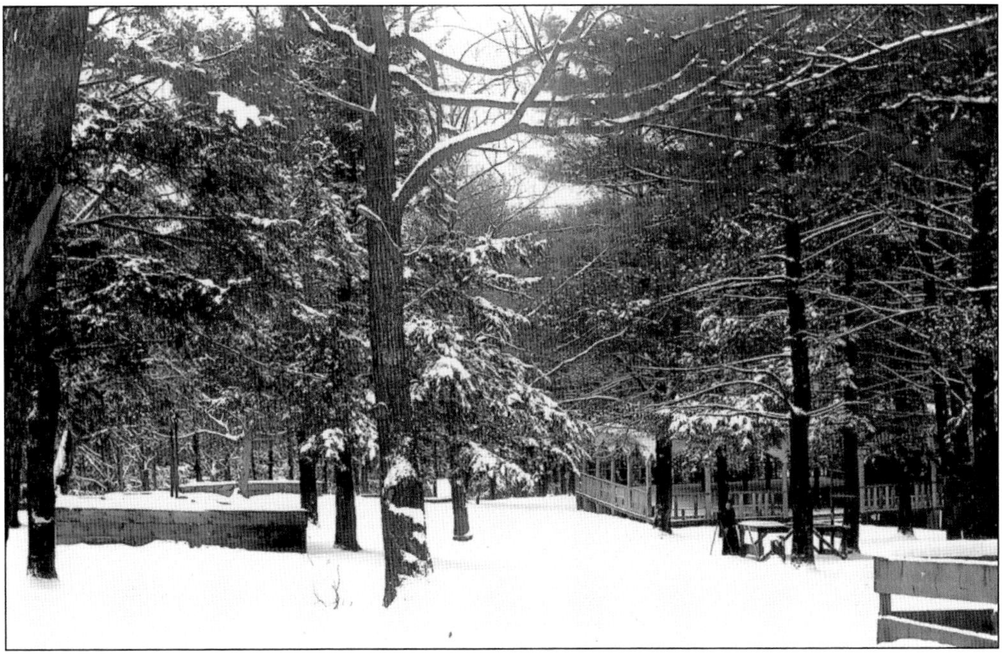

Another popular recreational facility was found at Agricultural Park, located on the eastern edge of the city of Pottsville in Mechanicsville. Agricultural Park had been a popular summer destination since the 1860s. In this *c.* 1890 scene, however, a blanket of snow has covered the park grounds, including the pavilion where performances by the Third Brigade Band were popular.

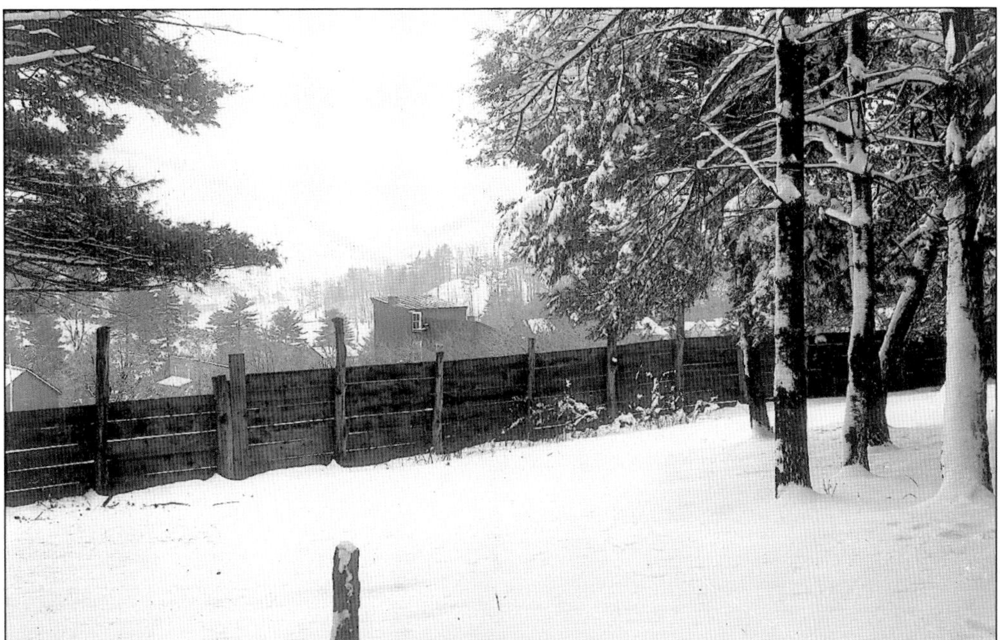

From this vantage point, Mechanicsville is seen in the foreground, while in the distance, a snow-covered Sharp Mountain is almost lost on this cloudy winter day. Agricultural Park was located at the present site of the United Cerebral Palsy facility, where the Pottsville Children's Home operated during the 20th century.

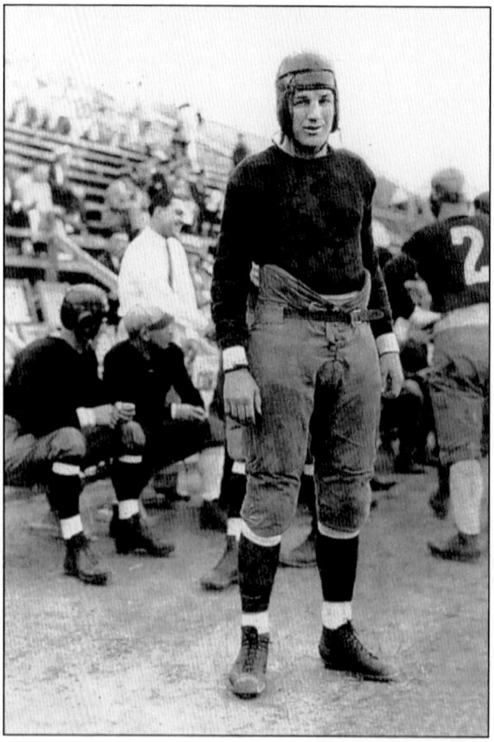

The Pottsville Maroons football team was part of the National Football League (NFL) from 1925 to 1928. The team played its games on Sundays at the Minersville Ball Park not far from Pottsville. The quarterback was Jack Ernst, pictured here. Duke Osborne, sitting on the bench, did not like to wear a helmet and wore a baseball cap instead.

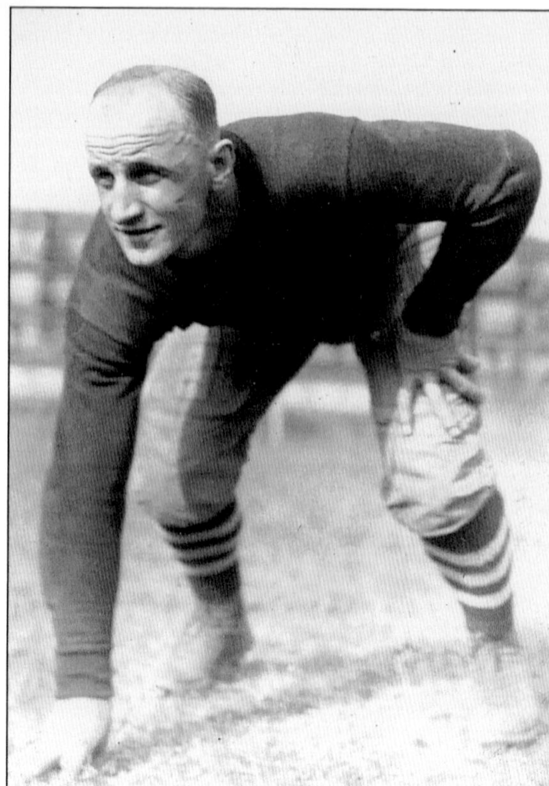

Harold "Red" Grange came to Pottsville to play against the Maroons on November 11, 1927. Grange said that Maroons fullback Tony Latone, shown here, was the greatest football player he had ever seen.

The Maroons beat the Chicago Cardinals in a frigid Comiskey Park on December 6, 1925, in a game for the league championship. The following week, the Maroons played the Notre Dame All Stars in Shibe Park. Charlie Berry, seen here, drop-kicked a field goal to win the game for the Maroons 9-7. The game became very controversial, and the league stripped Pottsville of the title that it had won in Chicago.

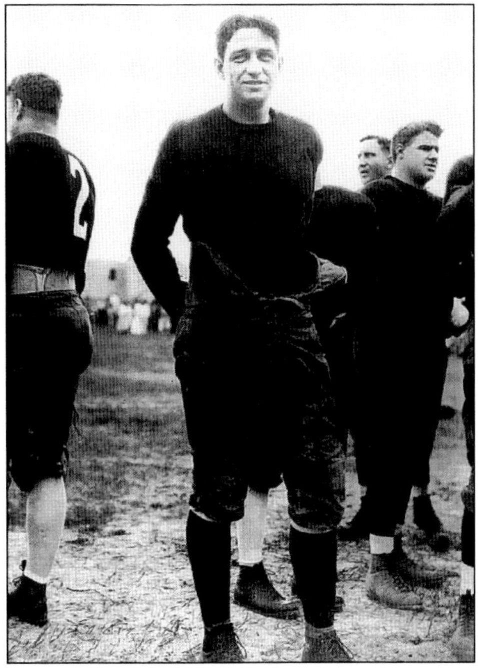

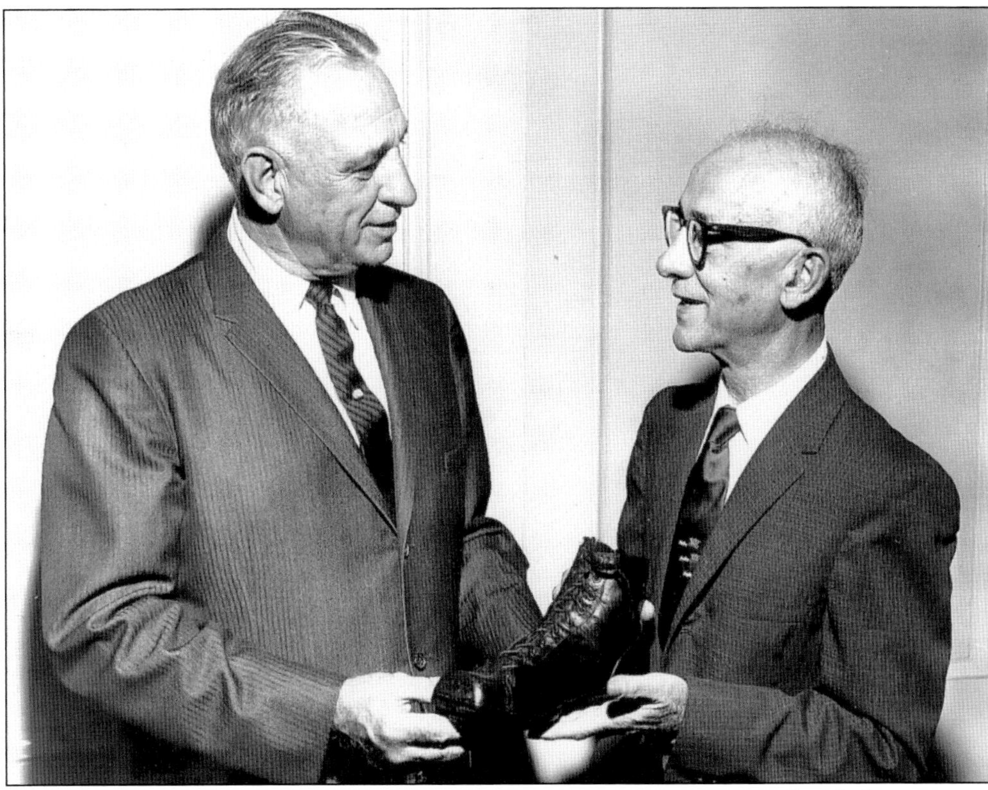

At the Maroons reunion in Pottsville in 1961, sporting-goods store owner Joe Zacko presented Charlie Berry with the famous shoe that Berry wore when the Maroons beat Notre Dame. Zacko had the shoe bronzed, and it is now on display in the Historical Society of Schuylkill County.

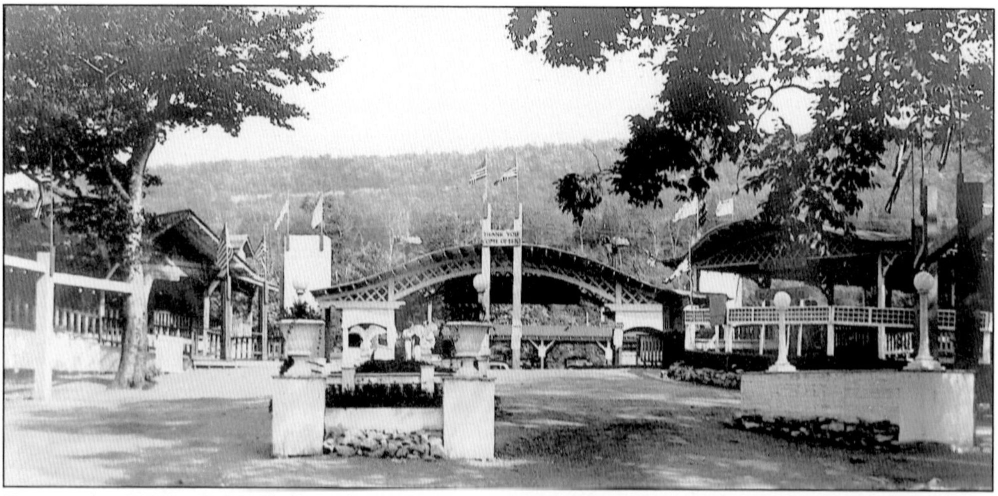

During the 1920s, Schuylkill Park emerged as one of the most popular local attractions in the county. Schuylkill Park, or what was later called Dream City, was located along Route 209 between Port Carbon and Cumbola. The park operated from the second decade of the 20th century until the early 1930s.

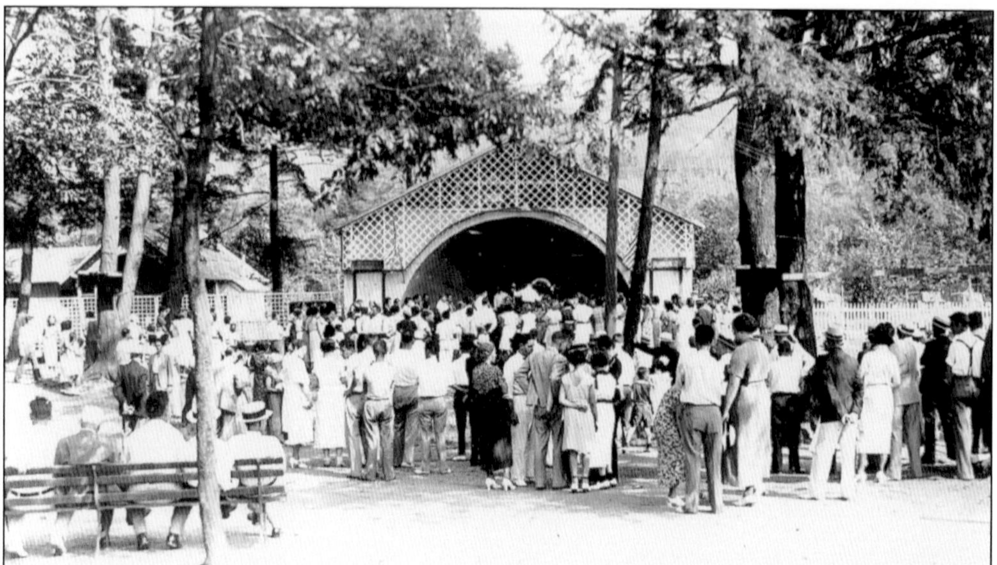

A crowd has formed around the bandstand to hear one of the many bands perform during the summer of 1926. Schuylkill Park replaced Tumbling Run as the most popular summer destination for Pottsville and its surrounding communities. Amusement rides, dancing, band concerts, movies, and circus acts all provided entertainment from May through September.

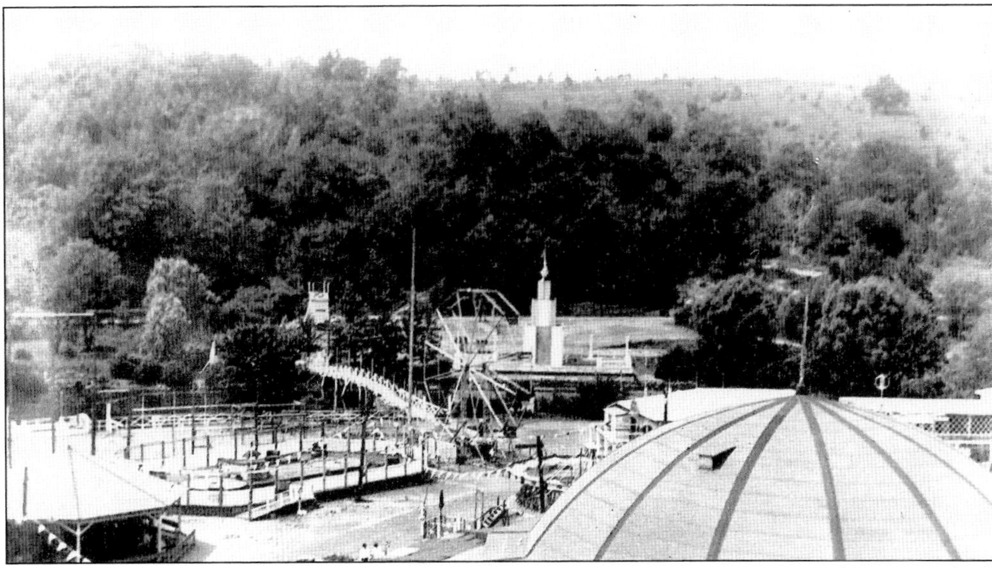

Schuylkill Park featured a swimming pool, a picnic grove, and "amusement devices," which included the "World's Most Thrilling Coaster, Great Aero Swings, and a Carousel of Magnificence." One of the popular draws was Sharp's Dance Pavilion, where dance marathons, then called walkathons, were popular in the 1930s.

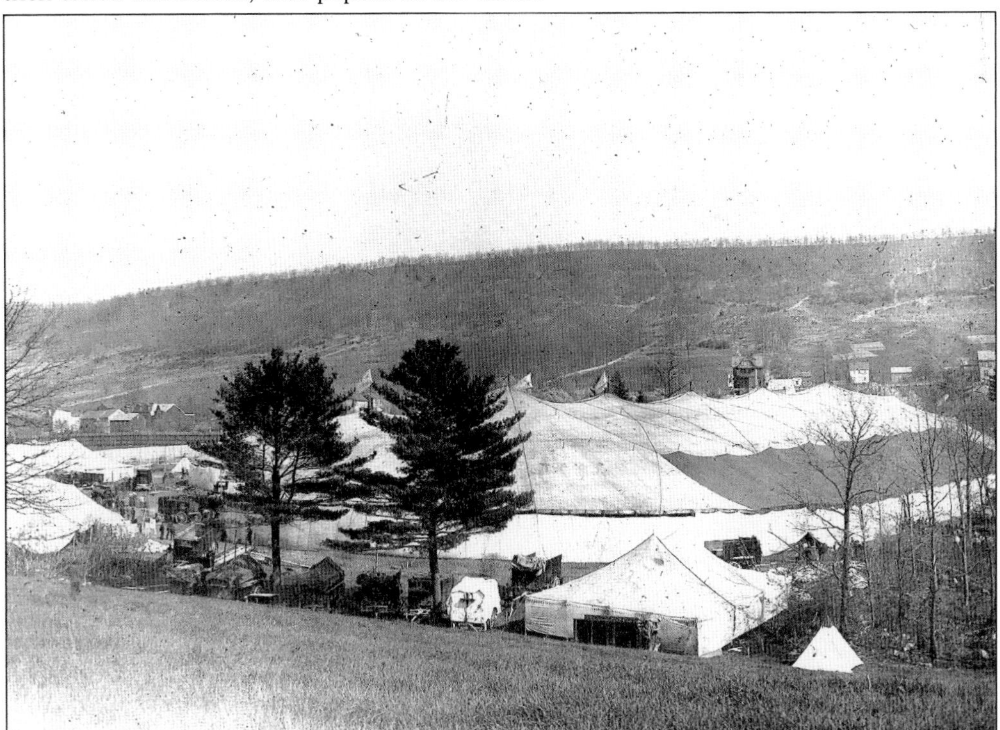

Another popular local park was in the Yorkville section of Pottsville, called Dolan's Park. Since the 1880s, Dolan's Park featured cricket matches, baseball games, and circuses. In 1889, the Buffalo Bill Cody Wild West Show was featured. This photograph was taken from around Third Street and Elk Avenue, looking across West End Avenue toward Sharp Mountain.

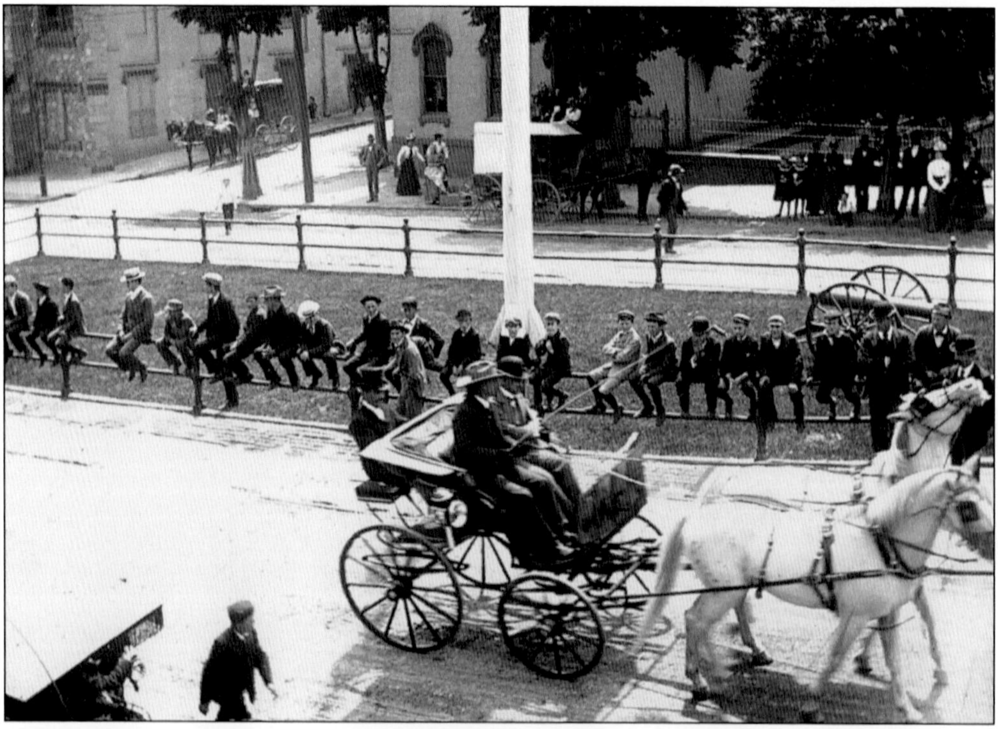

William "Buffalo Bill" Cody's circus was a popular attraction in Pottsville. In this image, Cody is driving his buggy through Garfield Square and is accompanied by Bench Miller of Pottsville. Miller was Cody's personal guard on the frontier and saved Cody's life during an American Indian attack.

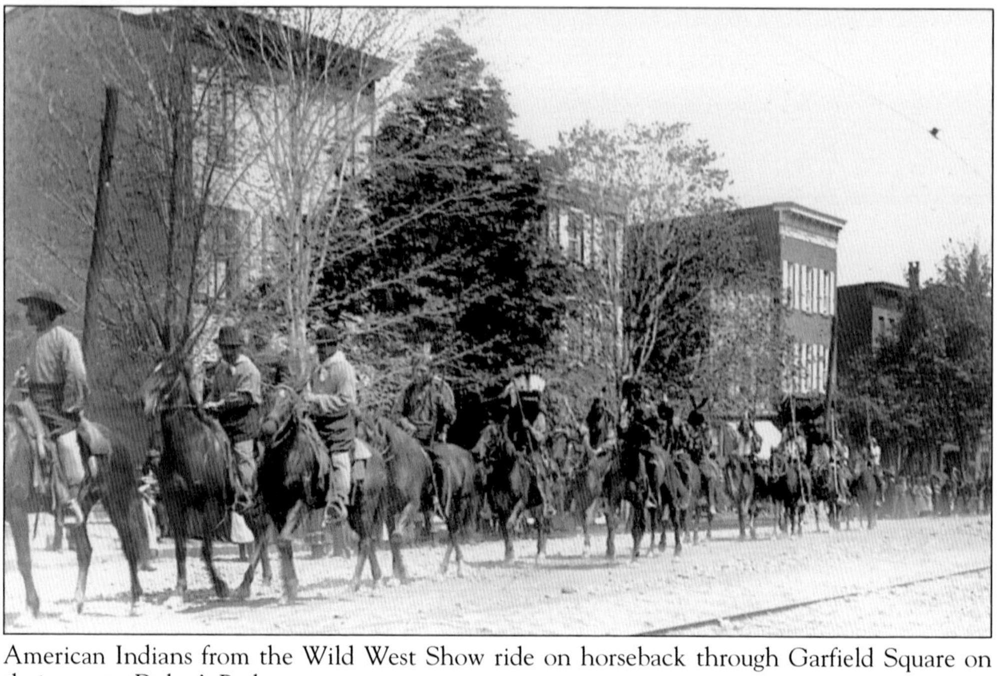

American Indians from the Wild West Show ride on horseback through Garfield Square on their way to Dolan's Park.

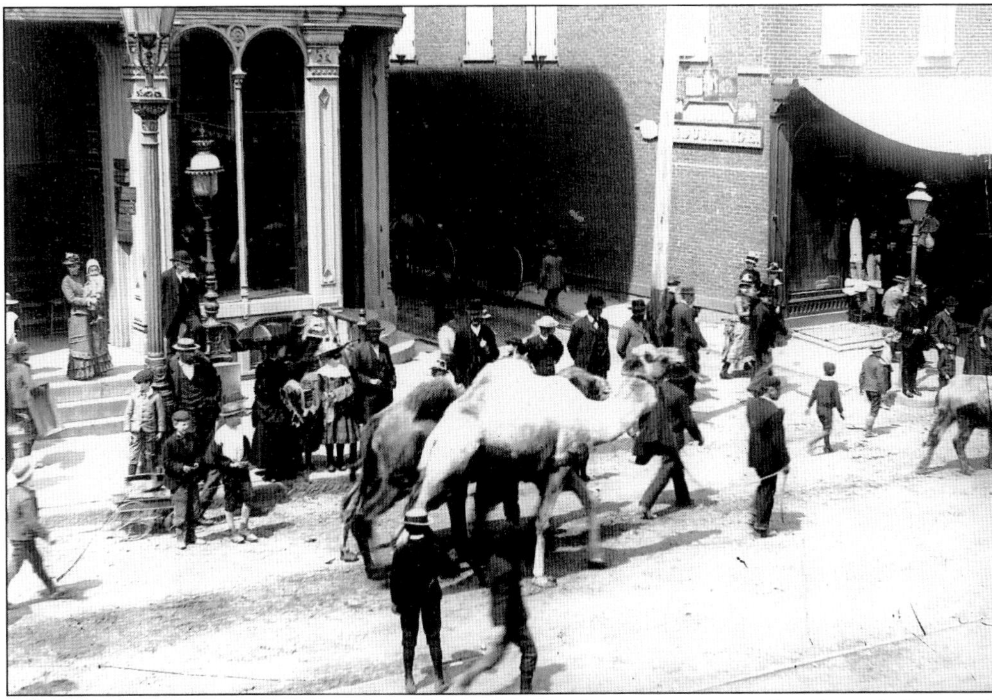

In this late-19th-century image, dromedaries, or camels, are being paraded through Pottsville on their way from the rail yard to Dolan's Park. This photograph was taken at the intersection of West Norwegian and Centre Streets in front of what was known as the Mountain City Building.

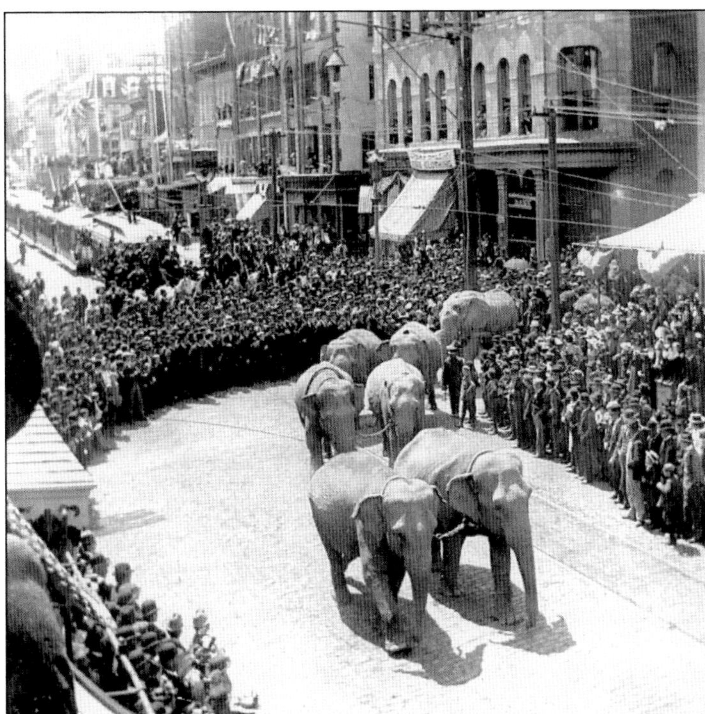

Elephants parade from West Norwegian Street onto Centre Street. The thick crowd separates the elephants from the line of trolleys that are delivering even more witnesses to the spectacle. The circus parade was always a popular attraction as it made its way through the streets of Pottsville.

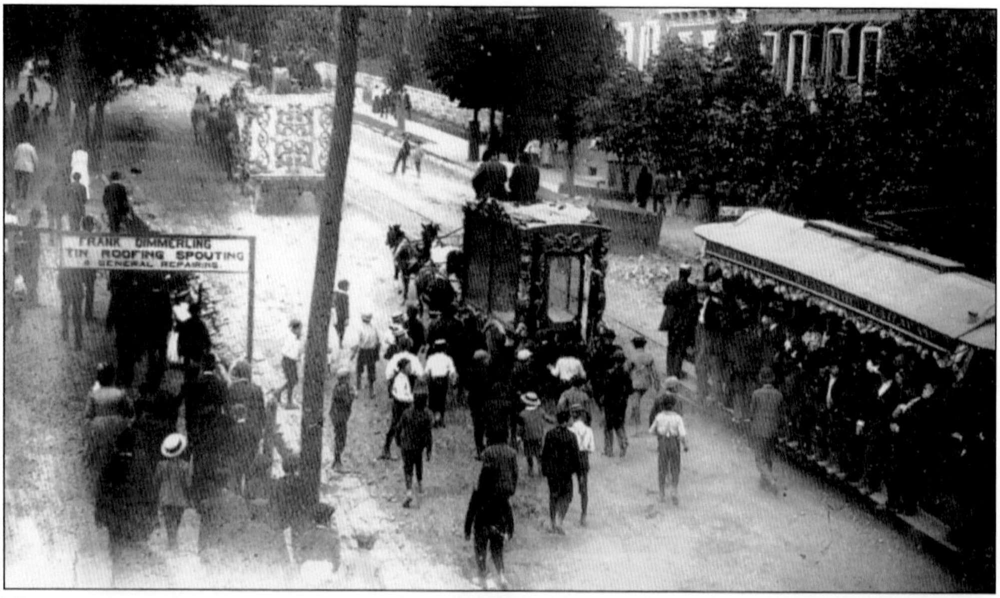

The circus parade continues westward on Market Street as the animals and circus performers continue on to Dolan's Park. The park was located on what was once the O'Connor farm in Yorkville. It was situated between Market Street and Third Avenue, between 18th and 22nd Streets. Dolan's Park was subdivided into building lots by the Inter-State Realty Company in 1906.

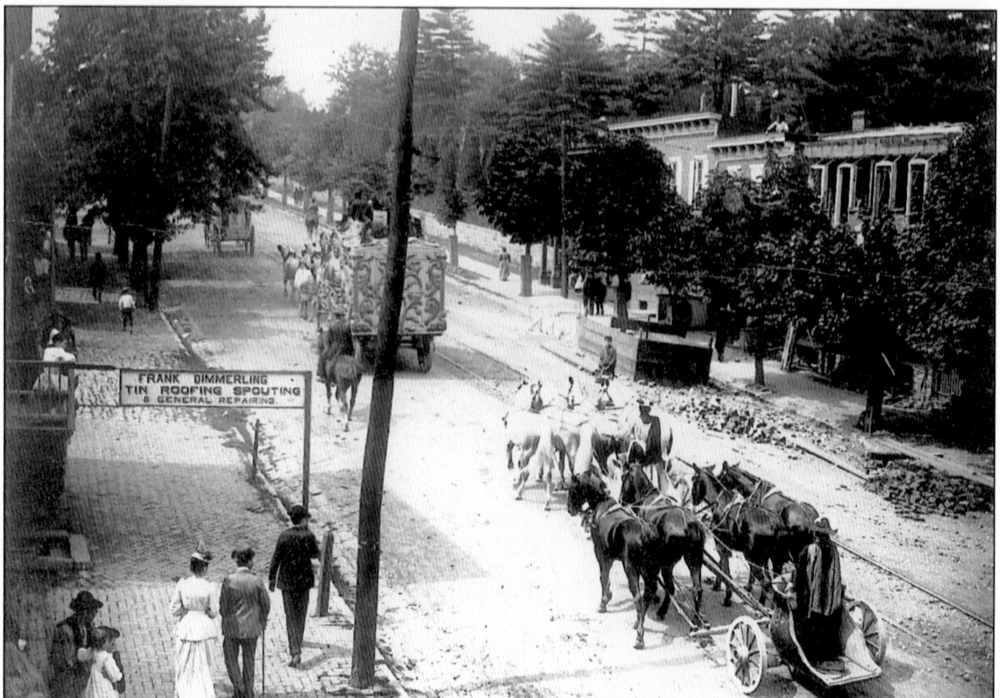

Circus chariots reminiscent of Ben Hur continue the uphill pilgrimage to Dolan's Park. The spectators, without the benefit of the usual trolley line, have undoubtedly followed the parade to its final destination on foot, as these folks seem to be doing.

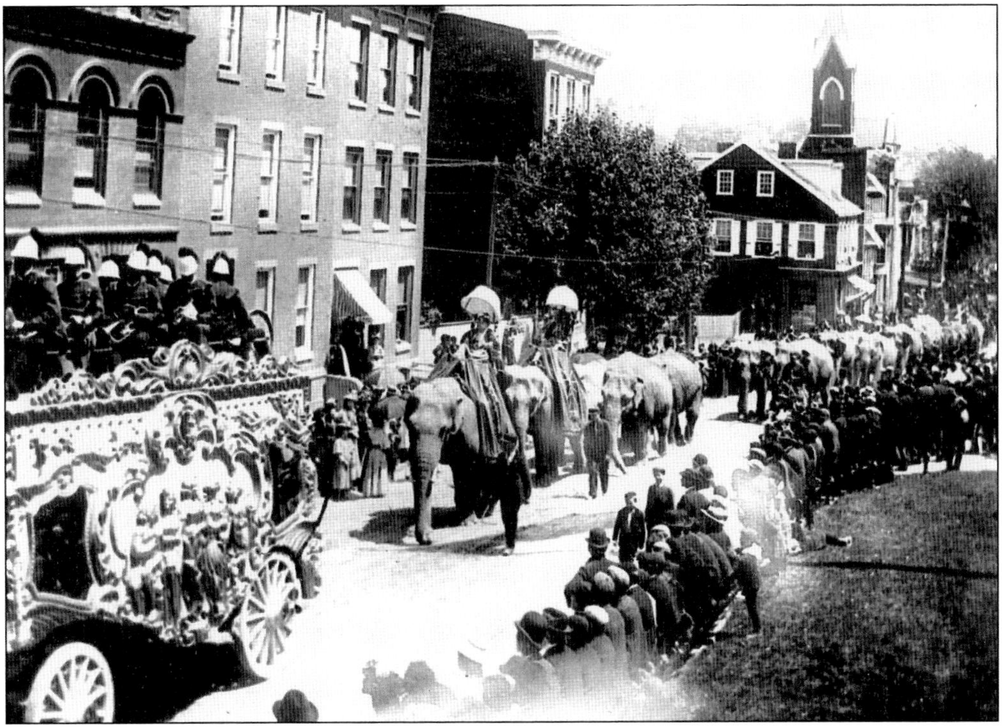

The ornate band carriage and shaded elephant riders of the Ringling Brothers and Barnum & Bailey Circus lead the rest of the parade through throngs of onlookers at Garfield Square. In this image, the steeple of the Trinity United Church of Christ is seen at 316 West Market Street. The steeple was removed years later.

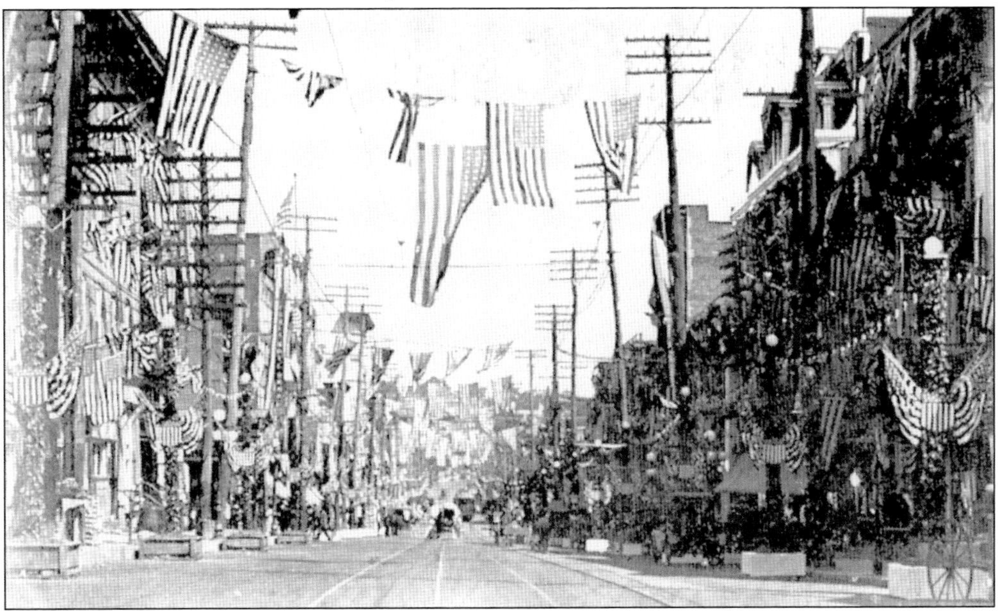

Centre Street is gaily decorated for the Pottsville Old Home Week and Centennial Celebration of 1906. This postcard view looks north from Mahantongo Street. The postcard souvenirs of Old Home Week were printed by Edward L. Long of Pottsville.

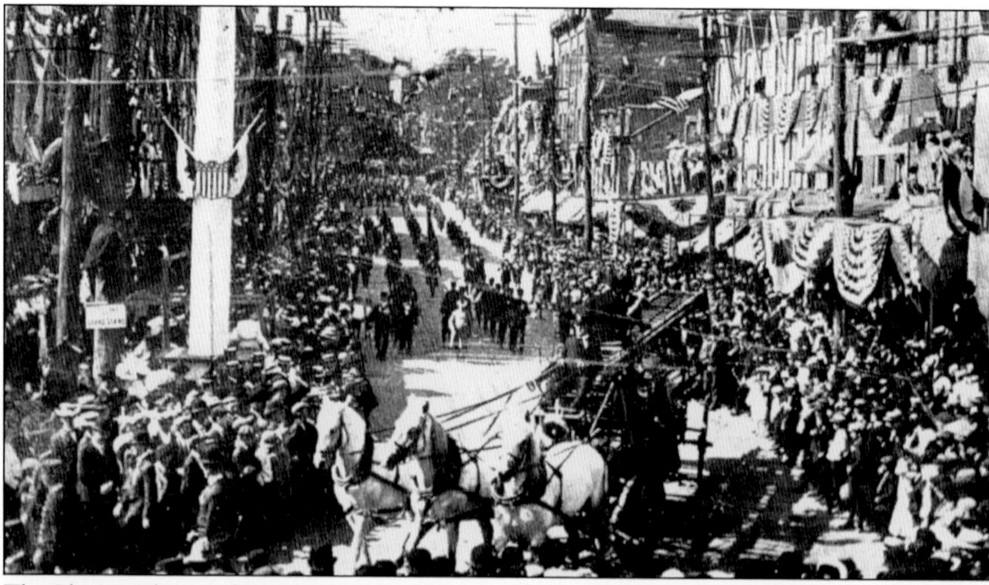

The Phoenix fire truck turns off Centre Street as a huge crowd watches the Old Home Week parade in 1906. The crowd jammed the street to watch the parade. Notice that the Phoenix truck has three white horses pulling it.

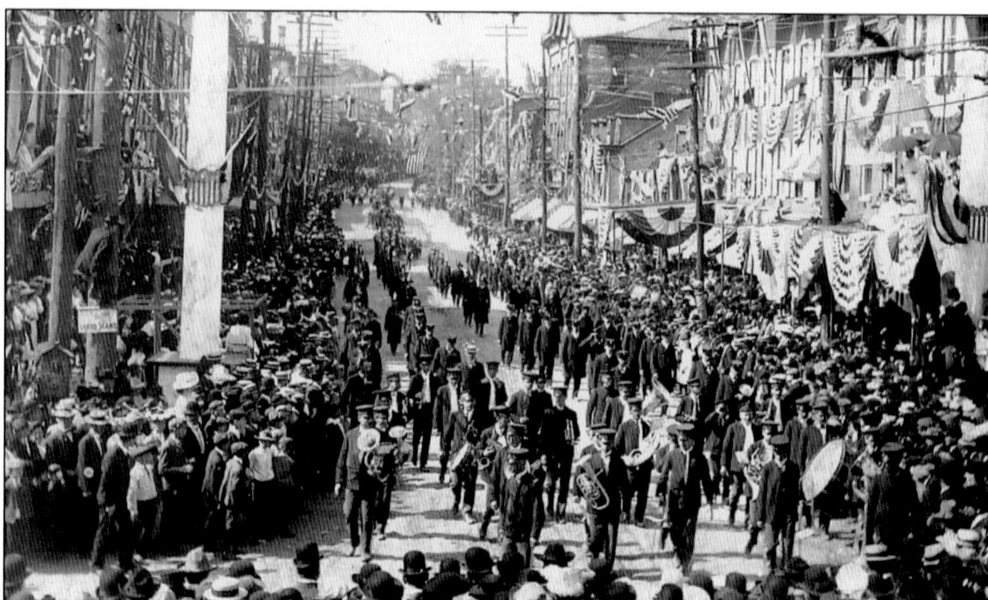

This postcard image was taken from the same spot where the postcard of the Phoenix fire truck was made. The band is following the Phoenix and is about to turn off to the left to follow the route of the parade.

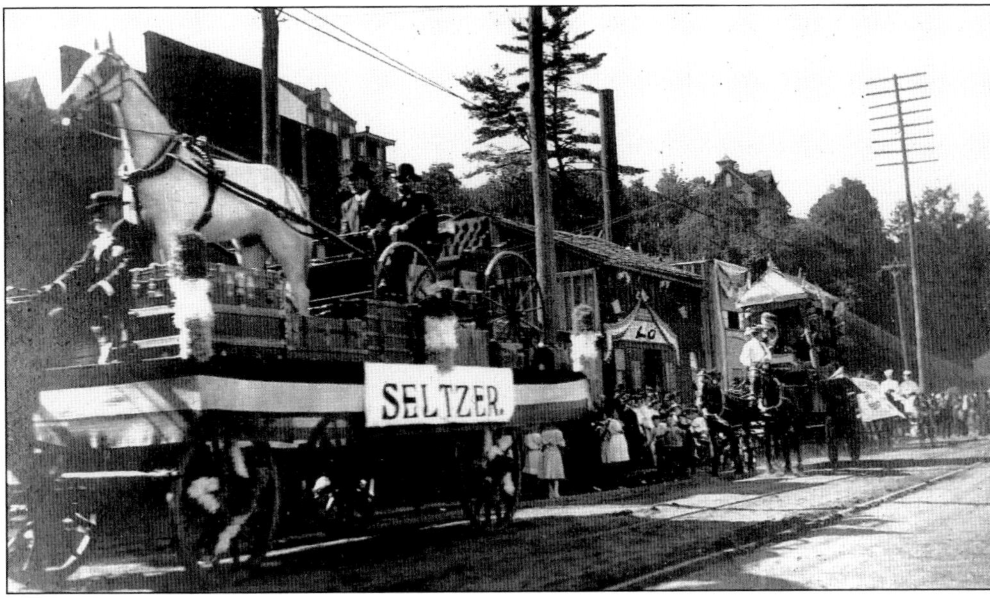

The 1906 parade travels down North Centre Street during the Old Home Week celebration. The borough of Pottsville was celebrating the 100th anniversary of John Pott's arrival in what was later to become the city of Pottsville.

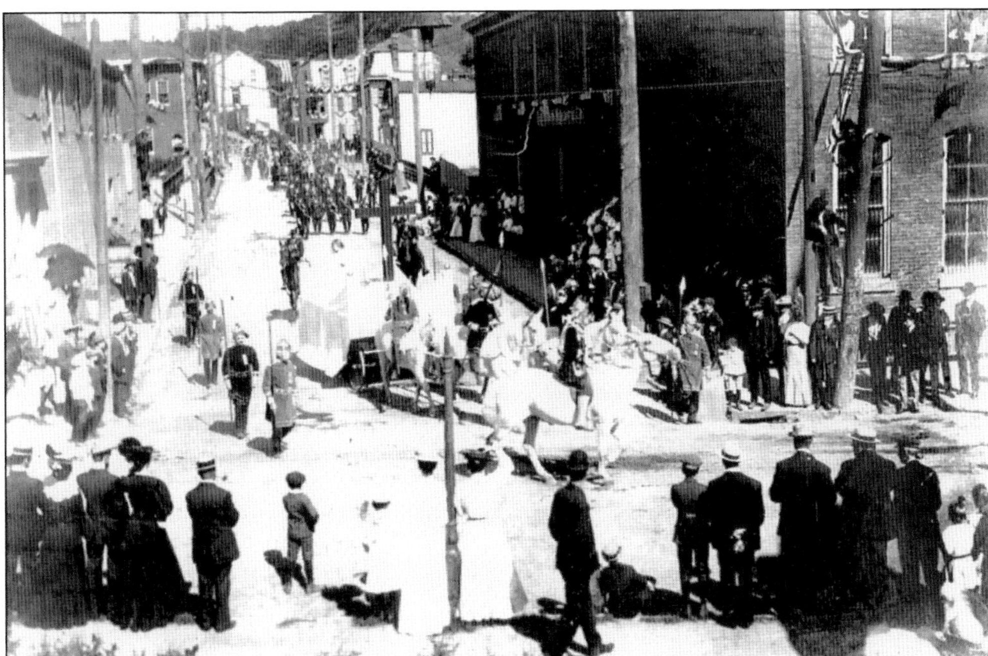

The Old Home Week parade of 1906 turns onto Centre Street from Nichols Street in this afternoon image. The Goodwill Hose Company is seen on the left, and the former Curious Goods building is on the right.

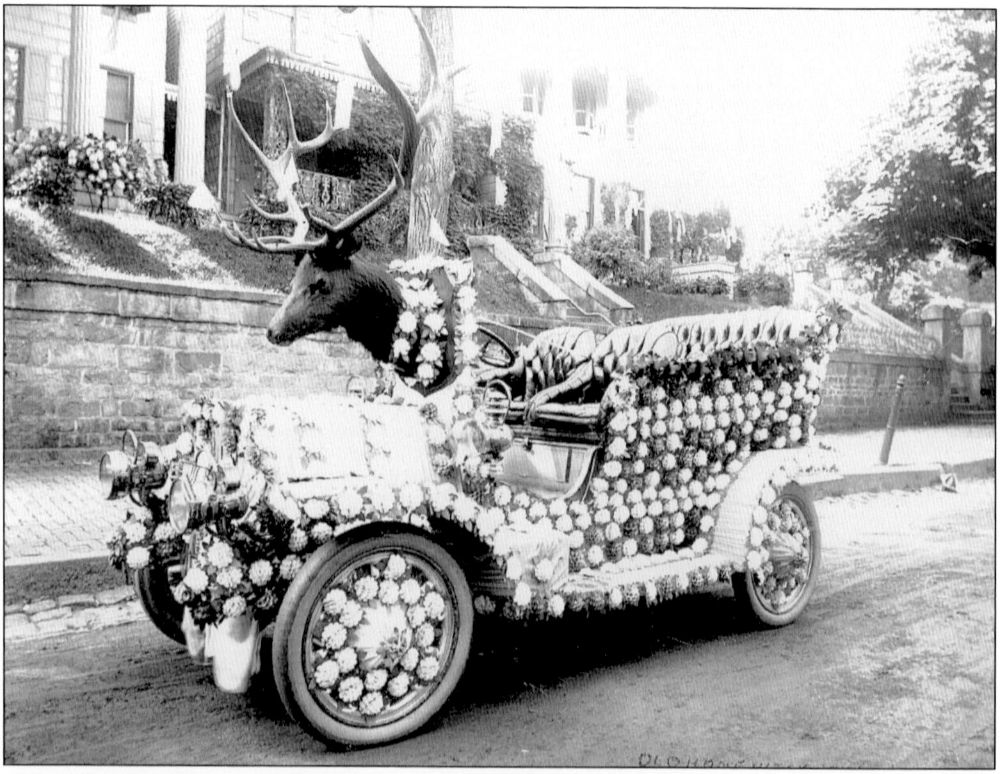

The Pottsville Elks parade featured this elk and flower-bedecked car on September 5, 1906, during Old Home Week. This photograph was taken at the corner of Sixth and Mahantongo Streets. The Braun School of Music is seen in the background.

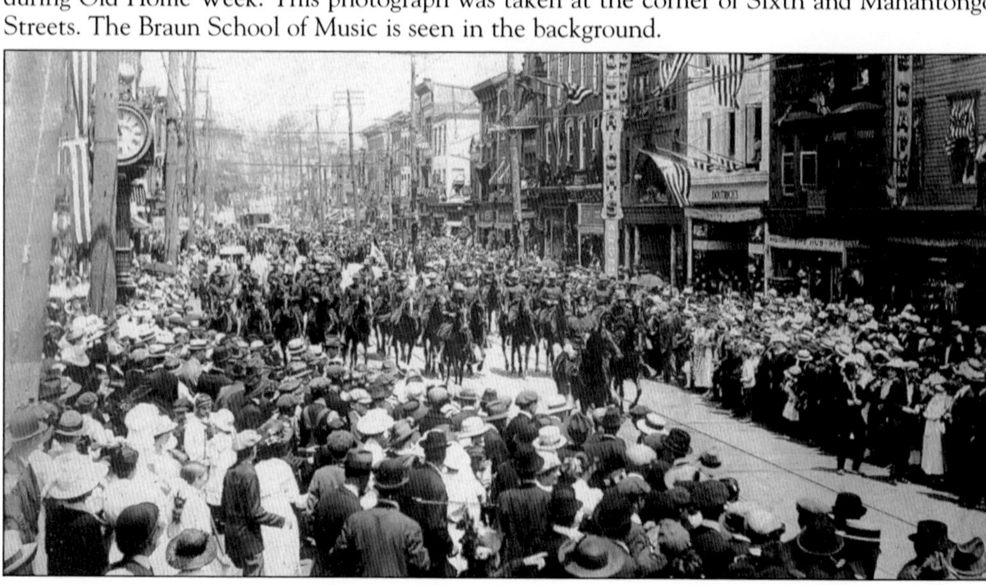

A cavalry company parades along Centre Street as soldiers prepare to embark for service on the Mexican border in 1916. Pancho Villa had made one too many incursions into Arizona, New Mexico, and West Texas, and local boys decided to participate in defending the southern border with Mexico. This photograph was taken from the intersection of Norwegian and Centre Streets.

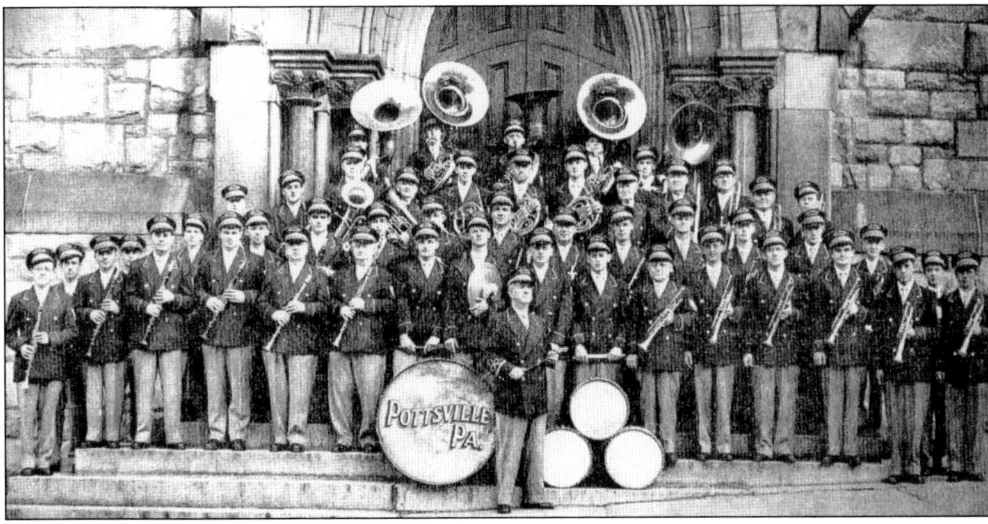

The Third Brigade Band is a Pottsville institution that continues today. In this 1949 image, the band has posed for a promotional image. Seen in the front is Dr. Robert Braun, the conductor. At the time that this photograph was taken, the Third Brigade Band was considered the best band in eastern Pennsylvania.

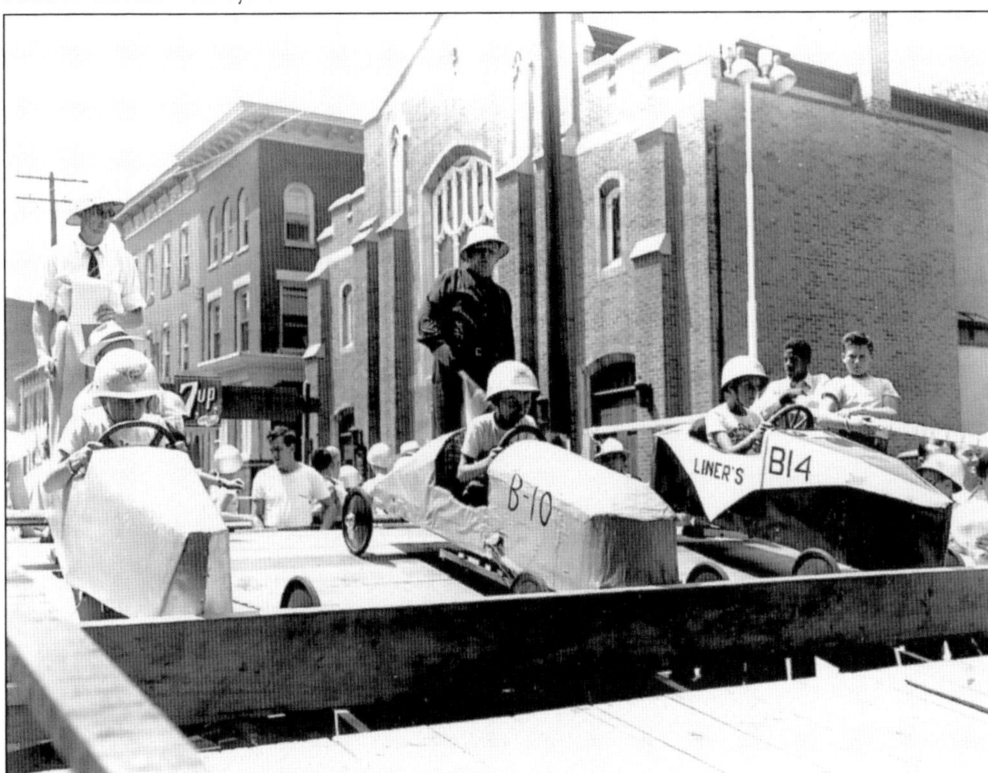

Three young men are ready to make their run down Market Street in front of the First United Church of Christ at the intersection of Ninth and West Market Streets. The soapbox derby racers competed at a variety of locations across the city, but the original races ran on this stretch of Market Street between Ninth and Sixth Streets.

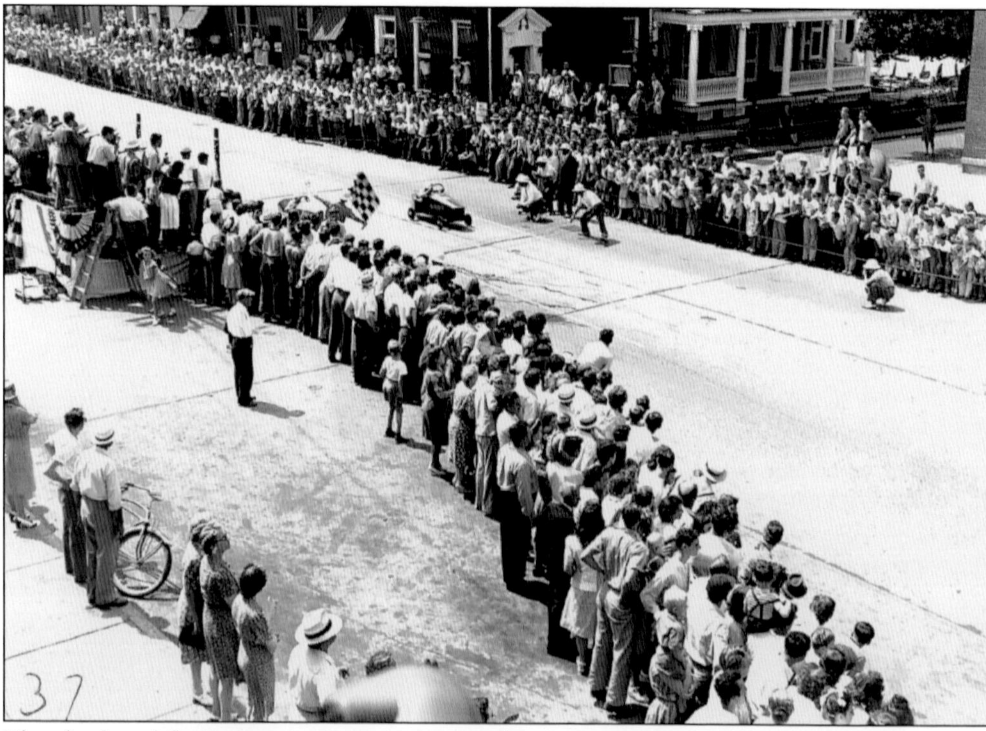

The checkered flag is raised in anticipation as the winner nears the finish line at Sixth Street in Garfield Square. Several judges wearing their pith hats look on in an effort to determine the winner. Long lines of amateur judges line the street as well.

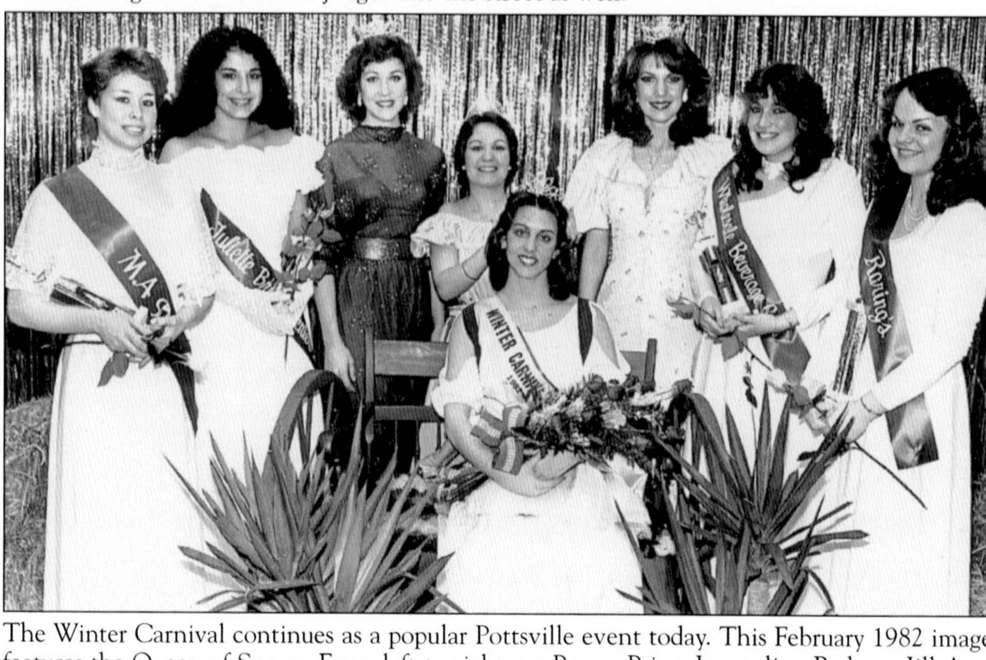

The Winter Carnival continues as a popular Pottsville event today. This February 1982 image features the Queen of Snows. From left to right are Penny Price, Jacqueline Bedway, Jill Ann Shaffer (Miss Pennsylvania), Denise Mirabella, Donna Davis, Sandra Truint (Miss Illinois), Sherril Brennan, and Karen Byrnes.

Five

TRANSPORTATION

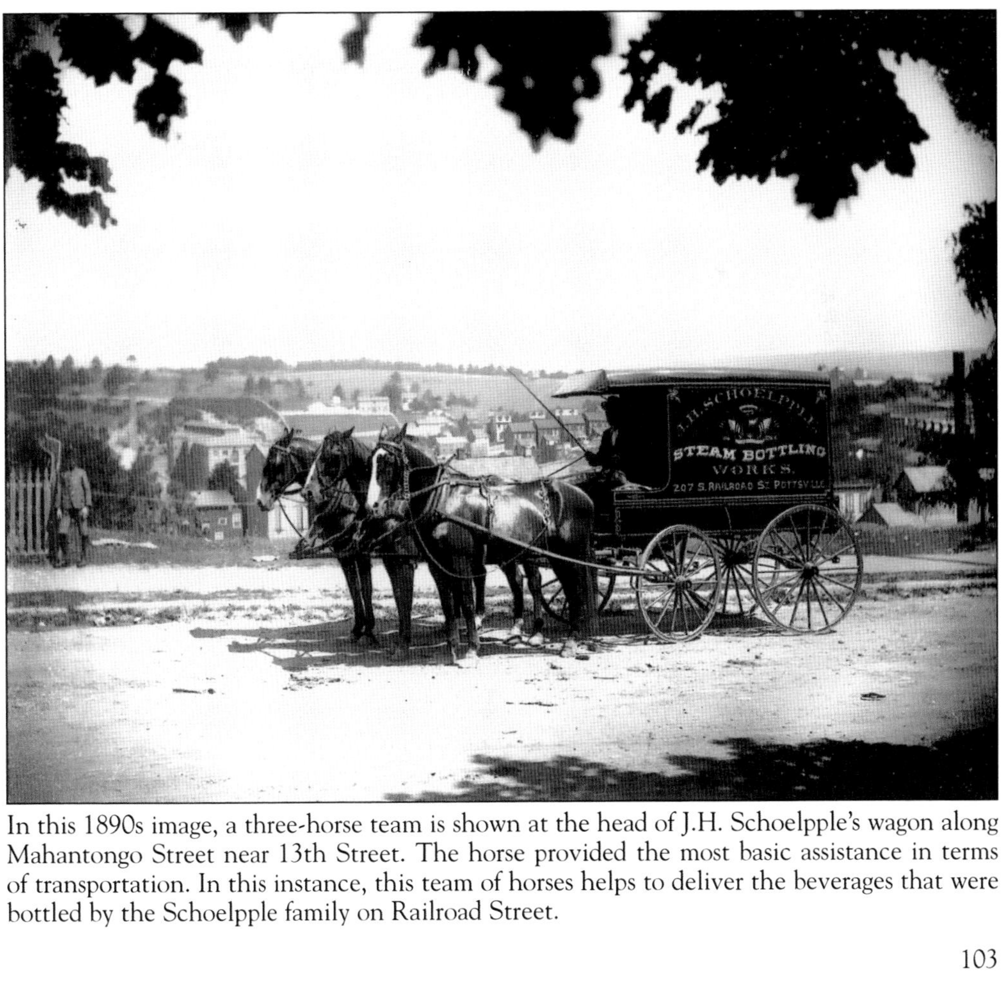

In this 1890s image, a three-horse team is shown at the head of J.H. Schoelpple's wagon along Mahantongo Street near 13th Street. The horse provided the most basic assistance in terms of transportation. In this instance, this team of horses helps to deliver the beverages that were bottled by the Schoelpple family on Railroad Street.

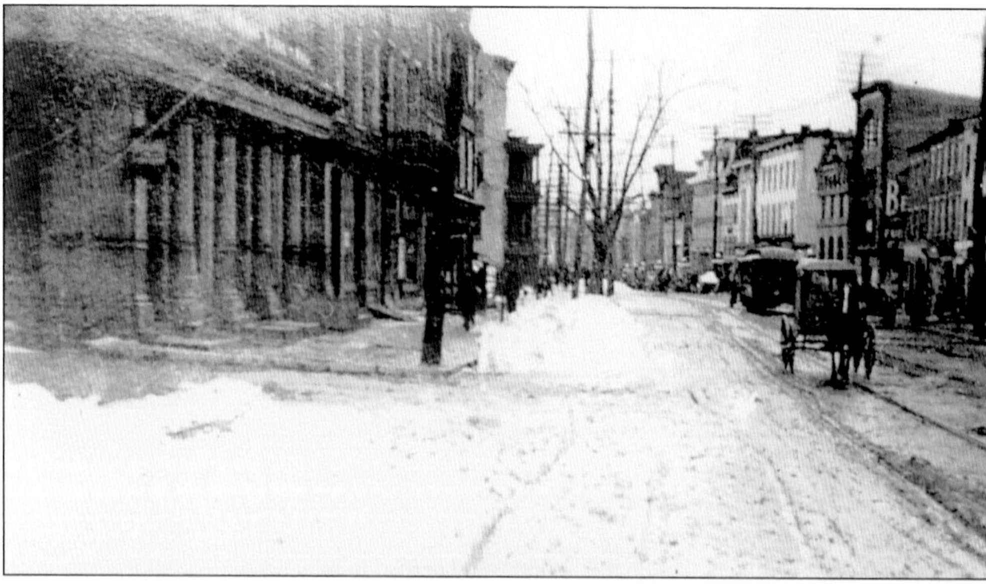

This Centre Street view, looking north from Union Street, shows a horse-drawn carriage heading south on a snow-covered street. Behind the carriage, a trolley makes its way into downtown Pottsville. The water authority building is on the left.

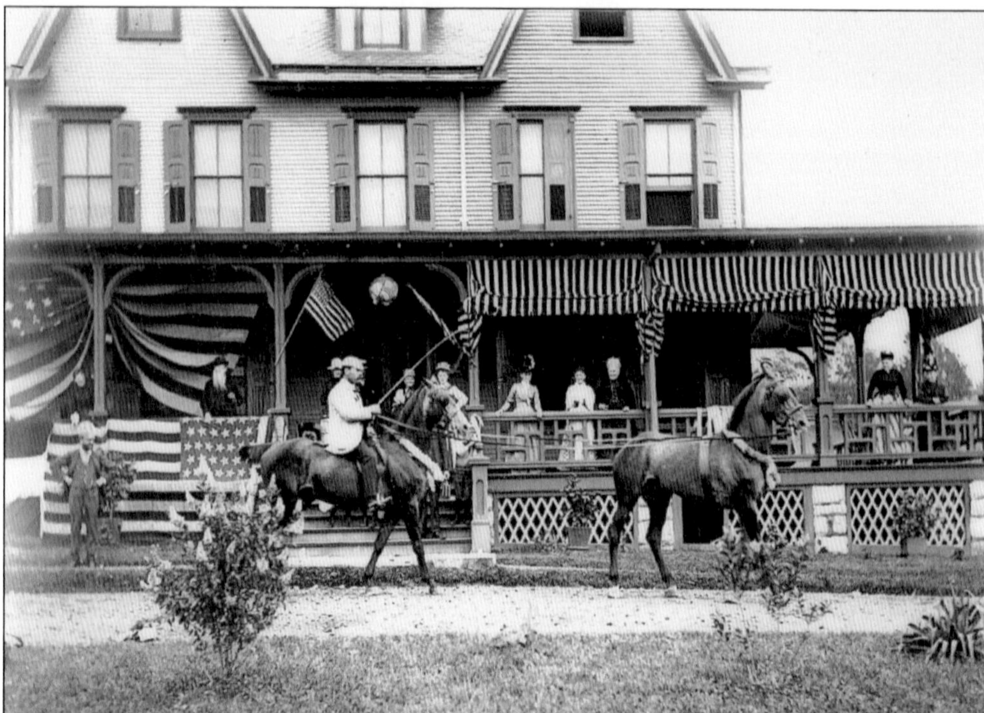

The Yuengling family farm, situated along Bull's Head Road in Norwegian Township, is the setting for this early image showing Frederick Yuengling on horseback. The 37-star American flag reveals that this photograph was taken sometime after 1876, but the Yuengling family used horse-drawn transportation into the early 20th century.

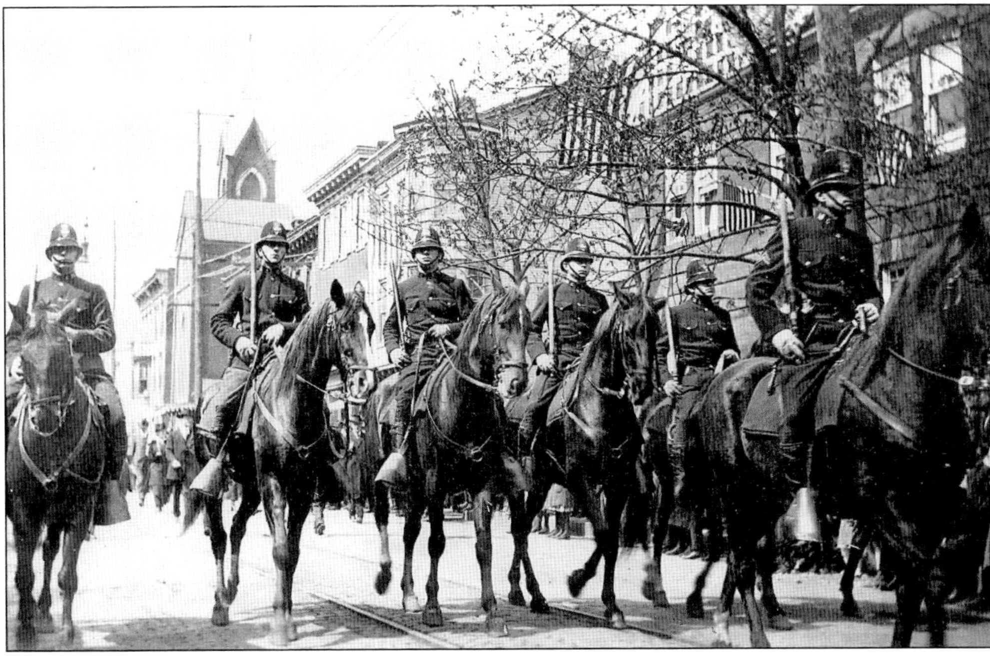

The state police are shown parading on Market Street in Pottsville. The steeple of the Trinity United Church of Christ is seen in this photograph, taken in the 1940s near what is now the Pottsville Free Public Library.

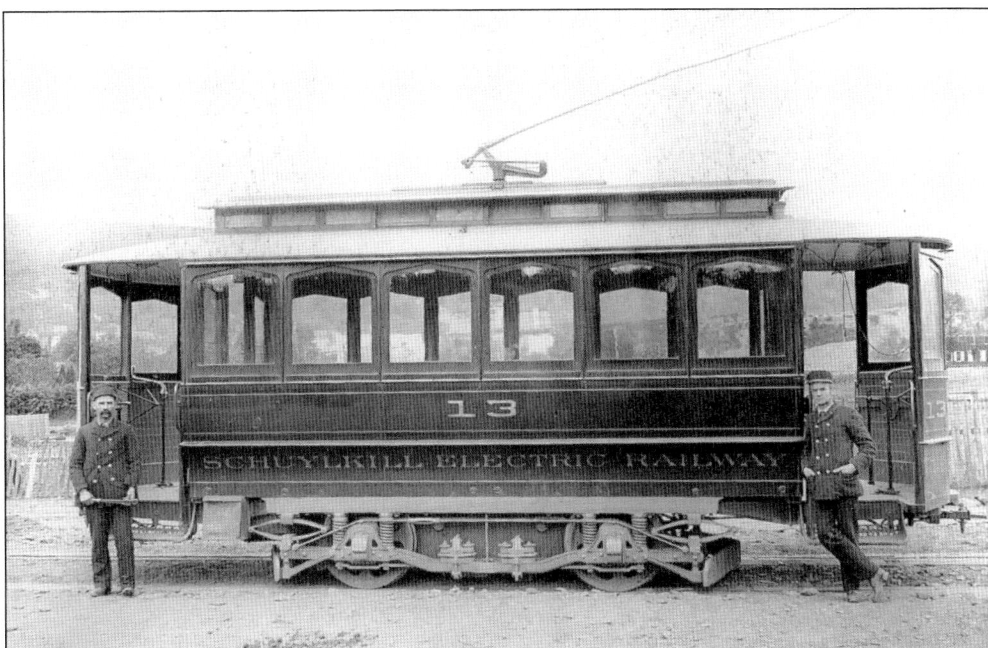

In this 1890s photograph, motorman John Conrad (left) and conductor Joseph Stichter pose with trolley No. 13 of the Schuylkill Electric Railway. Trolleys served Pottsville until 1932, when they were taken out of service permanently.

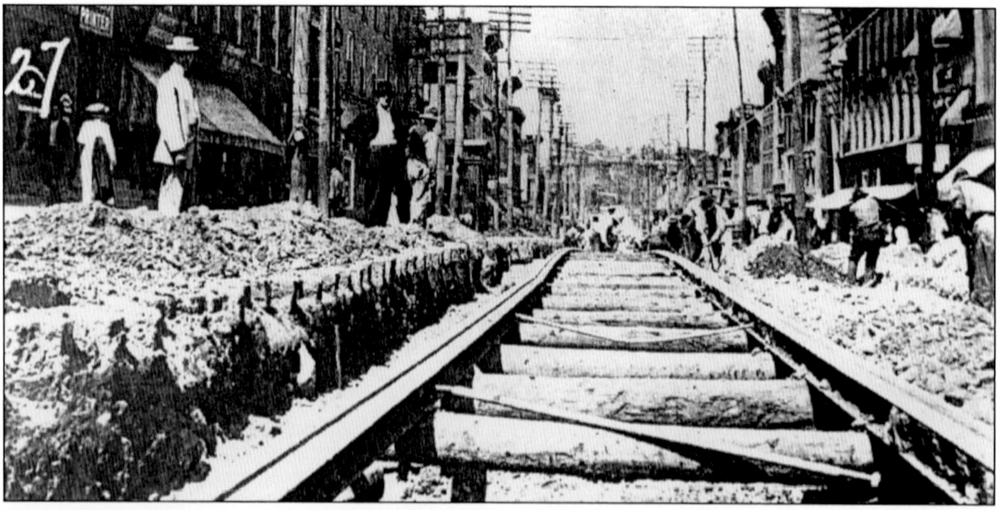

The workmen prepare to lay double trolley tracks along Centre Street in Pottsville. This image from 1910 was taken from Howard Avenue looking north along Centre Street. The old Hotel Allan is seen behind the man with his hands on his hips.

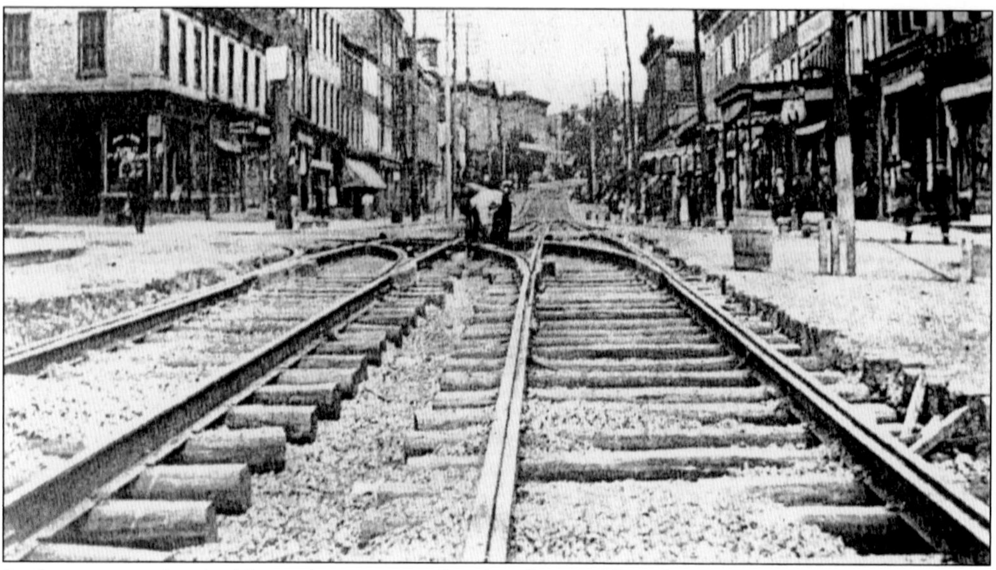

In this picture, the double tracking is completed in front of the Thompson Building at the corner of West Market and Centre Streets. Lewis C. Thompson's store stands on the left corner. The store was replaced by the Schuylkill Trust Company building in 1924. The trolley tracks still run along Centre and Market Streets, but they are covered by several generations of macadam.

This trolley is stopped along the tracks south of Pottsville at the "midway turnout," not far from where the trolleys turned east toward Tumbling Run near East Mount Carbon. This photograph was taken after a significant snowfall in February 1920.

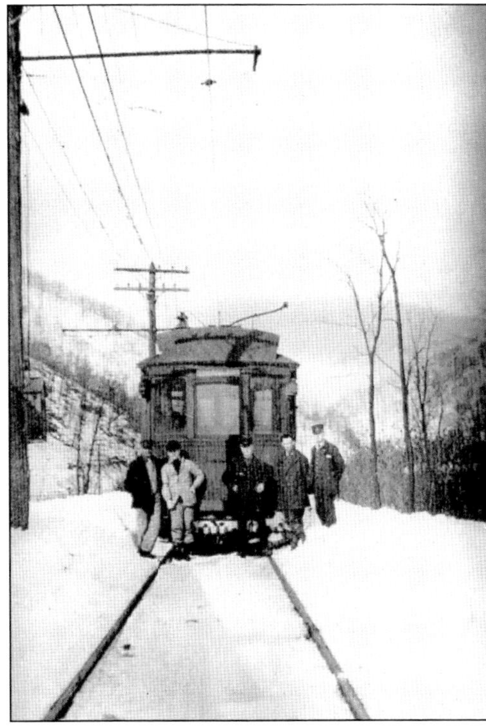

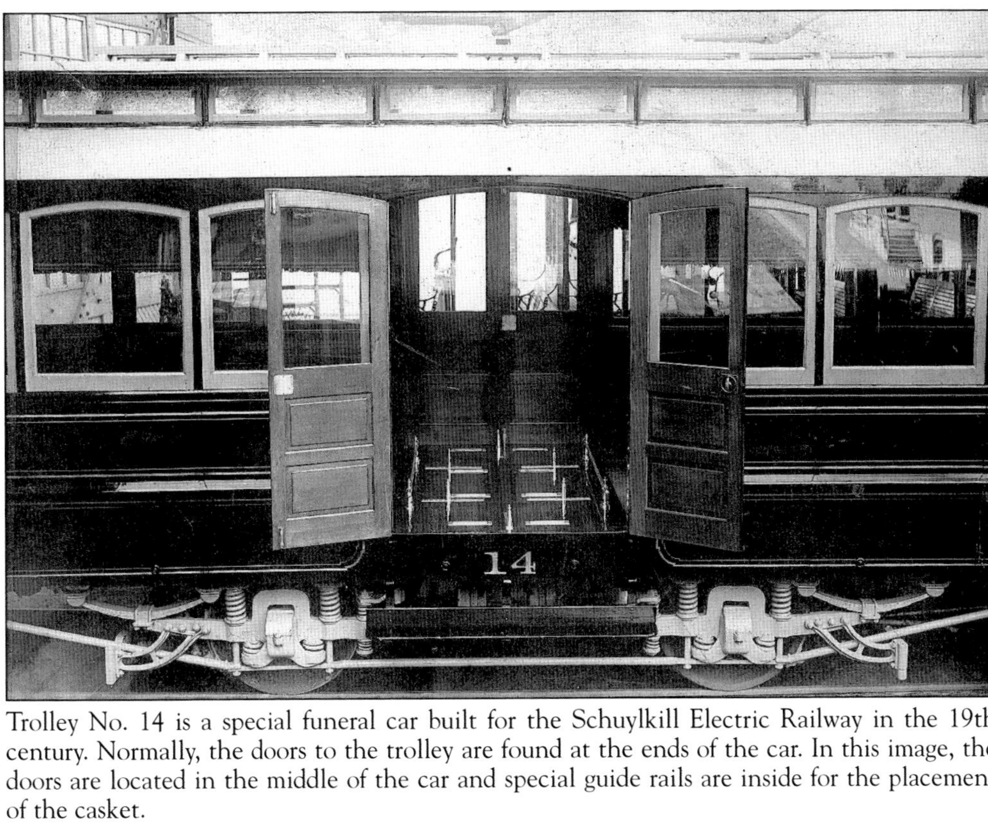

Trolley No. 14 is a special funeral car built for the Schuylkill Electric Railway in the 19th century. Normally, the doors to the trolley are found at the ends of the car. In this image, the doors are located in the middle of the car and special guide rails are inside for the placement of the casket.

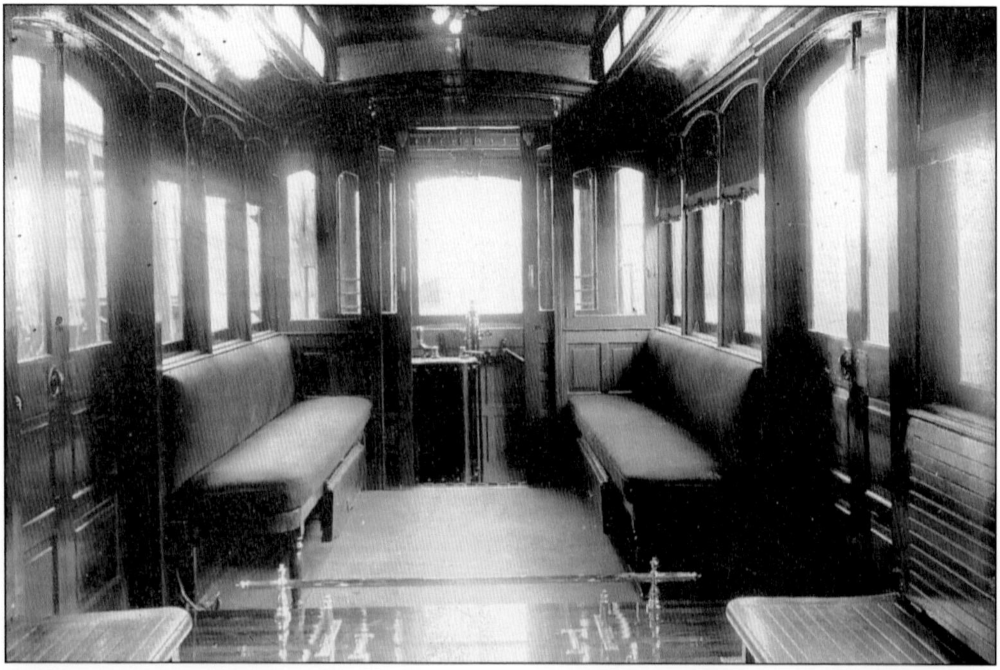

Here is an interior view of trolley No. 14 of the Schuylkill Electric Railway. Notice the privacy shades and cushioned seats for mourning family and friends.

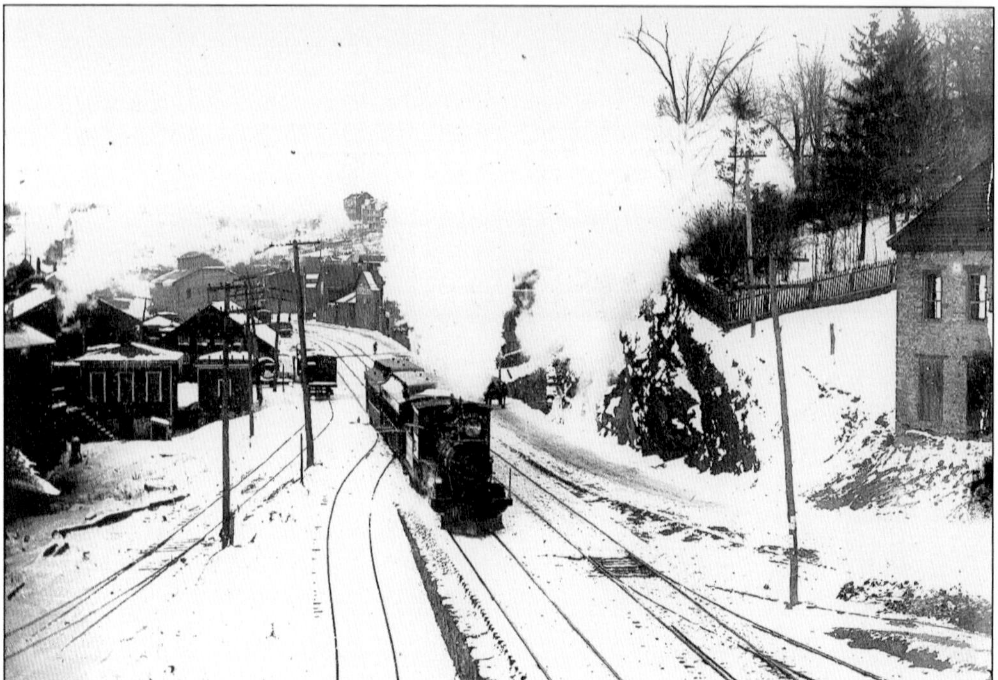

Along with the trolley, Pottsville also featured traditional rail service into the 20th century. Here, a Pennsylvania Railroad engine pulls passenger cars southward along what is today Claude A. Lord Boulevard near the Union Street intersection just north of where the Washington Street Bridge crossed the railroad and what was then Coal Street.

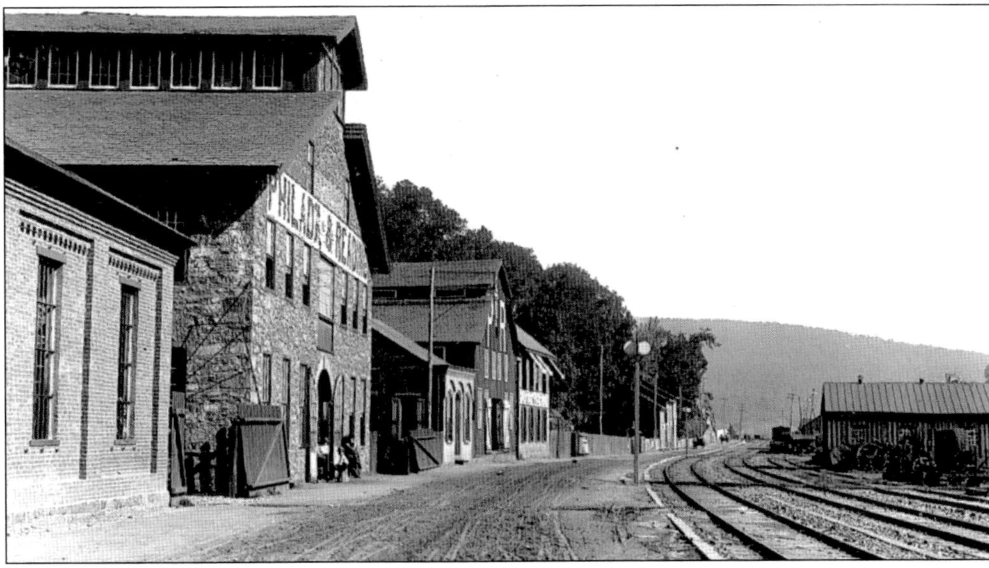

The Pennsylvania Railroad and Coal Street are clear on this summer afternoon. The view looks south from what is today the intersection of Norwegian Street and Route 61. Within the next 50 years, the landscape here changed drastically as the automobile and the railroad operated side by side.

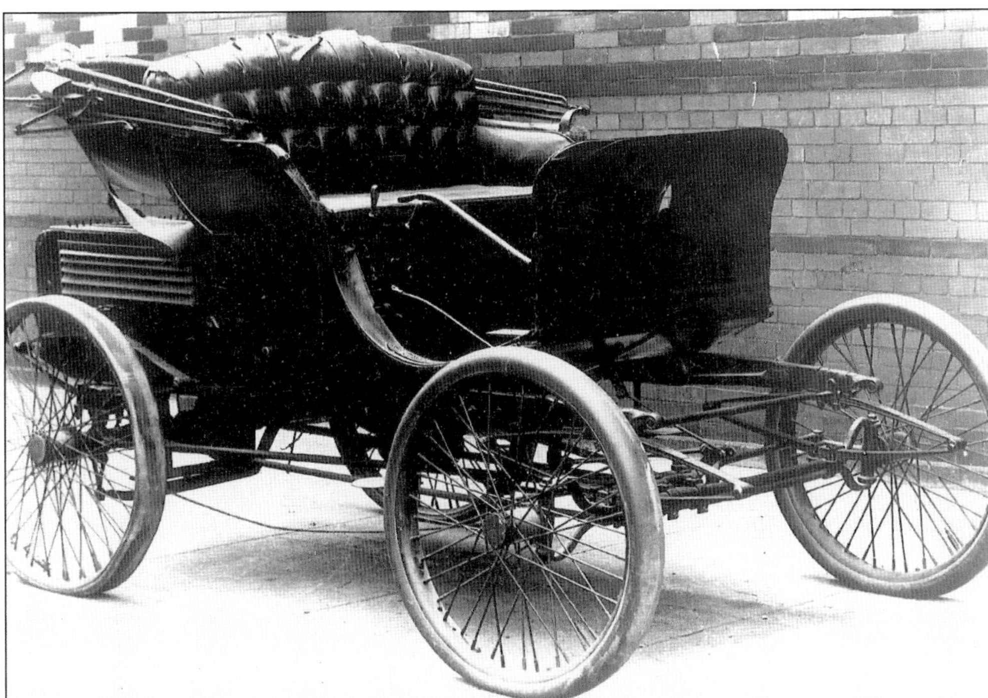

This contraption is the automobile that Robert Allison purchased in 1898. Allison is credited with being the first man to purchase an automobile for personal use when he bought this car from Alexander Winton of Cleveland. Allison's car arrived by rail to Pottsville, where it was unloaded and then driven to his home in Port Carbon.

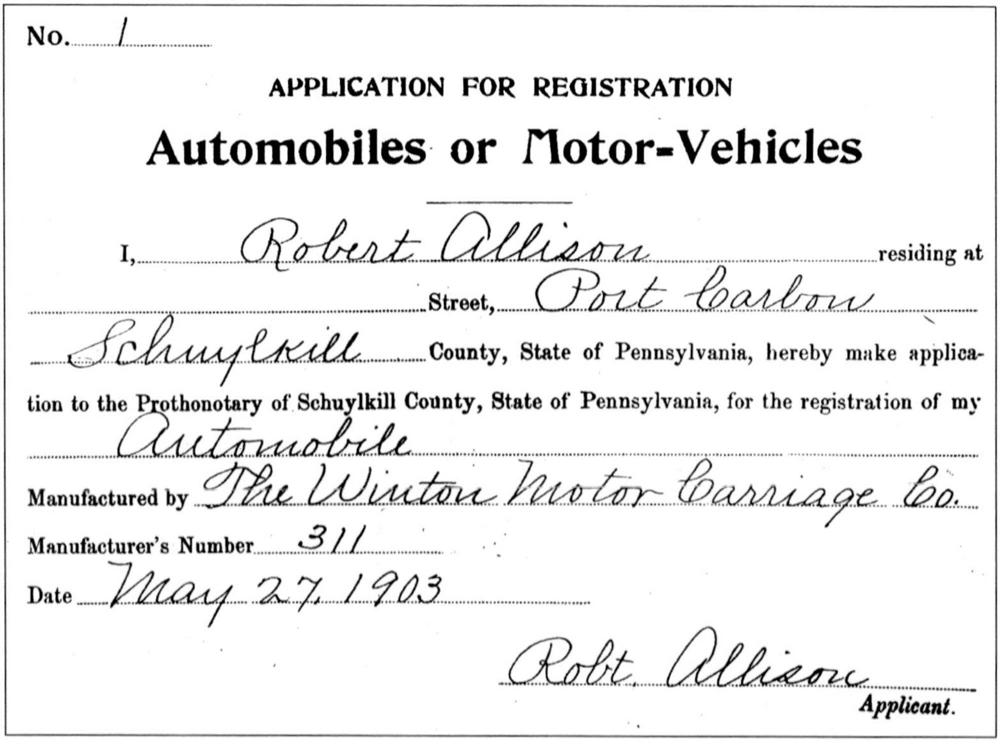

No. 1

APPLICATION FOR REGISTRATION

Automobiles or Motor-Vehicles

I, Robert Allison residing at Street, Port Carbon Schuylkill County, State of Pennsylvania, hereby make application to the Prothonotary of Schuylkill County, State of Pennsylvania, for the registration of my Automobile

Manufactured by The Winton Motor Carriage Co.

Manufacturer's Number 311

Date May 27. 1903

Robt. Allison

Applicant.

Allison was not only the first to purchase an automobile but also the first to trade one car for a newer model. Pictured here is his automobile registration for one of his early Winton vehicles.

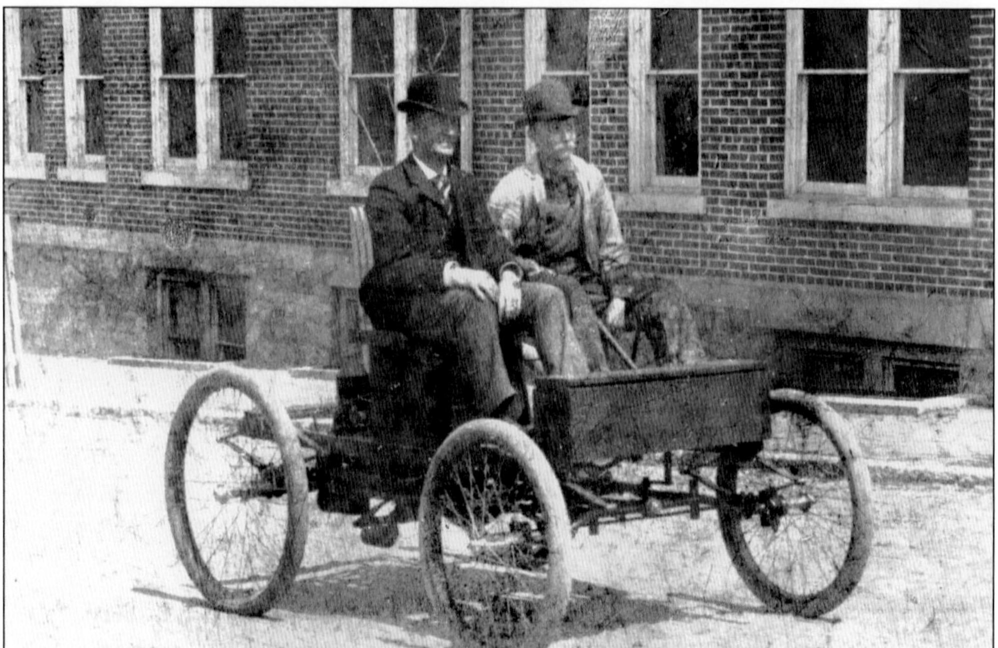

This image shows Pottsville's John Reber and Harry Bohler, who were local manufacturers of cars. The photograph was taken along West Market Street near 14th Street.

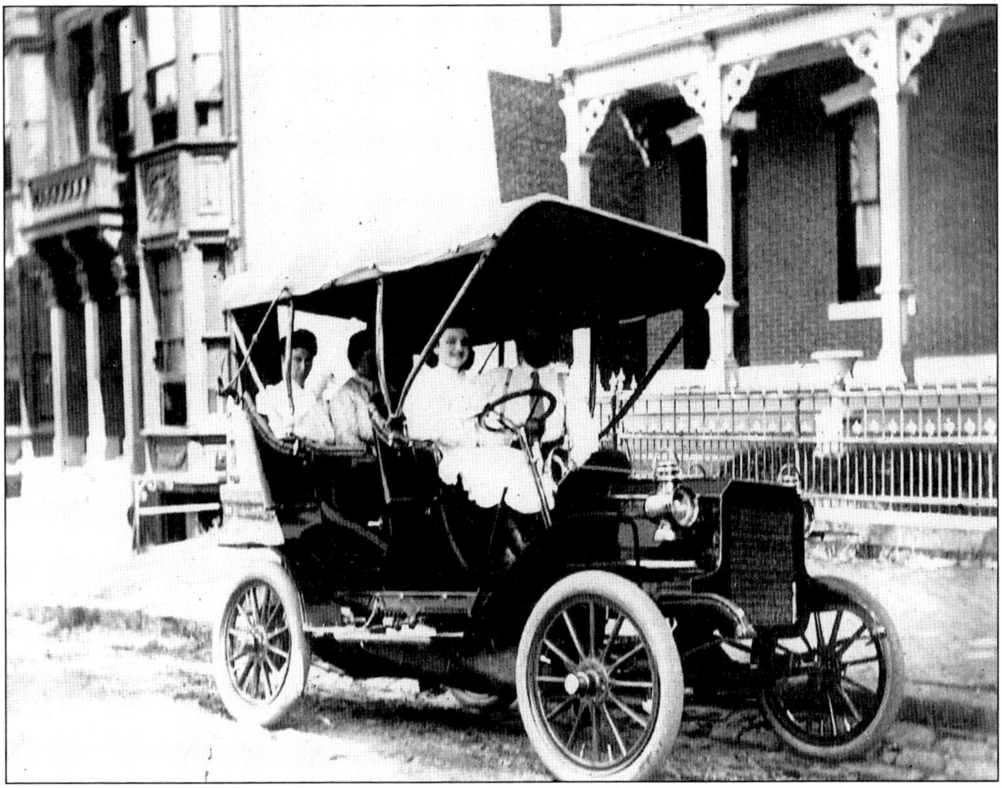

The Myers family on Market Street was the early owner of a horseless carriage. Members of the Myers family are seen in their vehicle on West Market Street.

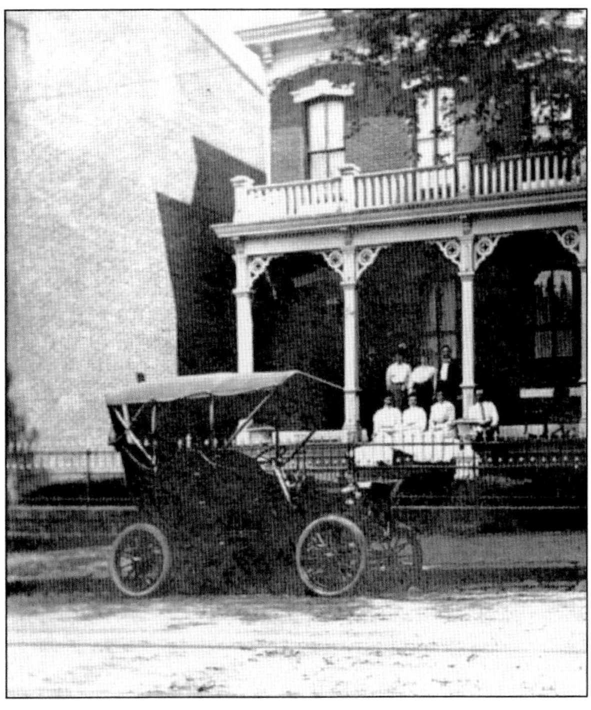

Here is another 1902 view of the Myers family car parked in front of their residence at 615 West Market Street in Pottsville. The house still survives today as a private residence, but the decorative porch and wrought-iron fence have long since been removed.

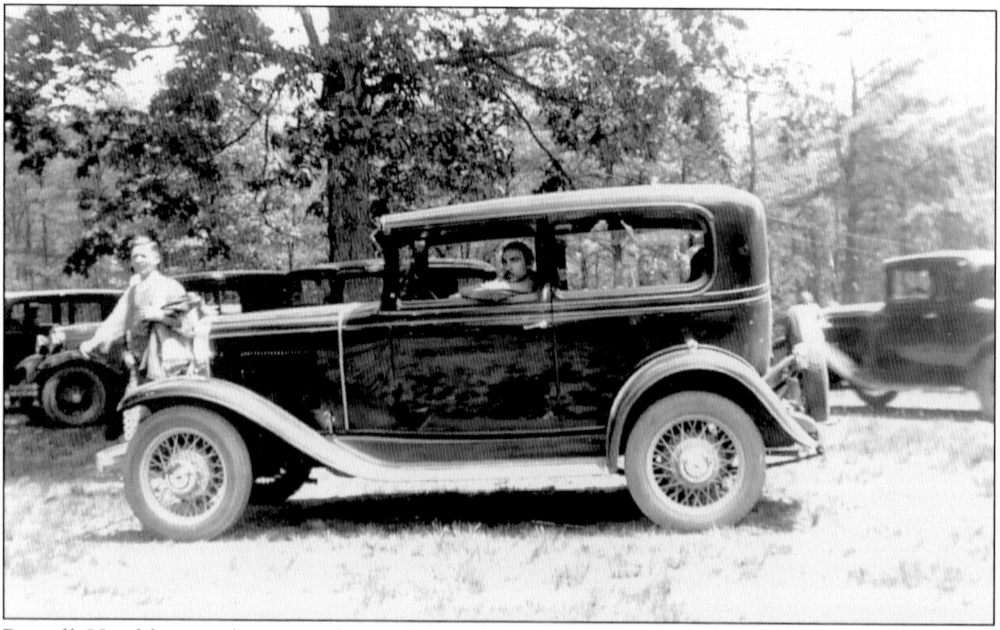

Russell Hershberger, late president of the Historical Society of Schuylkill County, is seen driving his 1931 Chevrolet in this 1932 photograph taken in Bushkill, Pennsylvania.

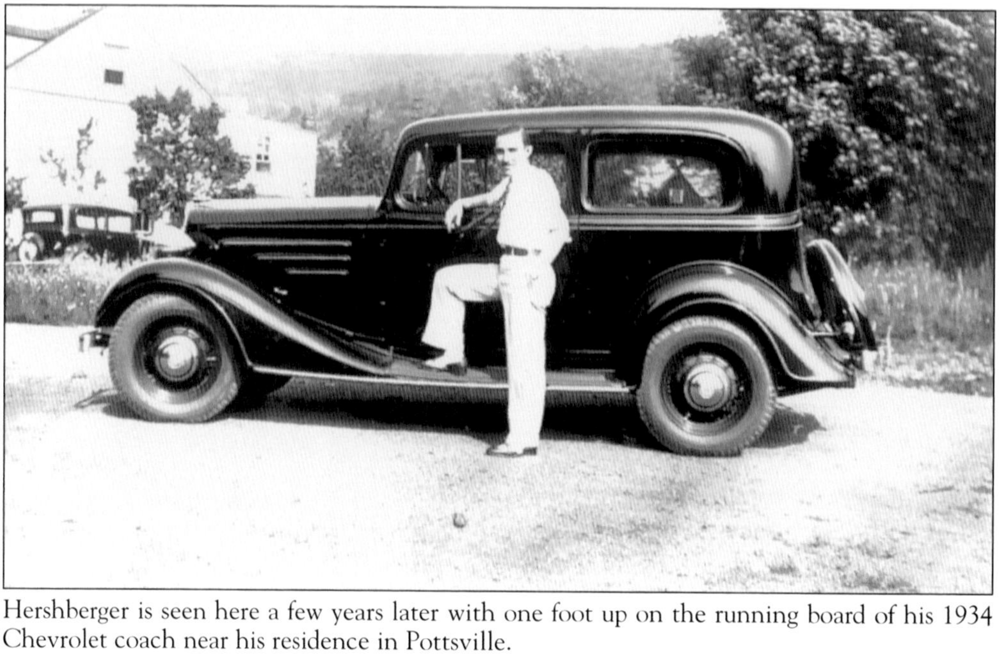

Hershberger is seen here a few years later with one foot up on the running board of his 1934 Chevrolet coach near his residence in Pottsville.

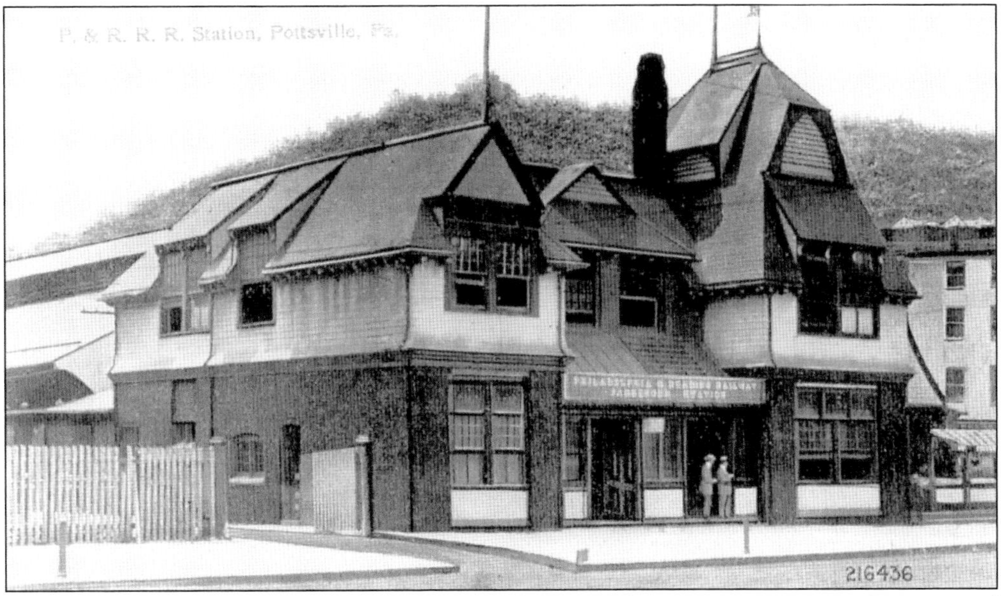

This early-20th-century image of the Philadelphia & Reading passenger station shows one of the railroad's most unique architectural structures built in the area. The Reading station was built in 1887 and survived until the early 1960s, when it last served as a bus terminal and train station.

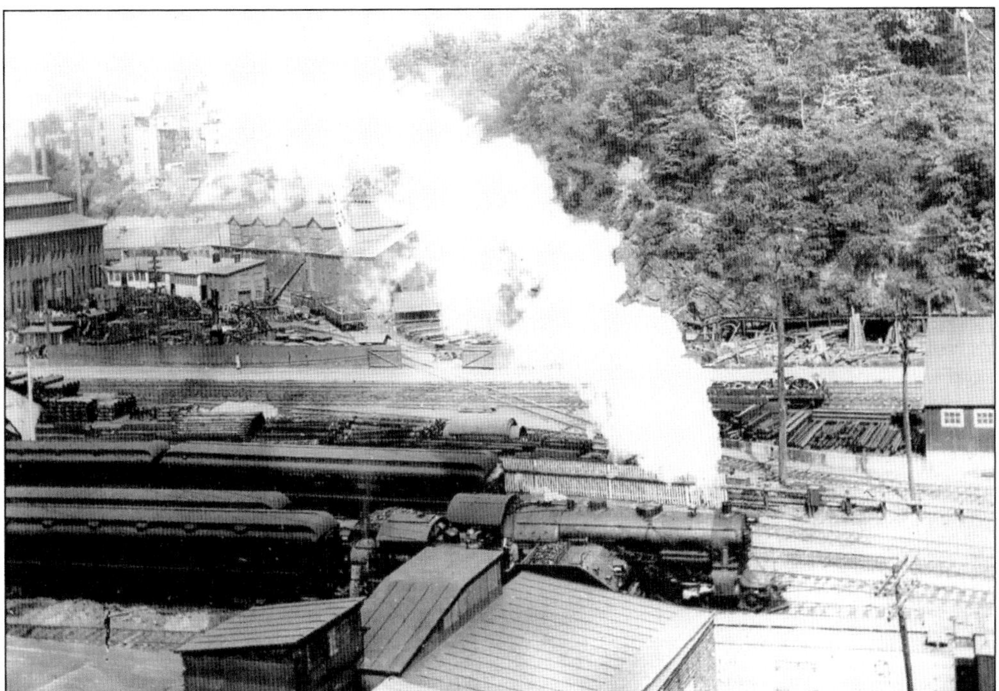

Another passenger train departs the Reading terminal in Pottsville in this mid-20th-century image. The Philadelphia & Reading shops are seen in the upper left corner. Coal Street, which was later widened and turned into Route 122, runs through the middle of the photograph.

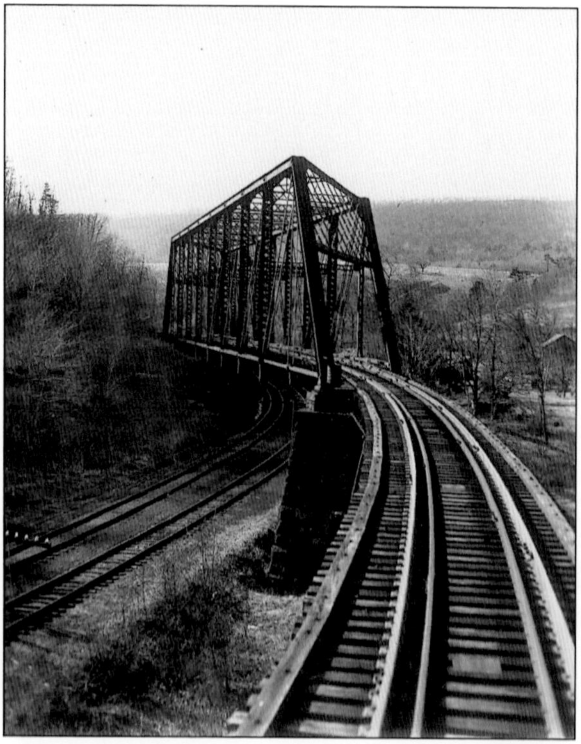

Pottsville was served by three railroad companies. In this image, the railroad tracks of the Lehigh Valley Railroad cross over the tracks of the Reading Railroad near Glenworth, or what is more commonly known as the Gordon Nagle Trail and Route 901 in North Manheim Township. Seiders Hill is to the right center of this image.

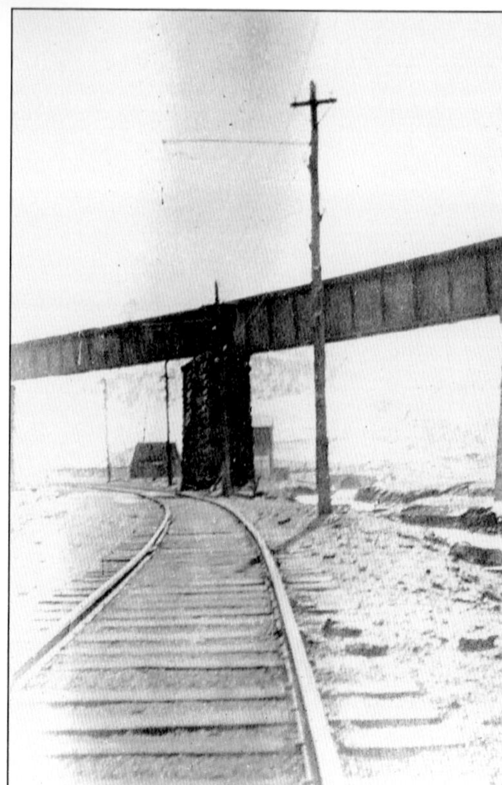

In this picture, the Pennsylvania Railroad trestle passes over the Reading Railroad and the Norwegian Creek near the Fishbach section of the city. While the tracks have been removed, many of these stone trestles are seen throughout sections of the city.

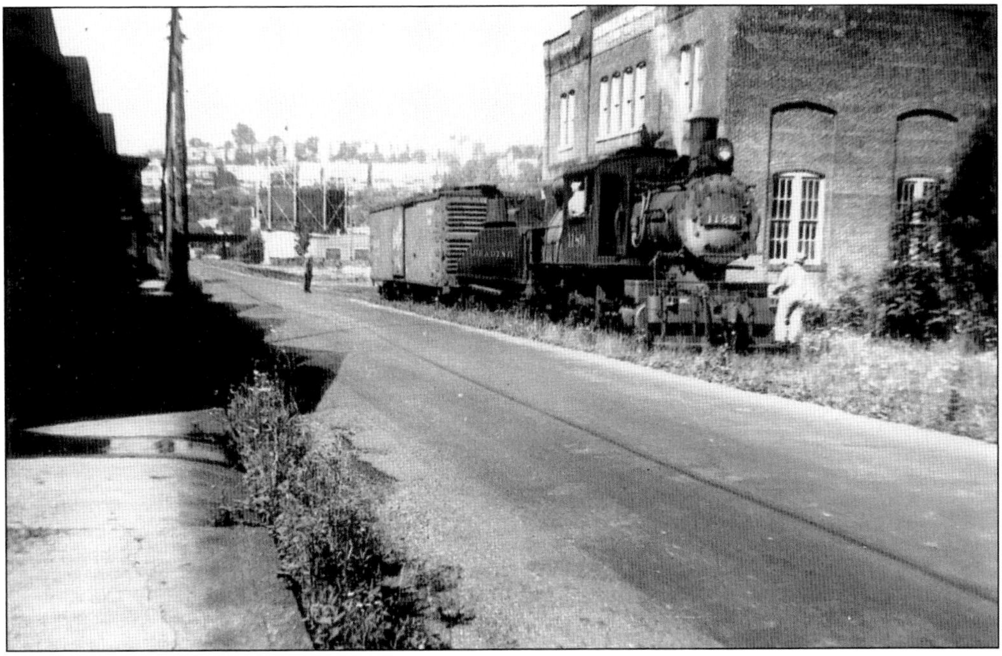

Engine No. 1189 of the Philadelphia & Reading Railroad appears to be shunting a boxcar in this 1940s photograph taken along East Railroad Street in the Jalappa section of the city. The large gas company tank located near the intersection of Railroad and Coal Streets can be seen to the left center of this picture.

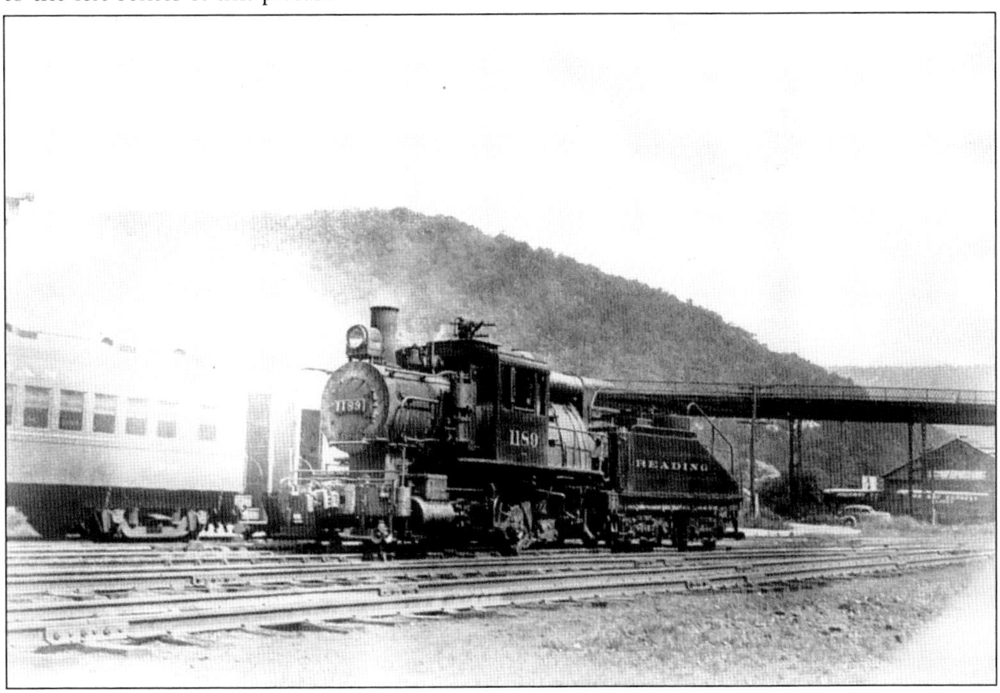

Engine No. 1189 heads north along the Reading Railroad tracks near present-day Union Street. In the background, the Washington Street Bridge is clearly visible. The city of Pottsville plans to return the railroad tracks to this same area of the city in the coming years.

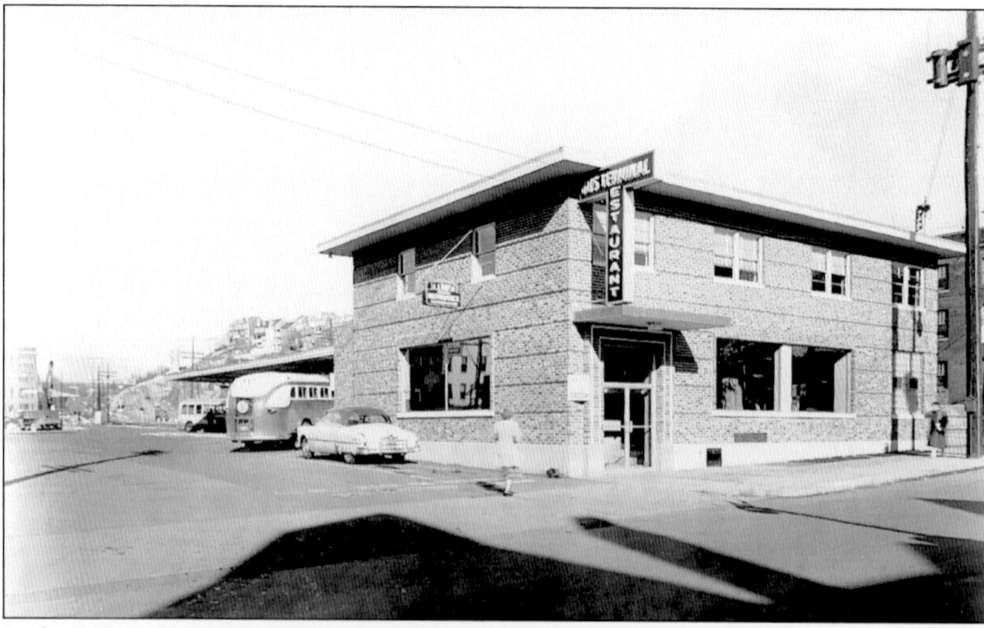

In this 1950s image, the shadow of the Reading passenger station creeps across East Norwegian Street toward the new bus terminal. In the coming years, the bus terminal took away much of the railroad's passenger business and the Reading station was converted into a municipal parking lot.

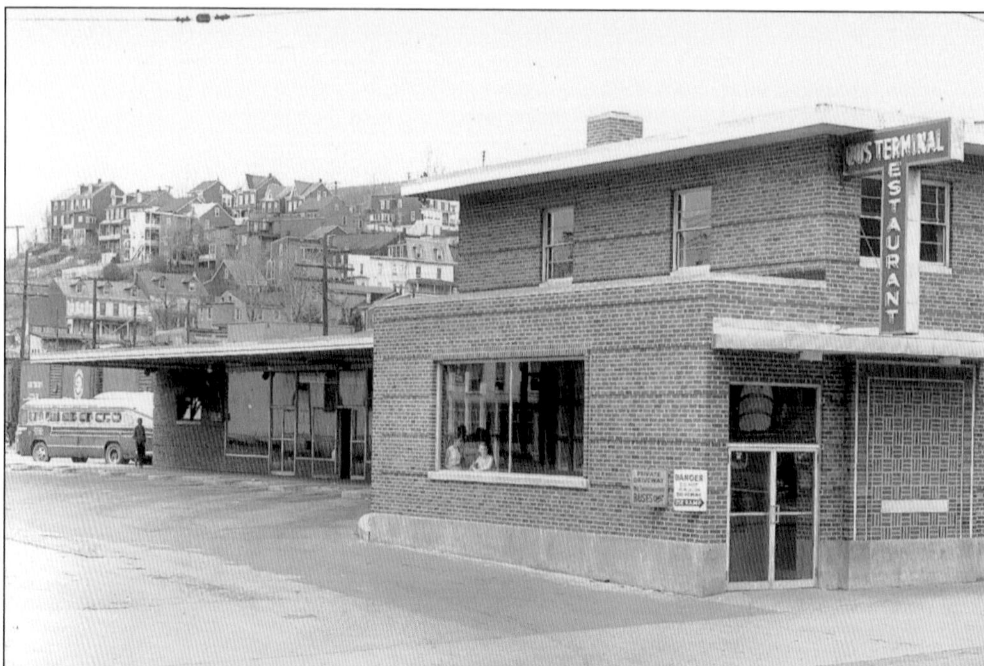

The bus terminal was constructed on the site of the former Pennsylvania Railroad station that faced Coal Street, or what is today Route 61. To the left of this 1956 image, the Pennsylvania Railroad boxcars line up between the station and the highway. The Bus Terminal Restaurant was one of the most popular eating establishments in Pottsville.

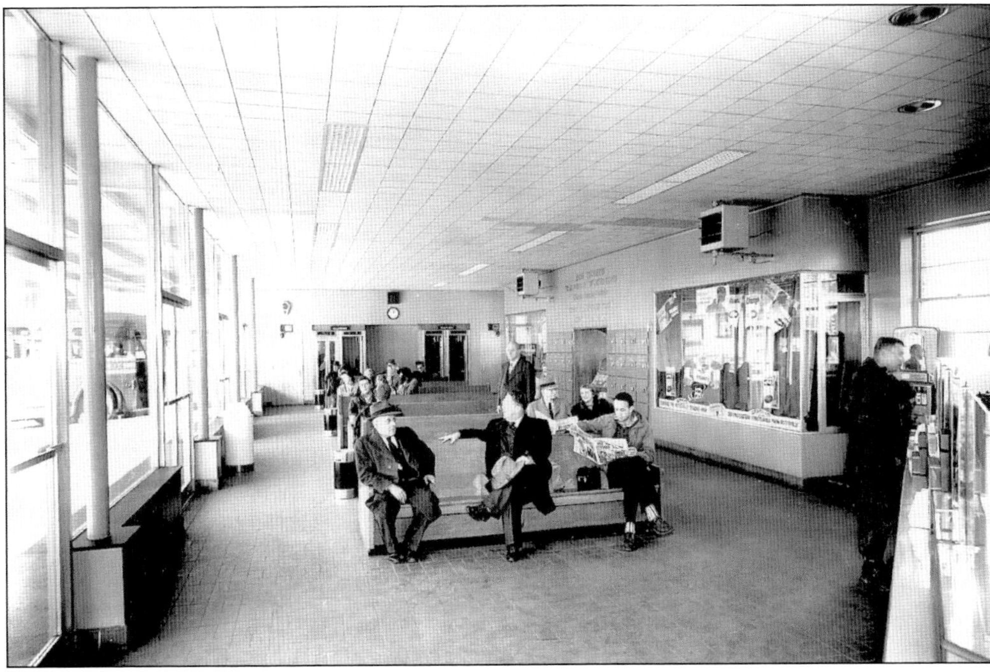

The bus terminal's lobby provides its customers with comfortable seating and amenities in this 1950s image. Today, much of the lobby has been converted into the Ryon Realty Company. The bus terminal's lobby is much smaller today than when the building was first laid out.

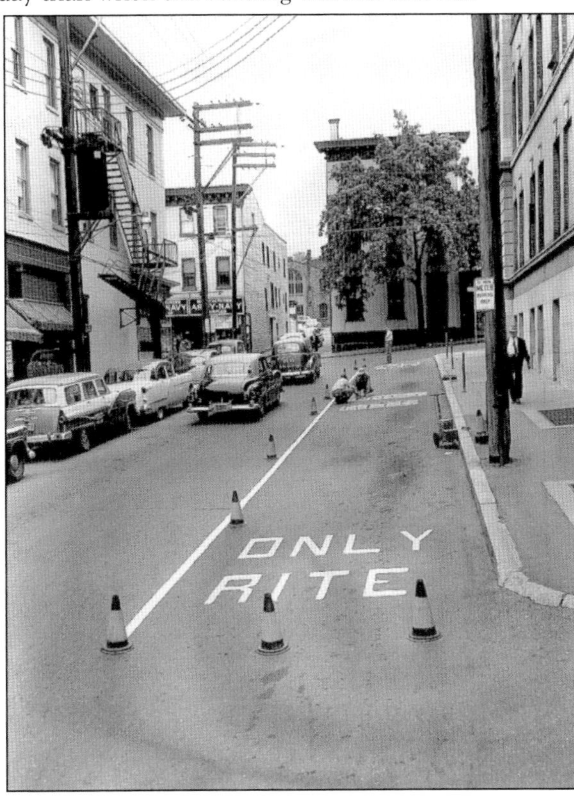

This post-1958 image shows a line of parked cars facing south on Second Street near Mahantongo Street. Note the spelling of "rite." The Army Navy Store stands on the southeast corner, but the building on the opposite corner was removed in the late 1960s when the city widened Second Street between Mahantongo Street and Howard Avenue.

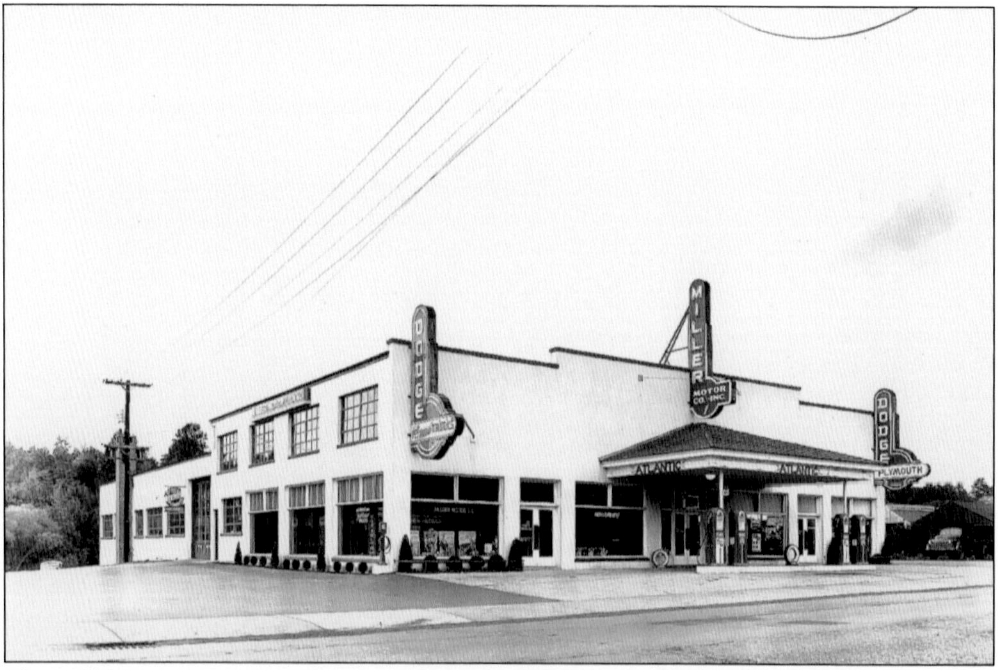

The Miller Motor Company, featuring Dodge and Plymouth automobiles, is seen in this 1940s image. The building was located at 22nd and West Market Streets. This is the present site of Bob Weaver Chevrolet.

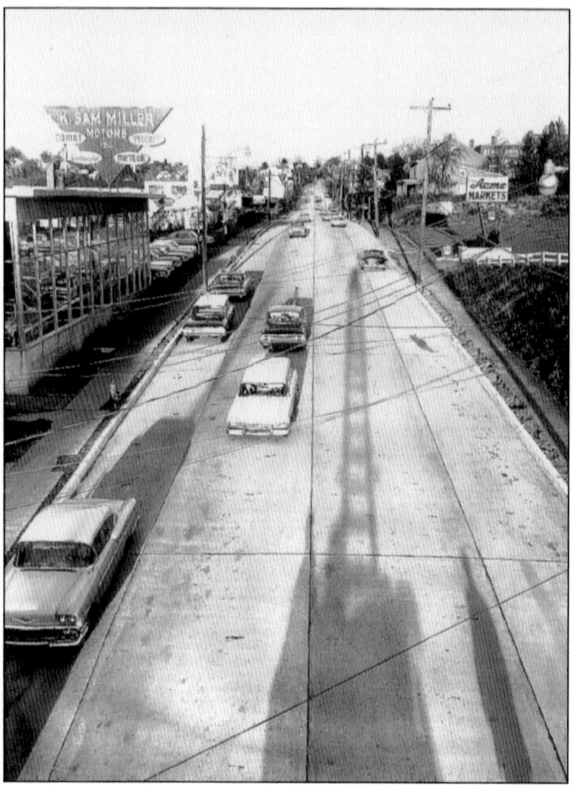

This early-1960s view, looking east along West Market Street, shows K. Sam Miller Motors selling Mercurys, Comets, Continentals, and Meteors. The photograph was taken from atop one of the city's ladder fire trucks. Burger King replaced the house beyond the Acme Markets sign nearly 10 years later.

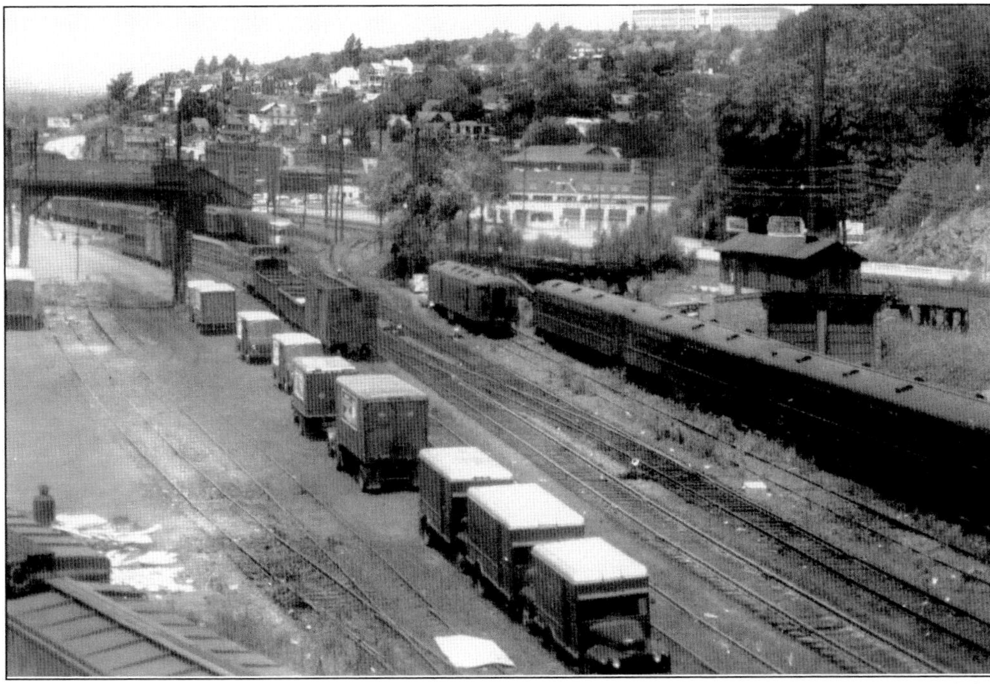

In this 1957 photograph taken from the Washington Street Bridge, the railroad and automobiles are operating side by side. Route 61 runs from the right middle of the photograph to the center of the picture, and the Reading Railroad yard is in the foreground just south of the Union Street station.

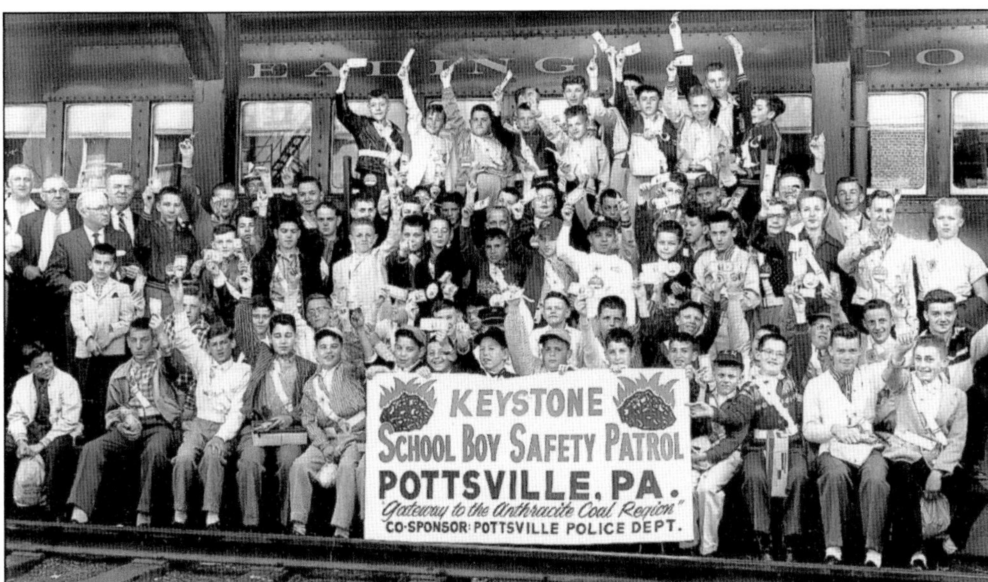

The Reading Railroad has provided the transportation for the School Boy Safety Patrol from Pottsville in this late-1950s image. Each of the boys is holding a crisp new dollar bill given to them as part of their reward for serving their community. The other part of their reward was a trip to a baseball game in Philadelphia. Years later, the boys (including this writer) went to the safety-patrol-sponsored game by bus.

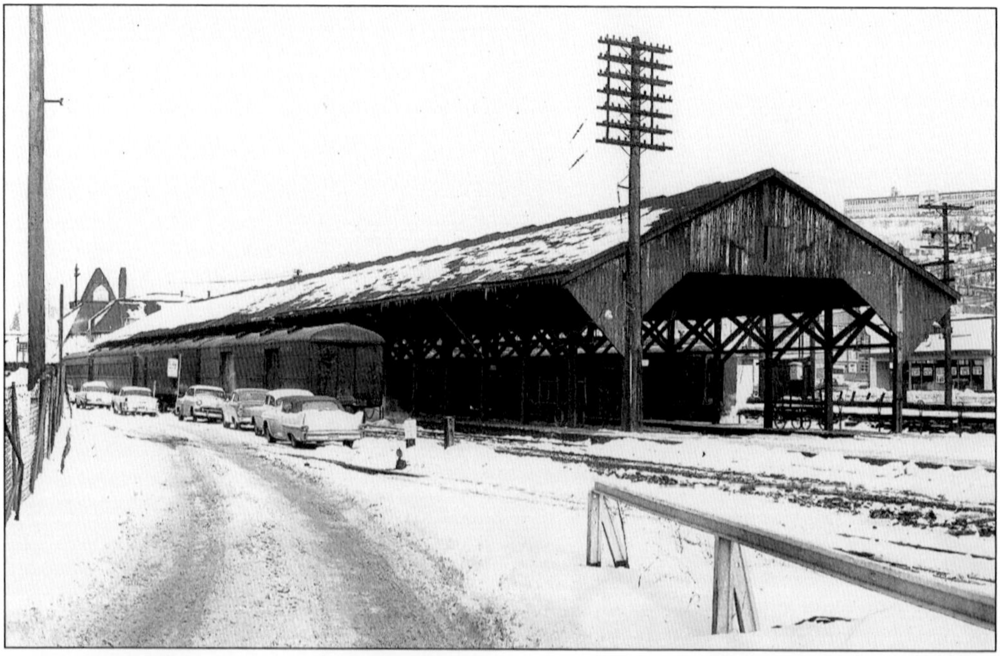

In this 1961 photograph, the Reading Railroad carbarn is seen parallel with Railroad Street. Within two years, the station and the barn were demolished to make way for the municipal parking lot.

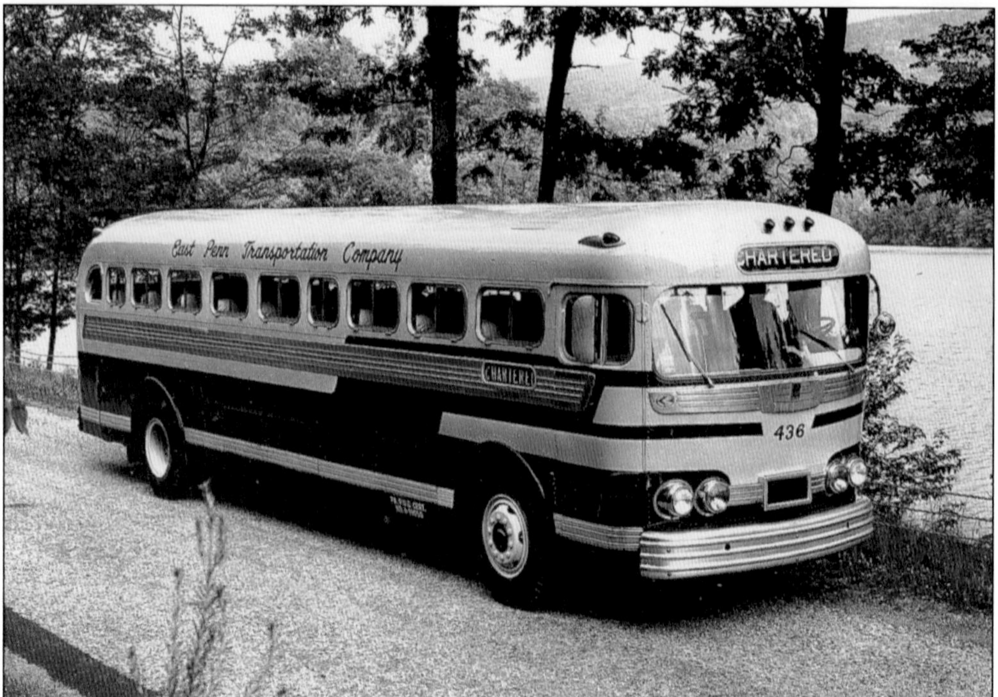

The bus challenged the railroad for customers since the 1930s. This East Penn Transportation Company bus is seen at a popular old resort spot along Tumbling Run Road, south of Pottsville. The Tumbling Run Reservoir is in the background.

Six

PRESIDENTIAL VISITORS

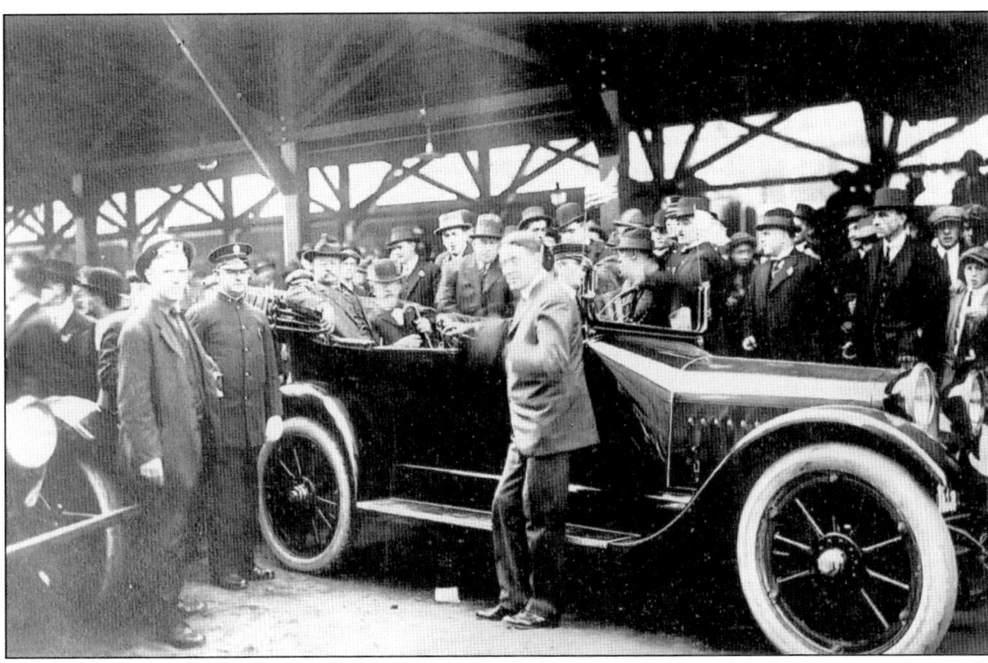

Seated in the touring car is Theodore Roosevelt, former president, during a visit to Pottsville in 1912. Roosevelt was campaigning again for president and represented the Bull Moose party. This photograph was taken at the old Reading Railroad terminal at East Norwegian and Railroad Streets, now Progress Avenue.

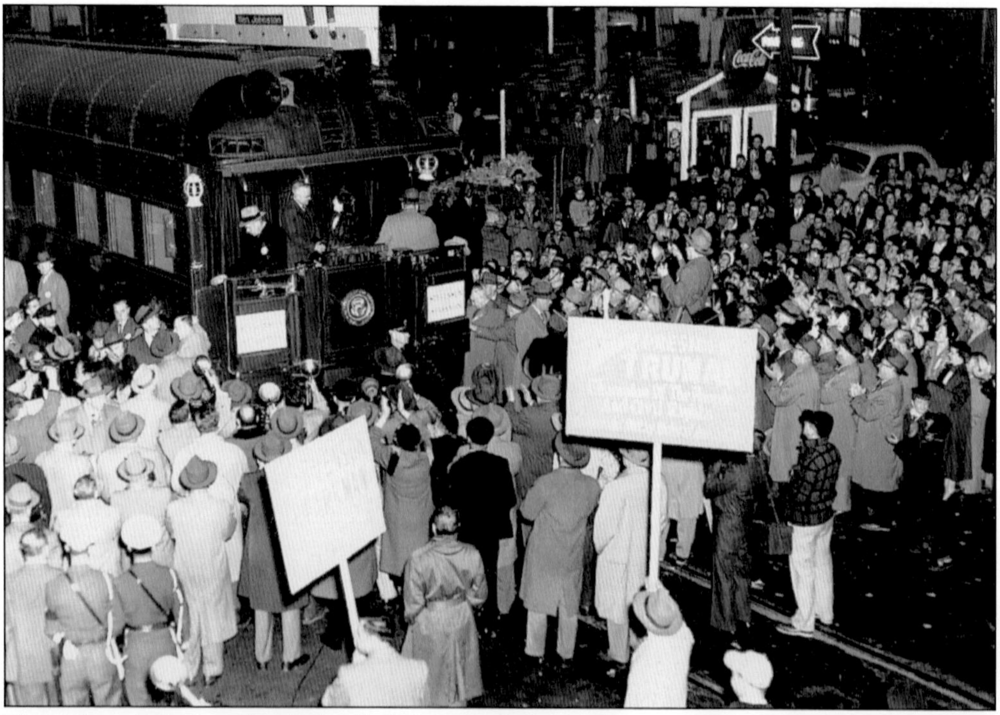

The only president to visit Schuylkill County while in office was Harry S. Truman. He visited Pottsville in October 1952. Seen here on the back of the train, Truman is being welcomed to the city at the Reading Railroad station.

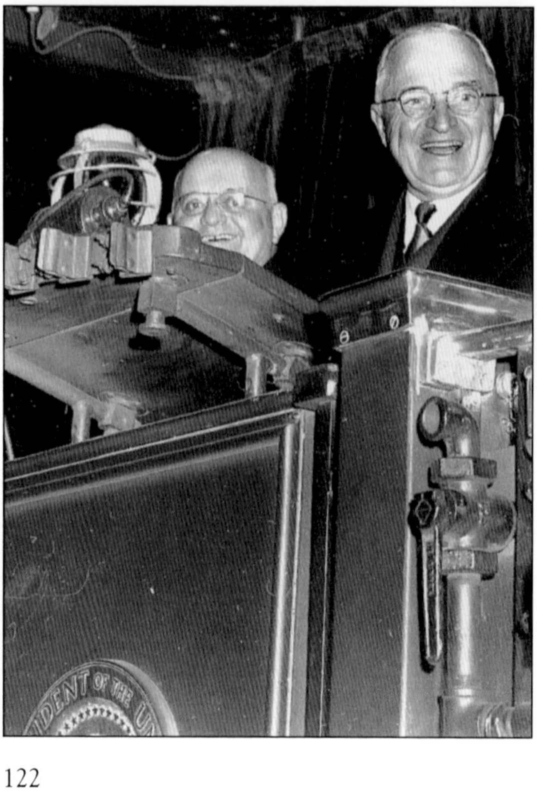

President Truman stops to make a few comments from the train car on his arrival. During Adlai Stevenson's run for the presidency in 1952, Truman's whistle-stop tour brought him to Pottsville.

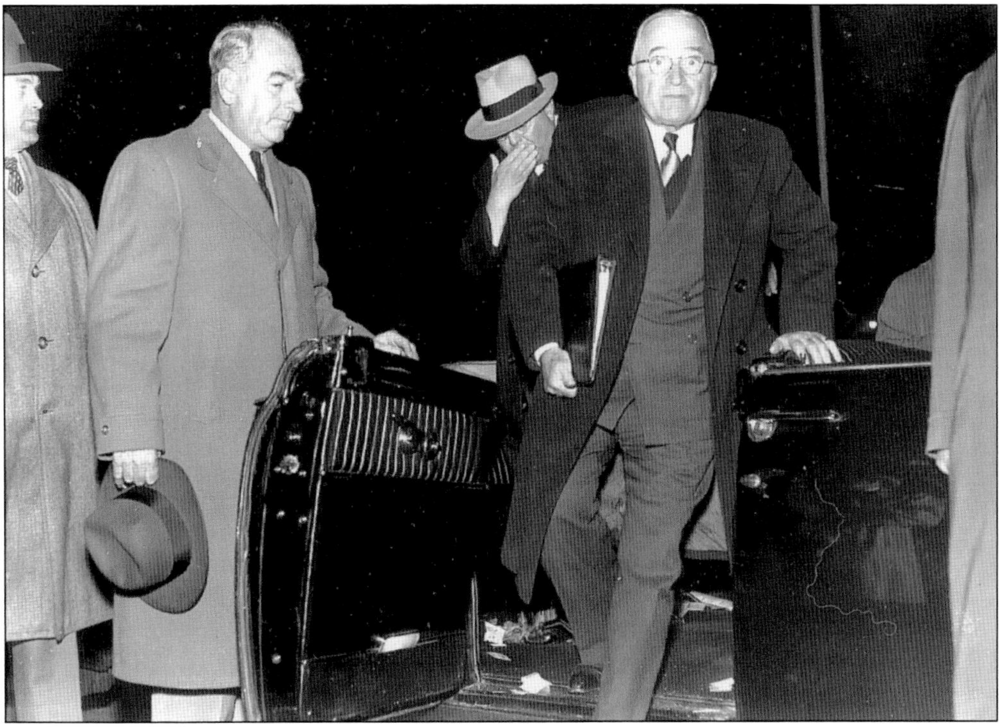

Secret Service agents and personal staff escort President Truman from his limousine as he arrives at Pottsville High School before his speech.

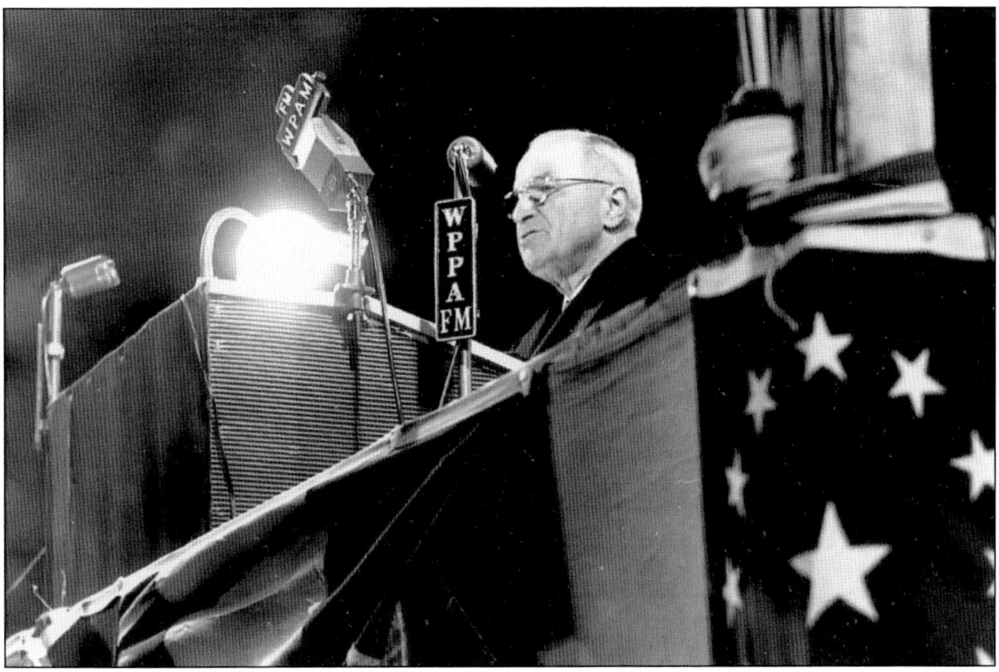

Pottsville radio stations WPAM and WPPA broadcast the voice of President Truman to listeners across the region in this photograph taken from the field at Veterans Memorial Stadium behind Elk Avenue.

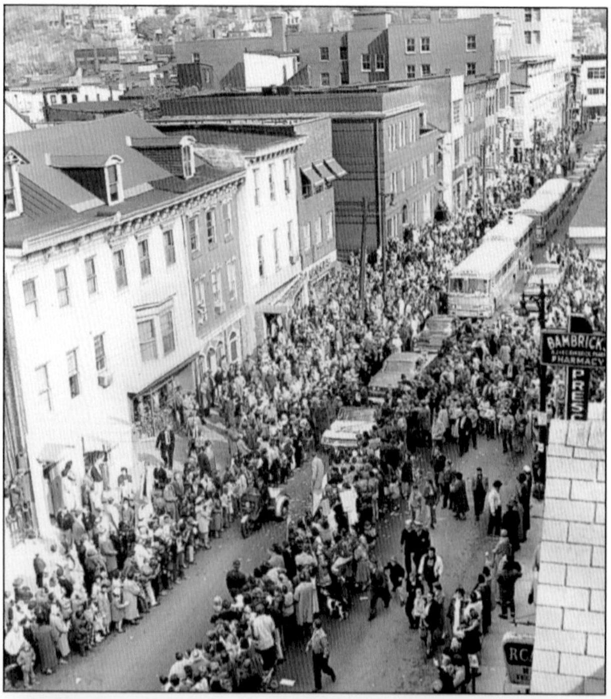

During the 1960 presidential election, Pottsville was visited by three more executive-office hopefuls. In this image, Sen. John F. Kennedy's caravan makes its way up West Market Street. The photograph, taken high above the intersection at Fourth and West Market Streets, shows the car and bus parade as it passes the Pottsville library on Third Street.

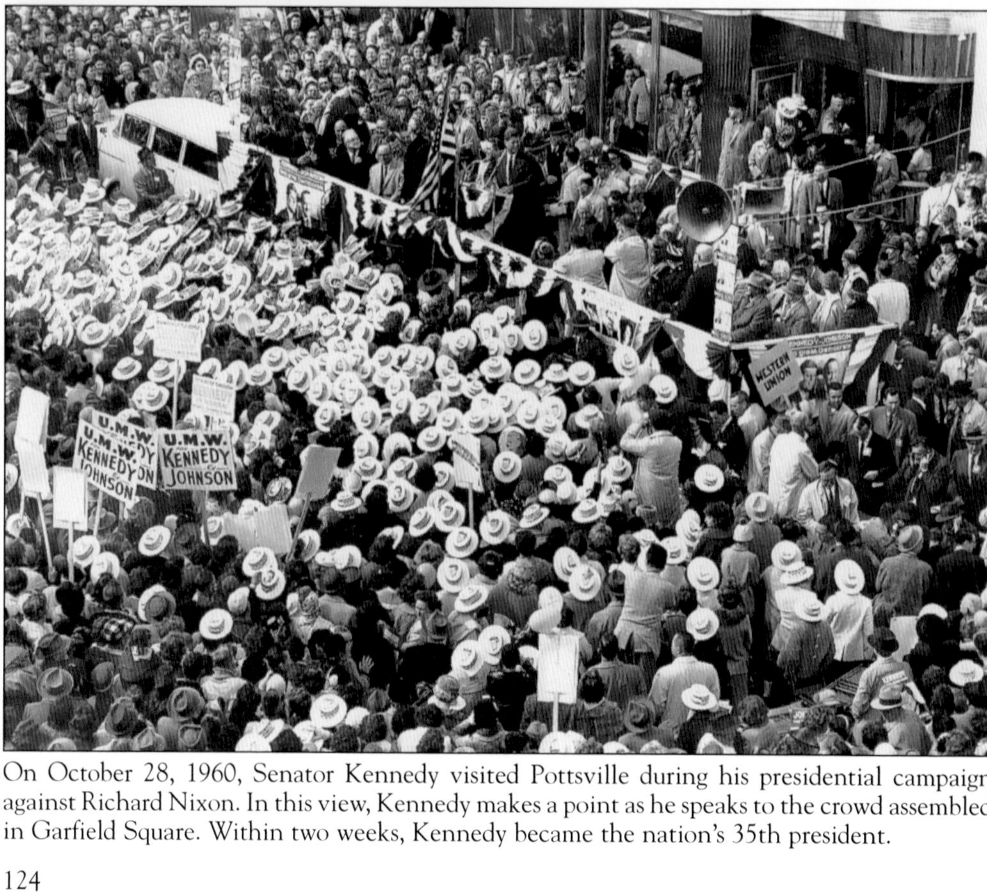

On October 28, 1960, Senator Kennedy visited Pottsville during his presidential campaign against Richard Nixon. In this view, Kennedy makes a point as he speaks to the crowd assembled in Garfield Square. Within two weeks, Kennedy became the nation's 35th president.

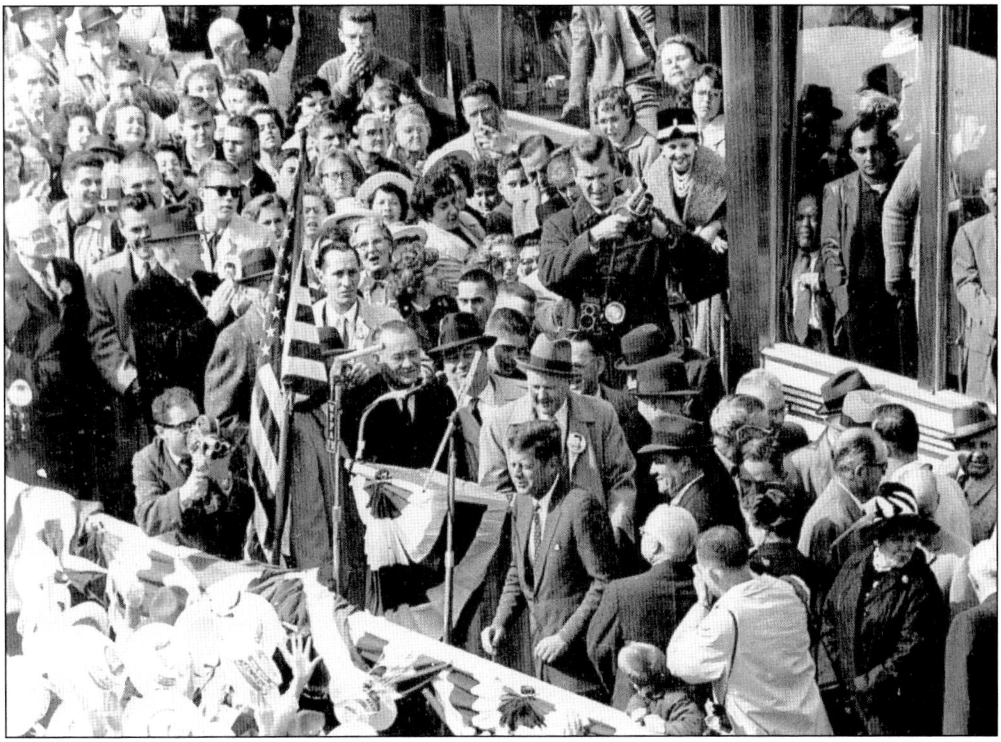

In this photograph, Secret Service agents, local democratic leaders, and the media surround presidential hopeful John F. Kennedy as he finishes his speech to the crowd in front of the Garfield Diner.

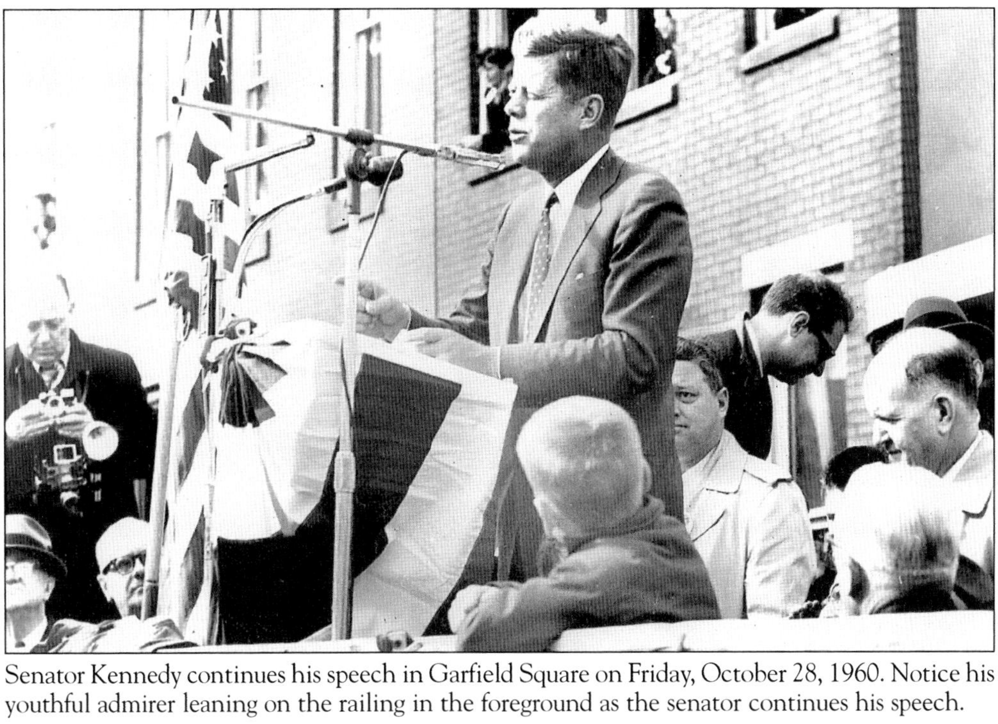

Senator Kennedy continues his speech in Garfield Square on Friday, October 28, 1960. Notice his youthful admirer leaning on the railing in the foreground as the senator continues his speech.

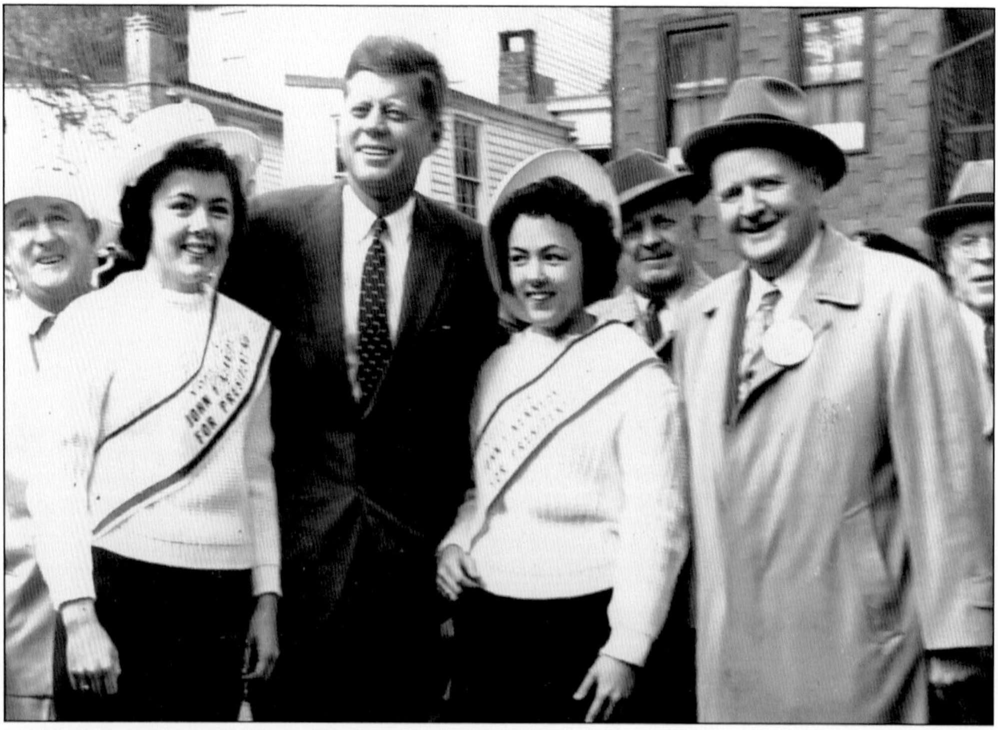

In this image, Senator Kennedy poses with the Kennedy twins of Girardville. Mary Rose and Theresa Jayne Kennedy flank the senator. On the right is James V. Ryan, the Schuylkill County Democratic party chairman of Heckscherville.

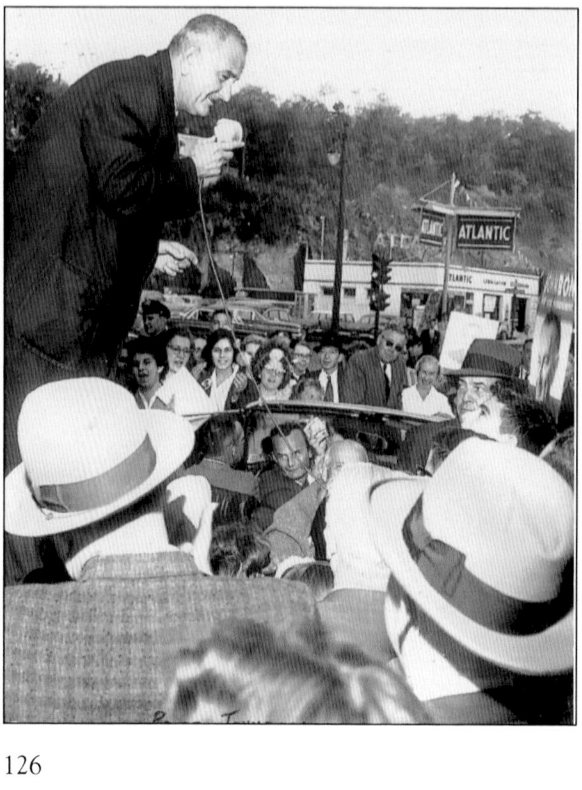

Two weeks before the Kennedy visit, vice presidential nominee Lyndon B. Johnson passed through the county while campaigning for the Democratic ticket. In this image, Johnson speaks to a crowd on Claude A. Lord Boulevard and East Norwegian Street. Johnson assumed the presidency in November 1963, after the assassination of President Kennedy.

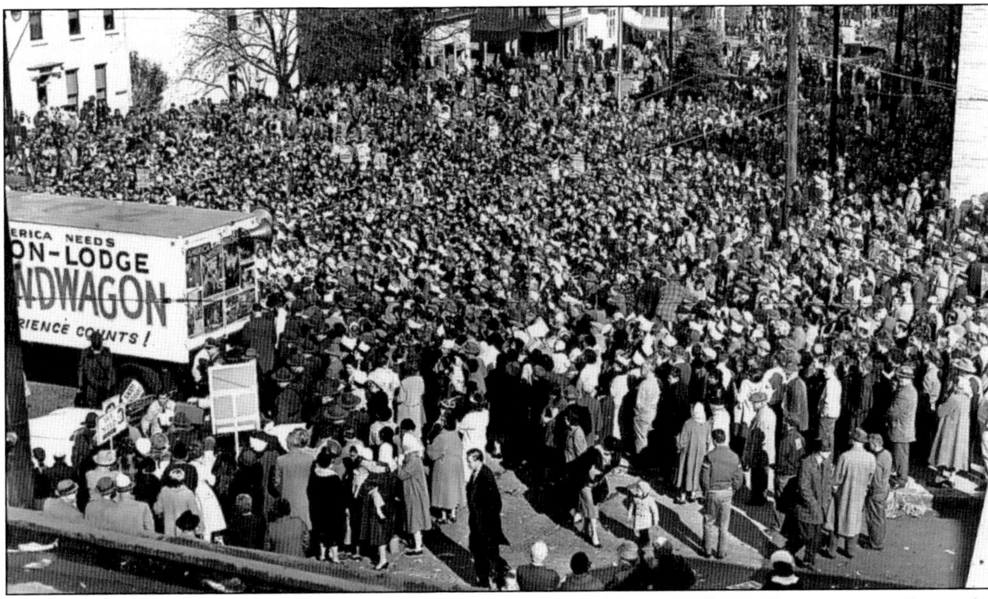

The 1960 presidential campaign would not pass through Pottsville without a visit from the Republican hopefuls. In this image, a crowd is gathered at Garfield Square, awaiting the arrival of Henry Cabot Lodge, who was running for vice president with Richard Nixon in 1960.

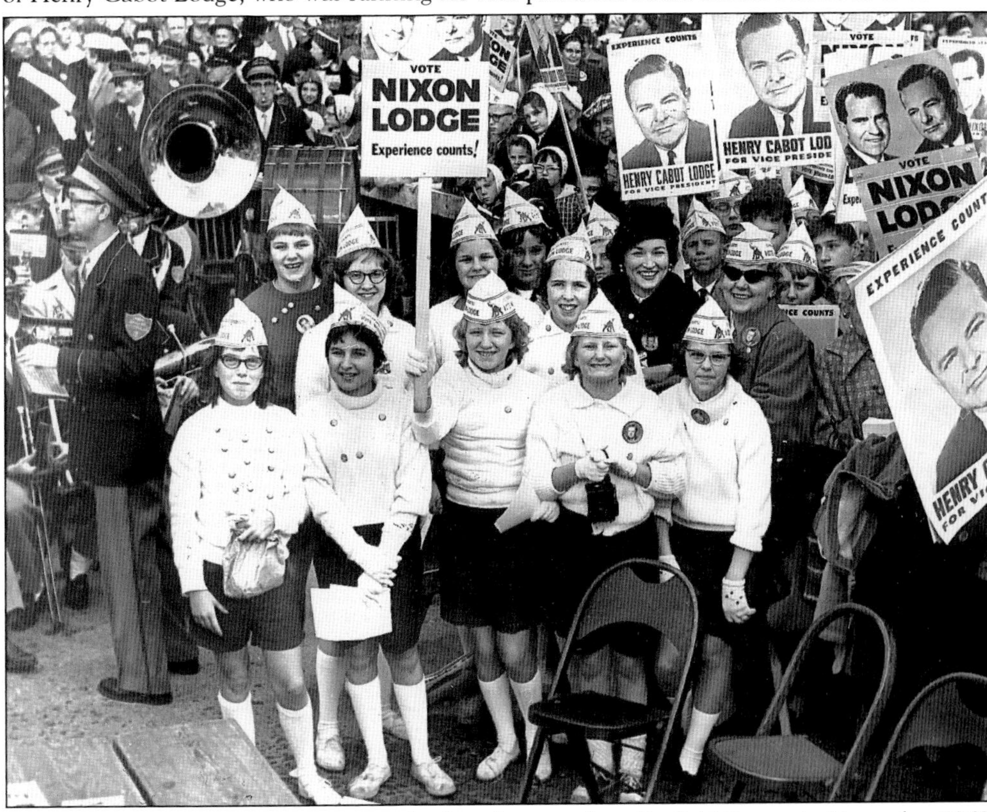

Youthful Nixon-Lodge supporters pose for this photograph at Garfield Square in November 1960, during Lodge's visit to Pottsville. The Third Brigade Band is also on hand for the festivities.

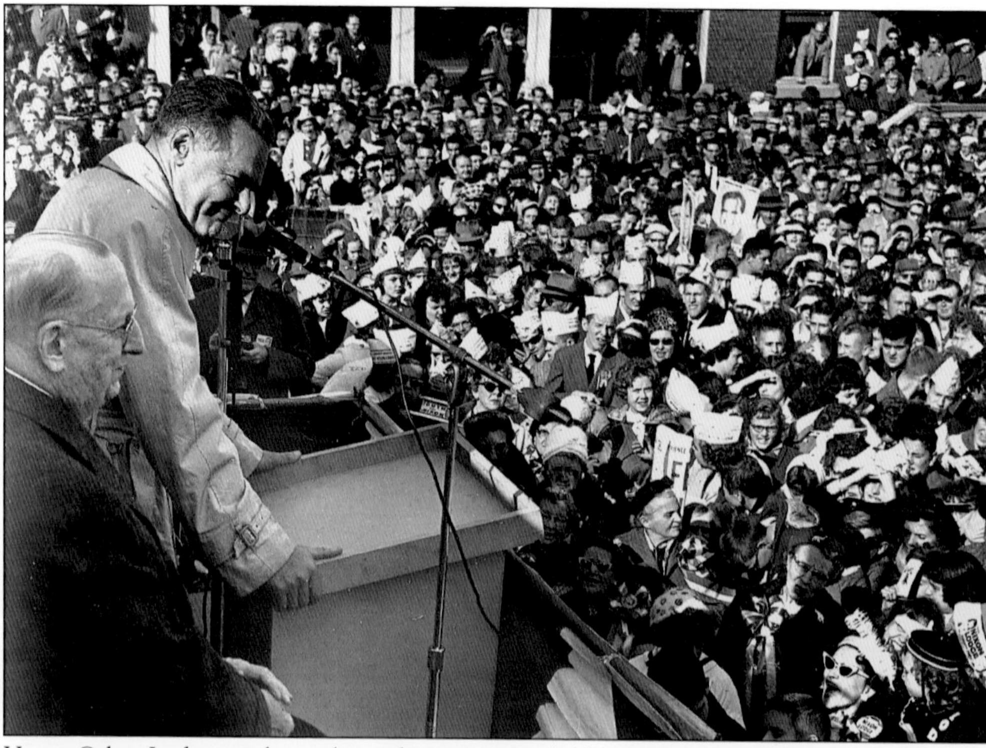

Henry Cabot Lodge speaks to the gathering at Garfield Square on November 4, 1960. Lodge and his presidential running mate, Richard Nixon, lost a close race against Kennedy.

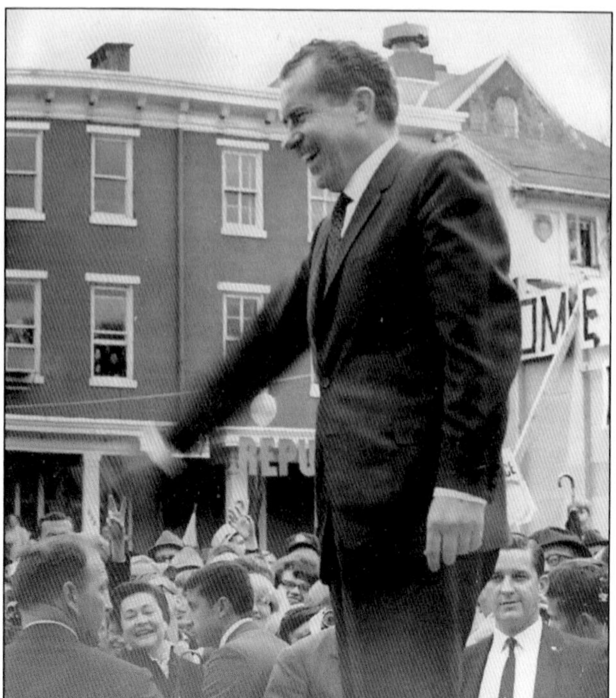

In 1968, Richard Nixon visited Pottsville during his presidential campaign against Minnesota senator Hubert Humphrey and Alabama governor George Wallace. Nixon reaches out to shake hands with his Pottsville supporters in this photograph taken at Garfield Square.